The End of Capitalism

Ulrike Herrmann was born in Hamburg in 1964.
She trained as a banker and later as a journalist, and
majored in philosophy and history. Since 2000, she
has been an economics editor at the left-alternative
national daily *Die Tageszeitung*, in Berlin. A member
of the Greens, she appears regularly on German TV
and radio, and often gives talks on economic topics
at foundations, institutes, and universities. She has
previously published four books, which all became
bestsellers in Germany.

The End of CAPITALISM

Why Growth and Climate Protection Are Incompatible— and How We Will Live in the Future

Ulrike Herrmann
translated by David Shaw

SCRIBE

Melbourne | London | Minneapolis

Scribe Publications
18–20 Edward St, Brunswick, Victoria 3056, Australia
2 John St, Clerkenwell, London, WC1N 2ES, United Kingdom
3754 Pleasant Ave, Suite 100, Minneapolis, Minnesota 55409, USA

Originally published in the German language as *Das Ende des Kapitalismus. Warum Wachstum und Klimaschutz nicht vereinbar sind – und wie wir in Zukunft leben werden* by Ulrike Herrmann
First published in English by Scribe 2025

Typeset in 12/16 pt Fairfield Medium by J&M Typesetting

Printed and bound in the UK by CPI Group (UK) Ltd, Croydon CR0 4YY

Scribe is committed to the sustainable use of natural resources and the use of paper products made responsibly from those resources.

978 1 761381 09 6 (Australian edition)
978 1 915590 93 0 (UK edition)
978 1 957363 92 9 (US edition)
978 1 761386 02 2 (ebook)

Catalogue records for this book are available from the National Library of Australia and the British Library.

scribepublications.com.au
scribepublications.co.uk
scribepublications.com

*For Xicu, Finn, Annika, Dorothea, Caroline,
and Johannes—the next generation*

Contents

Part III
The End of Capitalism

Preface to the English edition

Capitalism was invented in England. From around the year 1760, textile manufacturers there had an idea that had never occurred to anyone before in the history of mankind: to replace human workers systematically with machines. The first mechanical looms and spinning machines were water-powered, with steam power following later. Those industrialists simply wanted to maximise their individual profits, but they changed the world forever. They began the wave of industrialisation that swept first over Britain and then over the rest of Europe and North America, and now over large parts of the rest of the world.

We have all benefited from the resulting prosperity. To give just one example: in the 18th century, the average life expectancy in England, even for members of the nobility, was just 38 years. Britain's aristocrats enjoyed enormous privileges, but their lives were short nonetheless. Today, British men live 78.6 years on average, and women can expect to live 82.6 years. Life expectancy is similar in countries such as the US, Canada, and Australia, and the poorer countries of the Global South are catching up. In India, for example, the average person lived just 33.9 years in 1950; today, life expectancy has risen to 69.3 years.

But it has only been possible to attain and maintain this prosperity by burning coal, gas, and oil. Without energy, machines would simply be dead capital. Chemical factories, heating systems, computers, cars, planes—none of these could continue to function if we were forced to do without energy. Our vast technological complex would be nothing but an empty shell.

The British were the first to discover how coal can be used to power machines. Later, it was joined by gas and oil as additional energy sources. The energy density of such fossil fuels is extremely high—discovering them was like winning the jackpot for humankind. They have made the world richer by far.

But there is just one problem: burning those fuels releases huge amounts of carbon dioxide, which is heating up the Earth and threatening our future existence. That means we must turn away from oil, gas, and coal, and exploit green energy sources instead. That's easily said, but in fact it would mean the end of capitalism. Our current economic system is based on the need for cheap and abundant energy to power the world's huge fleet of machines. However, green energy will remain scarce and expensive rather than abundant and cheap, even if we install the largest conceivable number of wind turbines and solar panels.

At first glance, it may seem surprising that green energy will continue to be expensive. After all, the Sun radiates more energy towards the Earth than could ever be used by humankind. Proponents of solar power like to point out that 'the Sun sends no bills'. However, warm air alone is not much use to us. We have to concentrate the Sun's energy and convert it into electricity so that it can power our technology. And that's not easy to do.

In this book, the difficulties involved in the transition to green energy are mainly illustrated by examples from Germany. That country offers a prime example of the complexities involved in the transition—although there is no lack of political will to do so. Germany introduced a Renewable Energies Act as early as 2000, which earmarked billions of euros in funding for solar panels and wind turbines. But the results have been rather meagre. In 2023, only 6.2 per cent of the energy consumed in Germany came from wind power, with solar power providing only half that amount, at 3.1 per cent.

Germany is not the only country that is failing. Its fellow industrialised nations have similar climate records. In 2023, around 11 per cent of Britain's primary energy needs were filled by wind power, and only 1.9 per cent came from solar. The corresponding figures for the US are 4.0 and 2.0 per cent, respectively. For Canada, they are 2.1 and 0.3 per cent, and for Australia, 5.0 and 9.0 per cent. Gas and oil are the dominant fuels everywhere, while coal is also still an important energy source in Australia.

This failure is built into the system, as capitalism and climate protection are mutually incompatible. 'Green growth' is an illusion—what we need is 'green shrinkage'. Economic output must fall if we are to survive on just green energy.

But how can we quit capitalism? Once again, a look at the history of the United Kingdom gives us the answer. The British not only invented capitalism, but they also provided a possible way to organise its end. They faced having to shrink their civil production levels radically during World War II. In order to defend itself against the aggressions of Hitler, Britain had to free up huge capacities in its factories to produce urgently needed military hardware. The British did not starve, but everyday consumer goods became scarce. They invented a new economic system, which we can learn from today. It was a private, democratic, planned economy. That wartime British economic model can save our future.

Introduction

Many young people today despair of their parents. The climate crisis is jeopardising their future, yet the production of greenhouse gases continues unabated. 'We don't understand why our parents are at such a loss,' writes the young German climate activist Luisa Neubauer. She is equally baffled as to why the former German chancellor Angela Merkel spent 16 years doing next to nothing. 'Merkel is a trained physicist. Surely she must understand what it means when the climate graphs shoot upwards?'[1]

This feeling of exasperation is not exclusive to young people. The words of the primatologist Jane Goodall have become famous: 'How come the most intellectual creature to ever walk on planet Earth is destroying its only home?' There is no longer any doubt among scientists that the climate crisis poses a serious threat to humankind, and could even spell its total demise. The climatologist Hans Joachim Schellnhuber uses a dramatic image to describe this threat: 'We are shoving our children onto a global school bus that we know with 98 per cent certainty will suffer a fatal crash.'[2]

Another reason for the disappointment felt by young people is the common suggestion from scientists that protecting the climate is actually easy. The solar engineer

Volker Quaschning writes, for example, 'The necessary technologies and concepts have long-since been developed. And
we are also able to afford to make the necessary changes.
So, there are no insurmountable technological or economic
obstacles.'[3] And the meteorologist Mojib Latif alleges that
'corrupt politicians' and 'unscrupulous corporations' alone
are preventing the climate from being saved.[4]

Being told that protecting the climate can be achieved
so effortlessly, many young people conclude, quite logically,
that it is the political parties that are failing. Otherwise, the
planet would have been saved long ago. Therefore, politicians should no longer be left to make decisions, but should
rather listen to scientists. 'Follow the science' is a central
slogan. It was popularised by the Swedish climate activist
Greta Thunberg, and is now the motto of the Fridays for
Future movement.

The young climate-protection advocates presume that all
that is needed to avert a climate catastrophe is sufficient
funds. Phrases such as 'If the world were a bank, you would
have saved it long ago' are popular.[5] The impending climate
catastrophe is treated like a normal crisis, such as a financial
crash, for example. It may threaten our existence, but it can,
supposedly, be remedied quickly—as long as the necessary
millions are forthcoming.

Unfortunately, it's not that simple. The reason for the failure of climate protection is not the corruption of politicians
or their unwillingness to approve sufficient funding. The
will to save the planet is there. The German health minister,
Karl Lauterbach of the centre-left Social Democratic Party,
has remarked with distress, 'No one would heat their own
home so much as to create a 30 per cent probability that it
would burn down within the next 30 years. That's exactly
what we are doing with our home, the Earth.'[6]

The reason that humanity is torching its own home is that it is not enough to know the scientific facts. The problem goes far deeper than that. Climate protection will only be possible if we abolish capitalism.

Despite what critics of capitalism may believe, this is not good news. Capitalism has brought us extraordinary benefits. It was the first social system in history to generate wealth continuously. Before that, there was no significant growth. Humans eked out a relatively meagre living from agriculture, often faced famine, and had an average life expectancy of 35 years.

Capitalism was progress. Unfortunately, it has a fundamental flaw: it not only generates growth, but is also dependent on that growth for its continued stability. Without constant expansion, capitalism breaks down. But infinite growth is not possible in a finite world. Currently, developed nations are acting as if there were several planets available for them to consume. But there is, of course, only one planet Earth.

So far, governments have counted on finding some way to reconcile industry and climate protection. The typical slogans include such phrases as the 'Green New Deal' or 'decoupling' growth from energy. The great hope is that the entire industrial system will be able to switch over to green power—including travel and transport, manufacturing and processing, and heating.

Such 'green growth' is just an illusion, however, because the amount of sustainably produced energy will not be enough. That may seem surprising at first glance, since the Earth receives 5,000 times more energy from the Sun than would be needed by the eight billion people on the planet to maintain a standard of living typical of that in Europe.

So, there is no shortage of physical energy, but that solar energy must be collected before it can be put to use. Solar panels and wind turbines, however, provide energy only when the Sun is shining or the wind is blowing. Energy must be stored for use when there is no wind or sunlight. And that intermediate step is so costly that green electricity will continue to be in short supply. If green energy is to be sufficient, the only option is 'green shrinkage'.

The idea that permanent growth has no future is not a new one. Many climate activists have long been convinced that the natural world can only survive if capitalism ends. This is summed up in their catchy slogan 'System change, not climate change'.

There is also no lack of ideas for a green circular economy, in which only as much is consumed as can be recycled. This includes concepts such as exchange economies, economies for the common good, consumption reduction, shorter working hours, and a universal basic income, among others.

But how can a green circular economy be achieved? That remains unclear, since the vision is usually confused with the way to achieve it, conflating the desired result and the transformation required to attain it. How to actually leave a system of constantly growing capitalism without triggering a severe economic crisis and plunging millions of people into unemployment is a question that is seldom asked directly. The bridge leading from the dynamic present to a static future is missing.

Climate activists sense that letting go of capitalism will not be easy. Greta Thunberg was recently asked by a supporter what the system of the future will look like. 'I don't know,' she answered. 'It hasn't been invented yet.'[7]

To envision such 'green shrinkage', it helps to start by thinking of the end result. If green energy remains scarce, air travel and private cars will no longer be possible. Banks will also become largely obsolete, since loans can only be repaid if the economy is growing.

No one need starve in a climate-neutral economy, but millions of workers would have to reorient themselves. For example, far more agricultural and forestry workers would be required to alleviate the consequences of climate change.

Such a view of the future may seem radical, but there is literally no alternative. If we fail to reduce greenhouse gas emissions to net zero, we will end up living in a 'Heat Age', which will automatically lead to economic shrinkage. Such climate chaos would probably result in a dog-eat-dog situation and the end of our democratic system.

The dismantling of capitalism must take place in an ordered fashion. Luckily, there is a historical model for such a process: Britain's wartime economy, introduced in 1939. At that time, Britain faced a challenge of monstrous proportions. It had failed to see World War II coming, and had to militarise its economy at very short notice, without leaving its population to go hungry.

Almost overnight, a command economy arose, which worked remarkably well. Factories remained in private ownership, but the state controlled production — and organised the distribution of scarce goods. Rationing was introduced, but there were no shortages. Britain thus invented a private and democratic command economy that was far removed from the dysfunctional socialism of the Soviet Union.

Let there be no misunderstanding: not all wartime economies are suitable models. Not Hitler's policy of spoliation, and not Putin's attack on Ukraine. But Britain developed a model from which we can learn.

Climate protection can only succeed if it takes place globally, since greenhouse gases do not respect international borders. Nonetheless, this book describes a concept for Germany alone. This is not intended to promote any kind of national tunnel vision, but to provide a clearer understanding of the issue. The economics of climate change are already complicated enough in themselves. So it helps to at least to keep the scope manageable and familiar.

The problems with green energy are thus described here using the example of Germany. However, many people in Germany doubt whether there is any point in even considering climate protection at the national level. They fear that other countries could take advantage if Germany reduces its greenhouse gas emissions. The leading German economist Hans-Werner Sinn writes: 'If the Germans buy and burn less coal, crude oil or natural gas, the Chinese, say, will be able to buy and burn more.'[8]

Such caution is understandable, but it fails to recognise the fact that most countries are suffering far more from the effects of the climate catastrophe than Germany. It is also in their best interests to reduce greenhouse gas emissions. In the debate over the climate, there is always a suggestion that we already have the solution, and that all that is lacking is the political will to implement it. But in reality, we do not as yet have a concept for bringing capitalism to a peaceful end. The arguments always revolve around non-solutions.

There can be no understanding of the end of capitalism without a knowledge of its history. Therefore, this book begins with a description of the origin and development of our current economic system and the way it works. The inevitable conclusion is that it must come to an end. Capitalism is fascinating, but it has no future. The next age will be one of a 'survival economy'.

PART I

The Rise of Capital

CHAPTER ONE

A blessing: growth creates prosperity

Capitalism does not have a good reputation. Survey respondents around the world say it is in urgent need of reform. In Germany, only 12 per cent of people believe the current system benefits them and that they profit sufficiently from growth. By contrast, 55 per cent think capitalism in its current form does more harm than good.[1]

That sense of dissatisfaction is understandable, but capitalism is actually better than its reputation. Before the advent of industrialisation, famine was a widespread phenomenon. Death due to a lack of a sufficient food supply was common, even in Germany. The last major pan-European famine occurred in 1846–47, after bad weather destroyed a large share of the grain harvest and when potato blight was rife across the continent.[2]

There have been no food shortages in Western Europe since then, apart from during the two world wars. The only exception is Finland, where the last famine occurred in 1867, when a failed harvest led to the deaths of 100,000 people out of a population of 1.6 million.[3] Capitalism has conquered hunger and replaced it with overabundance, raising 'butter mountains' and filling 'milk lakes'.

In industrialised nations, everyone's life is now healthier and more comfortable than that enjoyed only by royalty in the past. The nobility may have lived in palaces and always had enough to eat, but they also often died young, carried off by the diseases that were rampant at the time—plague, typhoid fever, scarlet fever, diphtheria, tuberculosis, or smallpox, to name just a few. The same was true of monks. Monasteries were usually well supplied with food, but the well-nourished clerics did not live any longer on average than the laity.[4]

Even harmless ailments could become fatal. The eminent economist David Ricardo died in 1823 from what started as a simple middle-ear infection. And even the richest man in the world in his time, the banker Nathan Mayer Rothschild, succumbed to a boil on his buttocks in 1836.

Today, by contrast, newborn girls in Germany can expect to live to more than 83 years of age on average; the life expectancy for boys is just under 79 years. In the rich industrialised nations at least, life expectancy has more or less reached the maximum possible: even if a cure for all types of cancer were found, it would only add four to five years to our average lifespan.[5]

But it is not only our total lifespan that has more than doubled. Our quality of life is also significantly better now: worn-out knee and hip joints are replaced as a matter of routine, freeing patients from agonising pain, whereas in the past, a simple broken bone could leave patients with a serious, lifelong disability.[6]

Our everyday lives have also become far more pleasant. Even poor people now enjoy a more comfortable existence than royalty did in the 18th century. To name just a few modern conveniences that would have been unimaginable in the past: almost every household now has access to motor vehicles, mobile phones, computers, running water, heating, washing machines, fridges, television, bicycles, and electric light.[7]

Also, less and less work is necessary to be able to afford those conveniences. American workers had to put in around 1,800 hours to pay for a refrigerator in 1919. Little more than a century later, a new fridge now costs them the equivalent of fewer than 24 hours of work.[8]

At the same time, our devices are growing ever more powerful. Prices for normal smartphones now start at around 200 euros. That buys you not just a telephone, but also a computer, a camera, a pocket calculator, a GPS device, an alarm clock, a torch, a television, and a video camera. A modern smartphone has 160,000 times the processing power of the computer that successfully guided *Apollo 11* and its crew to the surface of the moon in 1969.[9]

Women in particular have benefited from the triumphal march of consumer goods, as domestic appliances have significantly reduced the time required for housework. A century ago, keeping a house and family was far more than a full-time job—requiring around 58 hours of work per week. Today, that has shrunk to an average of just 11.5 hours. Doing the laundry alone used to take almost 12 hours a week, while now it takes up just 90 minutes of our time.[10] It is scarcely an exaggeration when the South Korean economist Ha-Joon Chang pointedly asserts, 'The washing machine has changed the world more than the internet has.'[11]

However, housework and childcare are still divided very unequally between the sexes. In Germany in 2016, men living with a female partner took care of around 37 per cent of the housework.[12] However, precisely because family work is overwhelmingly carried out by women, they would never have gained an opportunity to participate in professional life without the help of domestic appliances.

The idea that capitalism is a blessing is not new. The best hymn of praise stems from Karl Marx, of all people. In *The Communist Manifesto* he wrote with powerful eloquence of the way the bourgeoisie had changed the world: 'It has been the first to show what man's activity can bring about. It has accomplished wonders far surpassing Egyptian pyramids, Roman aqueducts, and Gothic cathedrals.'

Karl Marx and Friedrich Engels had a lifelong fascination with the technological inventions of their time, and meticulously enumerated those 'wonders':

> [The] subjection of Nature's forces to man, machinery, application of chemistry to industry and agriculture, steam-navigation, railways, electric telegraphs, clearing of whole continents for cultivation, canalisation of rivers, whole populations conjured out of the ground—what earlier century had even a presentiment that such productive forces slumbered in the lap of social labour?

This shows that any claims that Marx and Engels rejected capitalism out of hand are based on a misunderstanding. They welcomed unbridled growth. The wanted a powerful increase in prosperity so that there would be more to distribute after the communist revolution.[13]

However, capitalism is far more than just an economic system that enables growth and prosperity. It shapes our thinking from the cradle to the grave and has long since penetrated even the most intimate spheres of our private lives. Who we marry, how we bring up our children, and how we spend our free time—our lives are completely different from those of our ancestors 250 years ago who grew up before the advent of capitalism.

People have always fallen in love, but for the most part they were unable to marry for romantic reasons. Throughout history, marriage has served as a way of ensuring that property remains and increases within an extended family. Peasants, craftsmen, and aristocrats all entered into marriages, often arranged for them by others, as a kind of life insurance. Fathers carefully chose marriage partners for their daughters and sons. Love matches did not become the norm until increasing prosperity meant young families were no longer materially dependent on their parents and could earn their own money.

Capitalism is a total system. It permeates not only our economy, but our entire lives. That's what makes it so difficult to conceive of alternatives. This dilemma is summed up by the legendary aphorism, 'It's easier to imagine the end of the world than the end of capitalism.'[14]

Added to this is the fact that the achievements of capitalism are so beneficial, and no one is keen to give them up. This material prosperity also has more intangible consequences. Capitalism has not only doubled our life expectancy; universal education, equal opportunities, and democracy are only possible in a richer society.

To return to Marx: when he completed his secondary education in Trier in 1835, only around 1 per cent of boys in Prussia attended grammar school.[15] Education was only available to the sons of the upper class, to which Marx also belonged. His father was an eminent lawyer and one of the dignitaries of the city. Most boys, if they enjoyed any education at all, attended elementary school for a few years, where they were taught a little reading, writing, and arithmetic in completely overcrowded classes. Girls often received no education at all. Children were needed as labourers in the fields or workshops, so parents were unable to afford to send their sons and daughters to school.

And, although academics were so few in number at that time, there were still too many of them. Theologians and law graduates often had to wait 12 years to receive a position as a clergyman or a judge—and were not allowed to marry or start a family until they did. Poor agrarian states have almost no need for academics, nor are they able to feed them.

The right to education is a human right, but it was not until the advent of capitalism that a large number of jobs were created that required well-trained workers to perform them. In Germany today, more than 50 per cent of school students in a given year will graduate from high school, with a slightly higher proportion of girls than boys gaining the qualification (called *Abitur* in Germany).[16] However, the education revolution was not restricted to grammar school students. All children now receive a significantly longer and better education than anyone could have imagined 100 years ago.

But it is also true that not all children have the same opportunities in life. Their background is a major factor in the qualifications they achieve by the time they leave school. Children of working-class parents are still very unlikely to study at university, while the offspring of university graduates almost always follow in their parents' educational footsteps.[17]

Capitalism is no paradise, and it certainly has not eliminated all inequalities. What is new about it, in the historical context, is that it at least allows protest against those inequalities. The issue of equal rights and opportunities only emerges when societies become more prosperous. Whether the demand is for equal rights for working-class children, women, LGBTQIA people, people with disabilities, or immigrants—it is only when prosperity becomes the norm that those demands have any chance of being heeded.

As long as a society remains poor, the ruling class can only enjoy wealth by exploiting the lower class. It comes down to a ruthless zero-sum game: those in power take ownership of scarce goods, leaving almost nothing for the vast majority. However, when the economy grows, that brutal contest is no longer necessary. The gains are enough for everyone to benefit from them. Inequalities remain, and the rich continue to get richer, but normal citizens also benefit. It is no longer necessary for the elites to forcibly subjugate the rest of the population.[18]

Thus, democracy was able to take hold only when industrialisation was quite advanced. Universal suffrage was introduced in Germany and Austria in 1918, and the right to vote was awarded to all British men in the same year, while suffrage was not extended to all British women until 1928.[19] Switzerland is a special case: the universal right to vote was introduced there for men as early as 1848, but the same right was not formally introduced for women until 1971.

However, it would be wrong to assume the reverse is also true. Democracies only flourish when they are prosperous, but that does not mean industrialised nations must inevitably become democracies. China is an interesting case in point: the per-capita income there is now almost as high as that in Australia in 1990[20]—still there are no indications that the ruling Communist Party might lose its grip on power.

The Chinese example also shows that capitalism has now reached the Global South and is no longer limited to the traditional industrialised nations. Life expectancy is increasing significantly even in poor countries. Newborn babies in southern Africa are now more likely to reach their fifth birthday than children born in England in 1918. People in India now live longer on average than those in Scotland did in 1945—although they are far less wealthy than British people were at that time.[21]

Global progress is impressive: extreme poverty around the world has been halved in the past 20 years, 80 per cent of the world's children are now vaccinated, and 80 per cent of families have access to electricity. 'Those are great achievements,' even the climate activist Luisa Neubauer concedes.[22]

Those success stories cannot, however, hide the fact that there is still extreme inequality in the world, and not all people profit equally from capitalism. Taking Germany as a starting point: the richest one-hundredth of the popula-tion—the top 1 per cent—own 33 per cent of the national wealth. The richest tenth of the population together own a not inconsiderable 64 per cent. That leaves little for the poorest strata of society; the lower 50 per cent own no more than 2.3 per cent of the national wealth.[23] Germany is a class-based society, despite the fact that many Germans believe they live in a 'levelled middle-class society'.

The differences between national states are even greater. Although life expectancy is increasing considerably around the globe, some countries are being left behind. There are still states in which more than 10 per cent of children die before reaching their fifth birthday. Those countries include Nigeria, Chad, and Sierra Leone, for example. Most infant deaths are not caused by exotic diseases, but by such routine illnesses as diarrhoea or malaria, for which effective treat-ments exist.[24]

At first sight, it seems strange that the Global South should have so much difficulty catching up with the tradi-tional industrialised nations. An obvious idea would be for them to simply copy the technology: Germany is well known for making a very large amount of money manufacturing luxury automobiles—so why doesn't Bangladesh just set up its own production lines and start exporting high-end cars, too?

Modern capitalism is complicated. It can be best understood by looking to its beginnings and at the conditions under which it originated: England from around the year 1760 onwards.

CHAPTER TWO

England, 1760: the invention of growth

Prosperity is a miracle. Western Europeans today are 20 times richer on average than their ancestors who lived 200 years ago.[1] Capitalism has also achieved far more than just producing more of what was already there—it has created a completely new world. A car with 50 'horsepower' (HP) is not simply a carriage drawn by 50 horses—it is a completely different product. And our modern lighting is not made up of millions of candles that need to be lit.[2] Capitalism was revolutionary.

However, this 'Industrial Revolution'[3] was not a sudden event. The transformation of the world occurred over several centuries and developed from very humble beginnings. Initially, just one branch of production in England was mechanised—the textile industry—and even there it was many decades before the last handlooms were replaced.[4]

There is no definitive answer to the question of why the Industrial Revolution began in England in 1760, rather than somewhere else. 'Although thousands of books have been written about this astounding phenomenon, it still remains something of a mystery,' adjudges the American economic historian Joyce Appleby.[5] This failure of their standard models to provide an answer irks neoliberal economists especially. They deem private property ownership, the division of labour, market forces, banks, and education to be particularly important in generating growth. But none of those phenomena can explain why capitalism began in England.

The textile factories of England were privately owned, but private property was also heavily protected in the rest of western Europe—without it having promoted growth there.[6] The comprehensive safeguarding of private property was also nothing new: even the ancient Romans devised legal constructs to limit the liability of property owners.[7] Clearly, private property ownership alone does not create wealth, otherwise dynamic economic growth would already have been a feature of the Roman economy.

The division of labour was also not an 18th-century invention.[8] The advantage of dividing production into smaller steps to speed up the work of each person involved in the process was already known in the ancient world. The Greek philosophers Aristotle, Plato, and Xenophon all mention the division of labour, and the Romans honed it to perfection. The Latin language has more than 500 expressions for different crafts and trades.[9] The advantages of the division of labour were also recognised early in other parts of the world. In Imperial China, more than 70 steps were required to produce the famous porcelain, and each job was carried out by specially trained craftsmen.[10] But it never took on an industrial scale. Just like the Ancient Romans, the Chinese never progressed beyond handiwork and craftsmanship.[11]

Nor can market forces explain why England's economy began to expand in the 18th century. Although capitalism is often described as 'the market economy', that phrase is misleading, because markets and trade networks have existed almost everywhere throughout history.[12] There were Turkish bazaars and Arabian souks, but they did not lead to industrial capitalism. Furthermore, Europe in particular was divided into many tiny states, each of which erected trade barriers by imposing high tariffs and customs duties.[13] Trading was difficult rather than easy.

If it were the case that markets bring about wealth, then huge empires, especially, would have flourished. The Russian tsars, the Turkish Ottomans, the Moguls of India, and the Qing Dynasty in China ruled over vast territories with barely any tariffs on trade.[14] Nonetheless, the economies of those empires stagnated, and famines were a regular occurrence. In the 18th century, China had a population of around 300 million, compared to just seven million in the United Kingdom. Despite that difference, it was on the tiny island that the first industrial machines were developed.

It is often stressed that Britain developed an efficient banking system early. And that is true. But those banks were not involved in financing the first factories.[15] As astonishing as it may sound, modern capitalism barely required any capital at the beginning. The earliest machines were so small and cheap that textile manufacturers were able to borrow the necessary funds from family and friends. The later socialist Robert Owen, for example, set up his factory in Manchester with just £100, which he had borrowed from his brother.[16] So a lack of funding cannot have been the reason for the failure of other nations to industrialise as early as England did.

Incidentally, the British also did not possess any special knowledge. Seventeenth-century Europe saw many groundbreaking discoveries in fields such as astronomy, mechanics, and optics, but that 'scientific revolution' was not limited to England. It resulted from the work of researchers across the European continent — from Galileo Galilei in Italy to Otto von Guericke in Magdeburg. Nor did those new scientific discoveries play any part at all in the establishment of the first factories. The early textile machines were not built by scientists, but, for the most part, by craftsmen who could barely read and write. These men kept tinkering with their inventions until they eventually worked as required.

The major milestones of the Industrial Revolution may be summarised as follows: In 1733, the inventor John Kay patented his 'flying shuttle'. This shuttle was still designed for use with handlooms, but it allowed the production of much broader textiles while requiring only one weaver to operate the loom. This sped up the weaving process to such an extent that the spinners who produced the yarn to be woven could no longer keep up with demand. That prompted the handweaver James Hargreaves to invent his 'spinning jenny' in 1764. The initial model had eight spindles, already making it three times more productive than traditional spinning wheels.[17] The real breakthrough followed shortly after. In 1769, the wigmaker Richard Arkwright designed his 'water frame', so called because it was driven by a waterwheel. Two unskilled labourers were now enough to supervise the machine's 96 spindles. In 1779, a weaver called Samuel Crompton combined the two machines to create the 'spinning mule', which was able to produce perfect, ultrafine cotton yarn.[18]

These inventors of those new machines were not born into the families of textile magnates. John Kay was the son of a wool manufacturer and ran his father's business from an early age, but the other inventors came from very poor backgrounds. The handweaver James Hargreaves probably never attended school, and was illiterate, but he had 13 children to support. His first 'spinning jenny' was built using a pocketknife.[19] Samuel Crompton's father died when he was a boy, and Samuel had to start work as a cotton spinner at the age of five. However, he does appear to have attended school, at least occasionally, where he is said to have particularly excelled in mathematics.[20] It is not known whether Richard Arkwright was able to read. What is known is that he was the youngest of seven siblings and that his parents did not have the means to send him to school. Despite his start in life, Arkwright eventually built a textile empire, and his descendants became the richest commoners in the British kingdom.[21]

Those textile machines could theoretically have been invented in antiquity, as the early inventions 'were not based on much more science than Archimedes knew'.[22] The English were not even the first to invent spinning machines. In China as early as 1313, Wang Zhen described a 'machine for the spinning of hemp thread' that was astonishingly similar to Hargreaves' spinning jenny and Arkwright's water frame.[23] However, that knowledge dissipated in China, and there was no progression beyond manual labour.

Why, then, was it English craftsmen who constructed the first machines? It might be expected that Austrian or Italian weavers could just as easily have pulled out their pocket knives and built new spinning machines, since they also possessed the necessary knowledge. The most convincing explanation is that industrialisation first took hold in England because it was the country with the highest wages in the world at that time. In the 18th century, English workers earned at least three times more than their counterparts on the European continent.[24] It was only because day labourers were so expensive that it became economically expedient to mechanise manufacturing processes and thereby reduce the number of workers required.

The first textile machines were small, unspectacular, and made of wood, but they also cost money to buy. Hargreaves' spinning jenny' was 70 times more expensive than a traditional spinning wheel. Using these machines was only profitable because it saved on high wage costs.[25] In other countries, where labour was much cheaper, the sums did not add up, as the economic historian Robert C. Allen calculates: 'In the 1780s, the rate of return to building an Arkwright mill was 40 per cent in England, 9 per cent in France, and less than 1 per cent in India. With investors expecting a 15 per cent return on fixed capital, it is no surprise that about 150 Arkwright mills were erected in Britain in the 1780s, four in France and none in India.'[26]

Those high wages were a reflection of the general prosperity that had taken hold in England even before the advent of industrialisation and which astonished visitors from the continent. In 1737, the Frenchman Jean-Bernard, Abbé Le Blanc, visited the island, and in his letters home he reported that English peasants enjoyed 'an abundance of all the commodities of life', and that even a farmhand 'takes tea before taking up the plough'—although tea was considered a luxury at the time. Le Blanc was also impressed by the elegant attire of country landowners. He described them 'wearing a frock-coat in winter', and their wives and daughters as being 'shod and hatted like [women] of property'.[27] A Spanish ambassador is said to have remarked in 1778 about the markets of London that 'more meat is sold in a month than is eaten in the whole of Spain during a year'.[28]

Those personal impressions are supported by solid figures from the time showing the level of prosperity, since the British had already begun to keep records of income

levels in different parts of the country. The income of a
40-year-old gardener with a wife and four young children
in 1797 is one of those recorded, for example. He earned
around 30 pence a day,[29] and that average wage was enough
to feed his family very well, with wheat bread, cheese, half
a pound of meat, tea, sugar, and a pint of beer on the menu
every day. The family could afford to buy new shoes and
clothes, and to send the two eldest children to school. They
lived in a house with a garden that was heated with coal in
the winter.[30]

Later calculations showed that workers in London at
that time consumed 2,500 calories a day, with a daily protein
intake of 112 grams. That was more protein than necessary
for a healthy diet. According to the current World Health
Organization (WHO) recommendations, one-third as much
would have been enough.[31]

Workers had it better there than anywhere else at the
time. In Italy or India, for example, workers consumed 1,900
calories per day, which was not enough to sustain a full day's
physical labour. In France, too, many people were undernourished and were forced to eat the same gruel day in and
day out. An estimated 20 per cent of the French population
were too weak to complete anything more than three hours
of light work at most.[32]

The relative wealth of the English was also reflected in
their height. The average height of British soldiers in the
late 18th century was around 172 cm. That compared to
just 165 cm in France, and a scanty 162 cm in Italy and
Austria.[33]

But what made the English so prosperous even before the
advent of industrialisation? That's a long story that includes,
among many other things, the plague, sheep, international
trade, a revolution, and coal.

It all begun with the 'Black Death'—the plague that reached Europe in 1347 and killed around a third of the population within four years. And that wasn't the end of the pandemic, as the plague returned several times. England alone saw further serious outbreaks in 1361–62, 1369, 1471, and 1479–80, each of which claimed the lives of up to 20 per cent of the population. The plague struck one last time in London in 1665–66, where it hit the poorer sections of society hardest, as noted in contemporary sources. The merchant and author Daniel Defoe cheerfully wrote that the Great Plague of London was a 'Deliverance in its Kind' as it 'carried off in that Time ... these very People, which had they been left, would certainly have been an unsufferable Burden, by their Poverty.'[34]

The decimation of the lower classes by repeated waves of the plague had its price. Labourers were suddenly in short supply, causing wages to rise significantly, and effectively ending serfdom. From around the year 1400, English peasants were no longer bound to their feudal lord, completely without rights. The feudal system was replaced by one of long-term contracts for land use with fixed rents. As a result, tenants were able to keep any additional yield resulting from investing more in the land, rather than the surplus being claimed by their landlord. That legal security was unique in Europe. Leaseholder tenants became farming businesses with an interest in maximising their profits.[35]

Every new discovery was utilised. The tenant farmers immediately abandoned the medieval three-field system when a better form of crop rotation was discovered in the 18th century. The old system meant each field lay fallow every third year to allow it to recover after a year of growing winter grain and a year of growing summer crops. Now farmers realised there was no need for that fallow year, as the third field could be used to grow clover or turnips.

From our modern vantage point, the new crop rotation system seems simple, but it was a revolutionary breakthrough in a world that had previously always struggled with two absolute limitations: insufficient grain to feed everyone, and a lack of enough fodder to maintain the pack and draught animals on which everyone relied. The new crop rotation system instantly solved both problems. The clover and turnips it produced meant, for the first time, people could keep enough horses to plough every field. The topsoil could be turned over more deeply, which resulted in far better grain yields. Cows were a source not only of meat and milk, but also of manure, which was used to fertilise the grainfields, further increasing crop yields.

New products also became important — wool, for example. The plague had left the countryside depopulated, so less land was required to feed the people. Land that had once been used to grow crops could now be turned over to sheep grazing. English woollens became a much-sought-after luxury commodity, accounting for almost 70 per cent of Britain's exports in the late 17th century.[36] Thus, there was already a thriving textile industry in England before the introduction of machinery and the increase in profitability it brought.

Initially, those developments do not appear to have been peculiar to Britain. Wages also rose in the rest of Europe after the plague decimated the workforce. However, pay did not remain high in most countries, where real wages fell as soon as the population increased again. This was because more people meant more demand for scarce goods, which left each individual poorer. England was the only place to escape that demographic trap. There, the population grew — but so did average wages.

This astonishing phenomenon was thanks, in no small measure, to European maritime trade and the fact that London was its hub. England was a small country, but London was the biggest city in Europe. Its population already numbered 500,000 in 1700, which grew to almost one million over the next century.[37] London's rise was no accident; it was fought for and won in military battles. The British waged four wars against the Netherlands alone over exclusive control of trade in Europe. They also fought the French repeatedly, eventually taking control of almost all of France's North American colonies.

The United Kingdom was a highly successful military state—not least because it was governed by a parliament. The 'Glorious Revolution' of 1688 curbed the absolute power of the monarch and gave members of parliament the right to decide on matters of taxation and the right to refuse to finance wars. Those concessions are often seen as a reduction in the influence of the state and crown, but in fact the opposite was true. Precisely because of the existence of parliamentary control, the importance of the state grew in England.

After 1688, raising taxes to equip the army and the navy was no longer a problem, since only the top 3 to 5 per cent of the male population were eligible to vote. This meant parliament was filled almost exclusively with noblemen and rich merchants. They were well aware of the fact that it was in their interest to gain victories in the endless wars in Europe. And they knew that those who ruled the waves would also control the global markets.[38]

England's tax revenues grew rapidly. From 1665 to 1800 they rose from 3.4 to at least 12.9 per cent of economic output. In France in 1788, by contrast, tax revenues amounted to just 6.8 per cent of gross domestic product.[39] The result is well known. Tiny England won every war it fought against a much larger France, which had twice as many inhabitants at the time.

Those taxes were mainly paid by the lower classes, since the British army and navy were largely financed through indirect duties on the consumption of beer, sugar, and tobacco. This was a result of the fact that most parliamentarians were members of the nobility and the rest of the population had no means of resistance. However, although British workers had to pay duties on consumer products, they still lived far better than their European neighbours—precisely because their wages were significantly higher.

Foreign visitors were amazed that Britain was able to compete with the rest of Europe, although its day labourers were so expensive to hire. Travelling to England in the late 18th century, the head of the French glass manufacturer Saint-Gobain stated that the British would never be able to manufacture cheap plate glass as his company could: 'Our French eat soup with a little butter and vegetables ... Your Englishmen eat meat, and a great deal of it, and they drink beer continually in such a fashion that an Englishman spends three times more than a Frenchman.'

But the Saint-Gobain boss was wrong. The British could afford to pay those higher wages because they had access to cheap coal, while the French had to rely on wood as their fuel. The energy costs in the glassworks of England were one-sixth of those in equivalent French companies.[40]

Coal was a rare commodity in Europe at that time, as many deposits had not yet been discovered. Germany's Ruhr Valley was one such site. Until 1851, the Prussians believed their country was poor in natural resources. It was not until they managed to penetrate the upper marlstone layers and dig deeper that they discovered rich coal seams.[41] In northern

England, on the other hand, the coal deposits lay directly beneath the surface and close to the shore, meaning the fuel could be shipped cheaply. As early as 1600, England experienced a 'coal revolution' in which wood was replaced as fuel. Long before the advent of industrialisation, coal was already being used in energy-intensive trades. It was used to extract salt from seawater, to refine sugar, brew beer, bake bread, blow glass, make bricks, produce tiles, and heat dwellings.[42]

The English fully recognised that the coalmines around Newcastle represented a form of wealth comparable to the silver treasures of the Spanish colonial empire. The poet John Cleveland quipped, slightly ironically, in 1650:

England's a perfect world, hath Indies too,
Correct your maps, Newcastle is Peru.[43]

England had both the most expensive labour and the cheapest energy. This combination was unique in the world, and it explains why the Industrial Revolution began there. Only in England was it profitable to replace people with machines.[44]

Britain produced only 20 million yards of printed cotton fabrics in 1769, but by 1830 that had grown to 350 million yards: enough to encircle the globe seven times at the equator. Even dishcloths were made of cotton, which was a uniquely versatile fabric, equally useful for making durable work trousers and delicate ballgowns. Cotton was also easily printed with bright designs, whereas wool had always appeared somewhat dull in colour. Most importantly, however, cotton was comparatively cheap, so many people were now able to afford more than just one shirt. In 1800, there were already 14 different women's magazines on the English market with detailed reports on the latest fashions.[45]

Initially, only a small minority profited from this new boom, while many people in Britain actually fared worse. High wages had triggered the advent of industrialisation, but the living standard of the masses fell again in the 19th century. This strange phenomenon entered the economic history books as the 'early growth paradox'. The British economy grew richer, but workers grew poorer. Weaving and spinning had been skilled, specialised crafts, but the new factories meant those artisans were no longer needed. The repetitive work operating the machines could be carried out by untrained women and children, who were paid a starvation wage.

Working conditions in the new factories were often appalling, as documented even by the conservative press. Bourgeois sources were so full of lamentations of the hardship suffered by workers that Karl Marx was able to fill page after page with them in his most important work, *Capital*. He took one gruesome example from the pages of the *Daily Telegraph* of 17 January 1860:

> Mr Broughton Charlton, county magistrate, declared, as chairman of a meeting held at the Assembly Rooms, Nottingham, on the 14th January, 1860, that there was an amount of privation and suffering among that portion of the population connected with the lace trade, unknown in other parts of the kingdom, indeed, in the civilised world... Children of nine or ten years are dragged from their squalid beds at two, three, or four o'clock in the morning and compelled to work for a bare subsistence until ten, eleven, or twelve at night, their limbs wearing away, their frames dwindling, their faces whitening, and their humanity absolutely sinking into a stone-like torpor, utterly horrible to contemplate ...[46]

Many children died before reaching adulthood, which even liberal politicians found scandalous. Marx quotes with relish a speech made by Joseph Chamberlain, who was mayor of Birmingham at the time and later rose to become one of Britain's leading political figures:

> Dr Lee, Medical Officer of Health for Manchester, stated that the average age at death of the Manchester … upper middle class was 38 years, while the average age at death of the labouring class was 17; while at Liverpool those figures were represented as 35 against 15. It thus appeared that the well-to-do classes had a lease of life which was more than double the value of that which fell to the lot of the less favoured citizens.'[47]

This quote from 1875 is interesting not only for its social criticism. From our present perspective, it is also striking how self-evident it was for Marx and Chamberlain that even privileged people could also only expect to live an average of 35 to 38 years.[48]

Industrialisation began in the textile factories, but its significance was initially quite modest. Cotton fabric production accounted for only around 8 per cent of economic output in Britain in 1830,[49] and most of the early machines were water-powered. This technological progress had not yet reached other branches of industry, and perhaps the Industrial Revolution might have ended as soon as it began if it had remained restricted to the textile industry. But, at the same time as it was taking shape, another groundbreaking development was taking place: Great Britain discovered steam power.

CHAPTER THREE

Essential energy: capitalism goes fossil

The amount of coal burned in Britain increased steadily from the 16th century onwards. It was used to fuel salt extraction, beer brewing, domestic heating, and brickmaking. However, this 'coal revolution' did nothing to change the *way* the mineral was used. It was still basically just a source of heat and warmth. It was not until the advent of steam power that coal was used to produce kinetic energy and drive machinery. That technological advance fundamentally changed the world.

Steam power was initially only used to pump water out of coalmines. The deeper the mines went, the more they would fill with groundwater, until horse-powered pumps were no longer sufficient to transport the unwanted water to the surface. Once again, it was a tradesman who built the first functioning machine: ironmonger Thomas Newcomen.[1] He lived in the quiet port town of Dartmouth, where he was also a lay preacher in the Baptist church. Newcomen spent ten years perfecting his steam engine, finally installing the first model in a coalmine in Dudley in 1712.

The machine was a technological miracle, as it turned

air into money. It used the weight of the atmosphere to transport water out of the ground.[2] Essentially, the core of Newcomen's invention consisted of an open metal cylinder in which water was heated to push a piston upwards. The subsequent addition of cold water caused the steam to condense, creating a vacuum as it did so. Atmospheric pressure forced the piston back down into the vacuum, which is why the first such steam engines were known as 'atmospheric engines'. A wooden beam attached to the piston rocked on a central fulcrum, and its up-and-down motion drove the water pump.

This technical masterpiece had just one single, but crucial drawback: Newcomen's engine required huge amounts of energy to create the steam and recondense it. Twenty kilograms of coal were required to produce just one horsepower (HP).[3] This meant that the machine was only profitable when it was used in mines that produced enough otherwise-unsaleable coal rubble to power it.

Newcomen's steam engine was far too expensive for use beyond the coalmining industry, which was particularly bitter for the tin and copper mines of Cornwall. They also needed to be pumped free of mine water, but their nearest coal deposits were located in Wales. The difficulty and expense of transporting coal from there immediately spurred attempts to make steam power more efficient.

And that was accomplished with astonishing success. Over the following 150 years, engineers managed to reduce the coal consumption of such machines to around one pound per horsepower.[4] 'Energy conservation' is not a new idea that only emerged as a way to combat climate change. The capitalist system has always relied on technological progress to increase energy efficiency. However, this did not result in less energy being consumed. Quite the opposite, in fact. As machines became increasingly efficient, their use spread rapidly—resulting in an overall increase in energy use, despite the fact that each individual machine required less energy to run. This paradox, known as the 'rebound effect', was apparent even in the steam age. From 1830 onwards, steam power became so cheap that it was profitable to use it in the textile industry, where waterpower had previously been the principal energy provider.

At the same time, a completely new coal-consuming technology was emerging: the railways. It was another technological revolution; contemporary figures and historians alike have tried to put into words the impact this invention had on the world. It is perhaps best summed up by the French poet and philosopher Paul Valéry, who did so in just one sentence: 'Napoleon moved no faster than Julius Caesar.'[5] Now, however, Europeans were whizzing across their continent on trains. Just before the outbreak of World War I, trains travelled at an average speed of 90 kilometres per hour.

The history of the railways also begins with the coalmines. An age-old problem had always been finding a way to convey the mined coal to the nearest river or canal for transportation. Horse-drawn, track-bound trolleys were introduced very early on. The tracks were initially made of wood. Later, in the 18th century, iron was used. However, the breakthrough came with the invention of steam power. It soon became obvious that it could also be used to pull those coal trolleys.

The first real railway route was opened in 1825. It connected the Durham coalfield with the coast. The Stockton-to-Darlington line was initially intended to transport coal and grain, but it was soon realised that transporting passengers was a lucrative source of money. This sparked a 'railway mania', with much speculative investment in the technology on the stock markets. By 1850, £240 million had been invested in an increasingly large number of railway lines. That was an enormous amount, considering the fact that Britain's entire economic output was £572 million in the same year.[6] However, coming up with the necessary financial resources was never a problem, since money emerges 'from nothing'. (See chapter 7 for more.)

The railways changed the nature of capitalism. Unlike in the textile industry, capital was now required, and it was needed in unprecedented amounts. Not only railways were being built, but also the necessary engineering works, more coalmines, and large new cities.

With the advent of steam power, capitalism went fossil. Without coal there would be no capitalism today. Timber resources from forests would never have been sufficient to fuel all the machines and the constant growth. A hypothetical calculation shows that as early as 1850, it would have taken forests covering one and a half times the area of Britain to provide the amount of energy consumed in the country—which is a physical impossibility, of course. Today, Europe consumes more than 20 times the energy that could be provided by a forest covering the entire surface area of the continent.[7]

Steam power was invented without a real understanding of how it functioned. The proper theory of steam engines was only developed *ex post facto* by the Frenchman Carnot in the 1820s, notes the British historian Eric Hobsbawm.[8] Its significance also went unrecognised for a long time. The famous economist Adam Smith found the first steam engines so silly that he believed an important part of this invention to be the work of children. In 1776, he wrote in his most important work, *The Wealth of Nations*:

In the first fire engines, a boy was constantly employed
to open and shut alternately the communication between
the boiler and the cylinder, according as the piston either
ascended or descended. One of those boys, who loved to
play with his companions, observed that, by tying a string
from the handle of the valve which opened this communication to another part of the machine, the valve would
open and shut without his assistance, and leave him at
liberty to divert himself with his play-fellows.

That clever idea of connecting the valves is still one of
the most famous examples of automation—and Smith dismissed it as child's play.[9]

Smith should really have recognised the potential of
steam power, since he was personally acquainted with the
inventor James Watt. Smith took up a position as Professor
of Philosophy in Glasgow in 1715, but he also ran the university administration at the same time. He provided the
21-year-old Watt with a workshop to maintain and repair
the university's scientific equipment.[10] It was in this laboratory that Watt began his experiments aimed at optimising
Newcomen's steam engine.

Watt and Smith also had a mutual close friend in
the chemist Joseph Black, who entered the scientific
history books for, among other things, discovering carbon
dioxide—without of course realising that this gas would later
be responsible for climate change.[11] In hindsight, it seems
positively emblematic that Watt, Smith, and Black were so
well acquainted, since they not only became the founding
fathers of their respective disciplines, but also worked on
precisely those phenomena that form the core of modern
capitalism: fossil-fuelled technology, economic growth, and
greenhouse gas emissions.

Those personal encounters never coalesced into an overall picture. Technology was irrelevant to Adam Smith when he attempted to explain the wealth of nations. And he was not alone. The process of industrialisation was so modest in its early stages that it was simply ignored or underestimated by contemporary figures. After witnessing the first steam locomotives in 1828, the French economist Jean-Baptiste Say predicted that 'no machine will ever be able to perform what even the worst horse can—the service of carrying people and goods through the bustle and throng of a great city'.[12]

Capitalism was neither planned nor predicted. It developed out of the desire of some textile manufacturers and mine owners to become more efficient and more competitive. They did not intend to spark an Industrial Revolution; they were simply concerned with maximising their own profits.

In the 18th century, people had no vision of a technological Modern Age. The classical world was still their great role model. They were not interested in the future, but rather the past, as the curriculum at the elite private school Eton from that time shows. Of the 27 lessons per week, only three were dedicated to writing and arithmetic, three were devoted to religious education, and the remaining 21 were spent learning Latin, Ancient Greek, and classical history.[13]

Capitalism was an unintended development in Britain. Machines were only invented and employed because labour was so expensive. However, its consequences were enormous, as they included the widespread exploitation of fossil-fuel deposits. At first only coal was burned, later to be joined by gas and oil. Humankind realised it had a kind of natural battery at its disposal—solar energy stored over millions of years. Humans tapped into the plant remains of the past and broke the boundaries of the present. Since time immemorial, humans had been forced to restrict their consumption of resources to the amount made available by nature. That 'organic age' now ended, to be replaced by the 'fossil-fuel age'.

Fossil fuels are extremely practical: they are abundant, easy to extract and transport, available 24 hours a day, and simple to use. For the first time in their history, humans began producing a surfeit of energy, which made prosperity and liberty possible.[14] For a long time, the downside seemed irrelevant: burning one kilogram of carbon produces 3.7 kilograms of carbon dioxide, and unfortunately that natural law of chemistry is unchangeable.[15]

The British were the first to profit from the use of fossil fuels, as their per-capita income doubled between 1770 and 1870. However, that new wealth was distributed extremely unequally, as workers' real wages lagged far behind the profits raked in by factory owners, rising only by 30 per cent.[16] Nonetheless, the fact that even the lowest stratum of society could now afford more than the bare necessities was a momentous development. That mass purchasing power changed capitalism forever as it created the modern consumer society.

Modern capitalism is unthinkable without mass consumption, as consumer goods now account for almost 80 per cent of economic performance. If real wages had never risen, capitalism would have been finished by the 19th century and would probably have developed no further than the railways. It was the massive demand from workers that made new products and new impulses for growth possible, such as would never have developed as a consequence of the lifestyles of the wealthy alone. In the words of Hobsbawm, 'It was the Ford Model T and not Rolls Royce which revolutionised the motor industry.'[17]

Capitalism first arose in Great Britain, but it had consequences for the entire planet. All around the globe, it produced winners—and losers.

CHAPTER FOUR

Every country was suddenly a 'developing country'

It hit Indian workers first. Their cotton fabrics were soon unable to compete globally, as British spinning machines were constantly improved. By 1825, mechanised production was 16 times faster than in 1780. English textiles became so cheap that it was unprofitable even for the very poorest Indian women to spin cotton yarn.[1] India had been famed for its soft, light fabrics since antiquity, but nothing now remained of that traditional industry. Within the space of a few years, India regressed from being a highly developed country to a purely agrarian state only able to export raw cotton and rice to England.

India was caught in a paradox. Wages were low, and that was precisely why the country grew poorer. With labour costs so low, it was simply not worth buying expensive machinery. European states struggled with the same vicious circle because of their low wages. Britain's industrialisation suddenly turned all other nations into 'developing countries' that were automatically left behind, because buying expensive technology was not profitable for them.

There was no lack of knowledge or a will to catch up.

Competing European powers saw the unprecedented developments in Britain and tried to emulate this 'English miracle'. German princes immediately dispatched industrial spies to the island, and financed entrepreneurs who were prepared to copy the English machines. They shamelessly embraced the principle of plagiarism, and Germany's early capitalists admitted it openly. Prussia's first mechanised cotton spinning mill was established in Ratingen, near Düsseldorf, in 1738. It was cunningly named 'Cromford', after the English village where Richard Arkwright opened his first factory. The mill contained exact replicas of Arkwright's 'water frames', although the British had done everything they could to prevent their European competitors from stealing their ideas.[2]

But Prussia's Cromford was not economically successful, precisely because mechanisation was not profitable amid Germany's low wages.[3] Instead, large parts of Germany found it was more lucrative to supply booming England with agricultural produce—and otherwise continue to rely on manual labour rather than developing an industry of its own. Until well into the 19th century, Germany's role was similar to India's in this respect—primarily as a supplier of raw materials to the British.[4]

The Swiss, too, were not quick to adopt industrialisation, although their own cotton industry was even older than the British factories. After lengthy debates, the Swiss concluded that purchasing machinery would not be economically worthwhile, and that it would be cheaper to continue to rely on manual labour.[5]

Of all the countries around the globe, there was only one that was soon able to keep pace with the British. That was the US. In the 'industrial states' of the north, copying and using British machinery was profitable from the outset, since labour costs were very high there. Unlike in the southern states, there were barely any slaves in the north. The workers were free immigrants from Europe who had to be recruited into jobs by high wage offers. Rather than toiling away in companies, they could also choose to move at any time to the countryside and set up a farm of their own. Available farmland was plentiful until well into the 19th century, which drove up wages in the city.[6]

Such considerations of course ignored the fact that those lands only *appeared* to be ownerless. They were available for European immigrants to settle solely because the indigenous people who originally populated them had been driven away or wiped out completely. (For more on this, see chapter 6.)

Although the northern US states industrialised immediately, they were initially just imitating Britain and so lagged behind. They needed to find their own way of asserting themselves against their superior British competitors. Their strategy was to seal themselves off rigorously from the outside world. High import duties of 35 to 50 per cent ensured that British goods were overly expensive on the American market. The motto was protectionism, not free trade.[7] Those high US tariffs remained in place until World War II, and only began to fall consistently from the 1950s onwards. So it is a little disingenuous of the US to present itself now as the self-appointed chief advocate of free trade. The US did not remove its tariffs until it had grown into the undisputed economic superpower it is today.

Incidentally, this is a pattern that repeats itself all the time. Free trade is a concern of the powerful. Import tariffs are never voluntarily removed until a country becomes a world-leading economy that no longer has to fear foreign competition.[8]

The US became a model for other countries hoping to catch up with Britain's technological advances. Germans, who at the time lived in 38 different small states, also took inspiration from there. Twenty-two of those states joined together in 1834 to form the German *Zollverein*, or customs union. Their aim was to create a similarly uniform market to that in the US, and to close it off to trade from the outside world. However, its success was modest. It made the flow of goods easier, but production did not rise.[9] Once again, this showed that a market alone is not enough to drive growth. For that to happen, it also has to be economically advantageous to employ technology. But steam power was initially not profitable at all in Germany, as is shown by some very meticulous calculations from the time. In most areas of Germany, using machines was almost twice as expensive as using horses, which was partly due to the fact that coal had to be carted laboriously overland.[10]

Things did not pick up for Germany until the invention of the railways. The first line was built in 1835, and ran for six kilometres from Nuremburg to Fürth. The Franconians (the people in that part of Germany) copied the English within just a few years — although the locomotive they used was British, as was the first train driver. The railways revolutionised the steel and engineering industries. Until that time, Germany's ironworking industry had seen little technological progress since the late Middle Ages. In 1835, 95 per cent of Germany's pig iron was produced using charcoal as a fuel, while only 4.5 per cent came from modern coke blast furnaces. Initially therefore, every railway project threatened to push Germany's industry to the limits of its capacity. The line from Dresden to Leipzig was built in 1837, requiring 5,650 tonnes of coke-produced pig iron for the tracks. That represented more than 90 per cent of Prussia's annual production at the time. Not a single German factory was able to deliver that material, nor was any capable of delivering well-produced railway tracks.[11]

At first, everything had to be imported from England: pig iron, tracks, and locomotives. However, Germany managed astonishingly quickly to replace those imports with domestically produced items. While only 10 per cent of Germany's railway tracks were produced domestically in 1834, that proportion had grown to 58 per cent by 1854, and as much as 85 per cent by 1863. German locomotive production expanded equally rapidly. In 1853, the Prussian railways purchased 105 new locomotives, of which 99 were German-built.[12] Soon, Germany was exporting locomotive engines.[13] Not everyone at the time was enthusiastic about this new age. On opening the line between Berlin and Potsdam in 1838, King Frederick William III was heard to grumble, 'Everything is expected to career ahead, but calm and comfort suffer from it. Can't see much of a blessing in being in Berlin or Potsdam a couple of hours earlier.'[14]

As in England, capitalism in Germany began with almost no capital. The cost of setting up a spinning or weaving mill, for example, or a dye works, was between 15,000 and 50,000 Prussian thalers. Even iron and machine works could be established with little more than 50,000 to 70,000 thalers. Those whose personal fortunes did not stretch to that could turn to their extended families.[15] The electrical engineering company Siemens & Halske, which was later to become so well-known, was a typical example. The seed capital came from a cousin of the founder, Werner von Siemens, and the company's first employee was his brother of his.[16]

The 'family financing model' did not work in the case

of the railways, which devoured millions. But, just like in England, raising the necessary capital was no problem; indeed, the railway companies were positively showered with funds.[17] This once again showed that money is never in short supply; it is always plentiful. Soon, investors began to complain that they could no longer find profitable investment opportunities. In 1851, for example, the Bielefeld Chamber of Commerce stated, 'Our banks are groaning under the burden of moneys offered to them for an interest-bearing allocation of 2 per cent.'[18]

The construction of the railways necessitated an expansion of the steel industry, which saw huge leaps in efficiency when the British inventor Henry Bessemer patented a new process in 1856. Without getting into too much technical detail, the Bessemer process meant as much steel could be produced in 20 minutes as would previously have taken 24 hours to manufacture.[19] That enormous productivity changed not just the steel industry, but capitalism as a whole. It launched the era of large business corporations. That is because the introduction of the Bessemer process increased investment costs so quickly that only large companies could raise the necessary funds. It also meant that each blast furnace was able to produce considerably more steel, which in turn meant that rolling mills also had to be expanded.[20] Huge conglomerates emerged, which squeezed all competitors out of the market that were not able to expand at the same rate.

Furthermore, the few corporations that remained banded together to form cartels. In the period between 1879 and 1886 alone, the number of cartels that emerged in Germany was probably around 90, most of which were price-fixing cartels.[21] From the companies' point of view, those close agreements were rational, or even necessary. Their investment costs were extremely high, and they needed to ensure their sales and revenues added up. Unrestricted competition would have had a very negative impact on prices and driven companies into bankruptcy. That was the first emergence of the paradox that still characterises capitalism today: investments are only ventured when risk can be largely ruled out.

The steel industry was far from being the only sector in which cartels were formed. The 'Rhenish-Westphalian Coal Syndicate' is a particularly infamous example. Its members sold 90 per cent of all the coal from the Ruhr region at uniform prices in Germany and on the world markets. This price fixing was not clandestine, and was even placed under legal protection by the Supreme Court of the German Reich in 1897.[22] Germany soon had more cartels than any other country, reaching an estimated 3,000 by the start of World War I.[23] Companies had also discovered another strategy to increase their market power: mergers.

Jumping briefly to the present, we see this trend continuing today. Companies grow bigger and bigger to avoid competition as much as possible. Although cartels are now forbidden, Germany's industry is extremely concentrated, as can be seen from one single, dry figure that appeared in the government's latest Statistical Yearbook: large corporations make up only 0.7 of companies in Germany, but they account for more than 66.2 per cent of total sales.[24]

Returning to the early years: the age of plagiarism, in which Germany mostly copied other countries' innovations, came to an end around the year 1880, when German companies began marketing their own technological developments. They had particular success in the chemical industry, in which a way was found to 'turn dirt into gold' with the invention of a process for transforming coal tar into brilliant aniline dyes. Until then, coal tar had simply been an inconvenient waste product from coking plants. This discovery transformed it into a valuable raw material.[25] Recycling and the utilisation of industrial residues are not new ideas; indeed, they are as old as capitalism itself.

Coal was now more than just fuel; it became the basic object of study in organic chemistry, which resulted in entirely new products and even new branches of industry. That included the pharmaceutical industry, which began producing medicines that were chemically very similar to coal tar dyes. The most famous result of that research was the painkiller aspirin.[26]

Enthusiastic patients believed the pharmaceutical companies carried out meticulous research according to the principles of science. After all, their advertisements often featured chemists in white lab coats. The truth was a little less impressive: their drugs were the result of a more or less random process of trial and error. Scientific analysis came much, much later. The same was true in the textile industry. Scientists had no idea why the dyes remained fixed to the fabrics — but that did not impede their use. Similarly, until the 1920s, steel producers also had little idea of the chemical processes taking place inside their furnaces and rolling mills.[27]

Methods in the electronics industry were similarly cavalier. The Siemens brothers engaged in what they called 'invention speculation'.[28] They did not set up a laboratory until 1873, long after the company had already matured into a large corporation. Siemens was still among the pioneers, however, since the only other companies to have their own laboratories at the time were the steel producer Krupp and the optics manufacturer Carl Zeiss.[29] Many companies realised that doing systematic science did not pay. For example, the Bayer dye factory in Elberfeld employed a number of chemists in the 1860s, only to lay them off soon after because they 'didn't invent anything new'.[30] Tinkering and trial and error remained the predominant research methods.[31]

By the start of World War I, German companies had overtaken their British competitors and were second in the world only to the US, which was the undisputed world leader. However, those superlatives obscure the fact that industrial corporations were still far from dominating the entire economy. German exports were rather rustic in nature, consisting mainly of beer, stockings, ironmongery, cutlery, musical instruments, salt, sugar, toys, woollens, and pharmaceutical goods.[32] German Christmas was also among the country's successful exports. Once the idea had spread abroad that a decorated fir tree in the living-room was an essential part of the festivities, hand-carved Christmas tree decorations from the Ore Mountains were in great demand.[33]

In today's parlance, Germany at the time was an 'emerging economy'. There were global corporations like Siemens, Krupp, and Bayer, for example, but they existed side by side with millions of farmers, most of whom led a very traditional existence.[34] The British economic historian Adam Tooze calculates that in 1933, around 12 million Germans still lived on farms that were too small to provide an adequate standard of living. That was 18 per cent of the total population at the time.[35]

Before World War II, per-capita income in Germany was approximately the same as it is today in South Africa, Iran, or Tunisia, for example. However, living conditions in those countries are better, insofar as the Global South benefits from the technological developments that have taken place since then. When needed, South Africa can import computers, cancer drugs, or modern aircraft—which was not available to Germany back then. Tooze therefore concludes that the comparison with South Africa is 'flattering to Germany's situation' up to World War II.[36]

Widespread prosperity did not reach Europe until 1950, when the entire continent began to experience an 'economic miracle'. Germans like to believe that only West Germany saw a massive economic upswing, but, in fact, all European countries recorded huge growth rates. Until 1973, the West German economy grew annually by 5 per cent per capita. But the same was also true of Austria and Italy, while Spain achieved 5.8 per cent.[37]

This boom was no 'miracle'. It was simply a process of catching up and bridging the technological gap that had opened up with the US due to the two world wars and the subsequent bouts of inflation.[38] Between 1914 and 1950, there was little per-capita growth in Europe, but when political stability was finally established, the economy was able to develop. Europeans were able to fulfil long-held dreams, buying themselves washing machines, fridges, television sets, cars, and holidays abroad.

The figures for car ownership show how great that divide had grown. In the US, there were already 204 passenger vehicles per 1,000 inhabitants in 1928. By contrast, one year earlier there were only 5,474 automobiles in entire metropolitan area of Munich.[39] It would take more than 40 years for West Germany to catch up.[40] When those gaps had been closed, the 'economic miracle' came to an end.

Germany did not become a truly industrialised nation until after World War II. By 1965, half of the country's employees were factory workers. However, it would be a mistake to look only at manufacturing. All other branches of industry were affected by technological advances, including the service and agricultural sectors. Banks, for example, replaced tellers with ATMs, and payment transactions are now handled by computers. The changes in agriculture are even more extreme: the sector now utilises more machines per human worker than heavy industries do. Tractors have replaced plough horses, and combine harvesters have made farmhands largely superfluous. Now a large farm can be run by just a small family.[41] The agricultural sector used to employ millions of people, but today there are only 287,000 people working full-time in agriculture.[42]

Between 1830 and 1970, Western Europeans managed to develop their own industries and catch up with Great Britain. But countries in other parts of the world still lagged; Peru, Malawi or Pakistan, for example, have still not managed to join the circle of wealthy states. Why is that? It is often assumed that the rich nations of the North are to blame for the Global South's lack of development. That's not entirely incorrect, but it is only part of the explanation.

CHAPTER FIVE

Left behind forever?
Why the Global South is barely
catching up

The situation the countries of the Global South currently find themselves in is reminiscent of that of Germany or France at the beginning of the 19th century, having to try to close the technological gap that separates them from the industrialised nations.

But the barriers seem to be insurmountable. Whether they are for the production of automobiles or high-quality medicines, the machines of the West require a huge amount of capital investment that poorer countries simply cannot afford. The Global South is caught in a vicious circle. Wages are so low that it is not profitable to invest in technology. But because productivity does not increase, those countries remain poor, and wages stay low.[1]

Bangladesh is a good example of this. About four million garment workers are employed in the country, sewing clothes for the West on electric sewing machines. These 21st-century workers are using a technology that was invented in Europe in the 19th century. Automated

51

textile-manufacturing machines could theoretically be installed in the factories. It is not a law of nature that jeans
must be tailored by hand. But those machines would be too
expensive because labour is so cheap in Bangladesh, where
the minimum wage is only $61 a month.[2] Some economists
believe, erroneously, that the textile industry is and needs to
be a labour-intensive sector that has been relocated to the
Global South.[3] In fact, the direct opposite is the case: the
garment industry does not use machines only because wages
in poor countries are so low.

The only way to escape this vicious circle is for the state
to intervene and manage the process of industrialisation centrally. Japan, Taiwan, South Korea, and China, for example,
are all places that managed to bridge that technological gap
within half a century, because their governments planned
and financed the enormous initial investments required.
The construction of power plants, blast furnaces, and car
factories was commissioned by the state. At the same time,
their governments erected customs barriers to protect their
own industries from Western products. People in Asia grew
prosperous in the 20th century by copying 19th-century
Western protectionism.

Thus, the relation between privately owned companies
and state planning changed. Initially, capitalism's development was exclusively private. The textile manufacturers
of England mechanised production to save on labour with
the simple aim of increasing their profits. But the longer
capitalism existed, and the further technology developed,
the more state control was necessary to make sure no one
was left behind in the race to catch up. Japan set up its
planning ministry, MITI, which soon gained legendary status as per-capita income rose in Japan by an annual 5.9 per
cent between 1950 and 1990.[4] Other states copied the idea:

Taiwan has its Industrial Technology Research Institute, Israel its Office of the Chief Scientist, and the planning body in Singapore is the Agency for Science, Technology and Research.[5]

However, it is becoming increasingly difficult for the Global South to catch up with the industrialised nations. Today's stragglers face a problem that did not exist for Germany or France 150 years ago: technological progress means factories have to become ever-bigger to remain profitable.

The automotive industry is a case in point. Producing cars is so expensive that it is only economically viable if a very large number of automobiles can be manufactured simultaneously and then sold to a huge market.[6] That puts China at a clear advantage, with its population of around 1.4 billion people. In such a situation, a country can still seal itself off from international markets to protect domestic companies against foreign competition. So China imposes high import duties, controls foreign-currency trading, and bans some imports altogether.

Smaller countries cannot isolate themselves to protect their manufacturing, because their internal markets are not large enough. They are in a catch-22 situation. They are reliant on worldwide trade to find buyers for their products. But at the same time, that very free trade favours the established industrialised countries that are technologically more advanced and so need not fear competition.

This is compounded by the fact that the gap between the industrialised nations and the Global South is growing increasingly wide. When Europeans were trying to catch up with Britain's economic progress in the 19th century, the technological gap between the richest and poorest countries was on a scale of four to one at most, as calculated by Ha-Joon Chang. The ratio between wealthy nations like the US and the poorest countries such as Malawi or Niger, for example, has now grown to around 60 to one. When it comes to economic productivity, the ratio is about five-to-one even for emerging economies such as Brazil.[7]

The technological gap was still small enough in the 19th century that Europeans just needed to wait until the price of British machines came down. In addition, imitators benefited from the fact that they were spared the many technological dead-ends that the pioneers in England had had to exclude laboriously by trial and error. When copying British inventions, the Americans, French, and Germans made immediate use of the most successful machines, bypassing various intermediate development stages.[8] However, that easy route is no longer open, because the technological gap is far too wide for the Global South to ever hope to leapfrog it by simply entering the competition at the same level as the West.

It does not follow from this that the Global South is stuck in the pre-industrial age. Capitalism shapes the entire world, and often has positive consequences even for poorer nations. Girls now attend school almost everywhere in the world,[9] almost all children are vaccinated against diseases such as polio and smallpox, and more than 90 per cent of the world's population have access to clean water.[10] Most inhabitants of the Earth now own a mobile phone with access to the entire world's stock of knowledge. The American progress optimist Andrew McAfee writes with enthusiasm: 'A Maasai warrior on a mobile phone in the middle of Kenya has better mobile communications than the president did twenty-five years ago. If he's on a smartphone using Google, he has access to more information than the US president did just fifteen years ago.'[11]

Poor countries can also develop and make impressive progress, as shown by Bangladesh, which became independent after a civil war with Pakistan in 1971. At that time, women gave birth to an average of seven children, life expectancy stood at just 52 years, and most of the population were illiterate. Today, almost every child completes primary school, and 60 per cent of both girls and boys attend secondary school. Life expectancy has risen to 74 years — and the average number of children per woman is now just two.[12]

The economic growth achieved by Bangladesh is also astonishing. It has remained consistently above 4 per cent per year since 1994, often even reaching more than 6 per cent. The country posted a plus of 3.8 per cent even during the Covid-19 pandemic. Bangladeshis are now more prosperous than their neighbours in India. Corruption is still widespread, but Bangladesh has got a lot of things right, investing systematically in healthcare, education, infrastructure, and women's rights.[13]

So the Global South *can* grow more prosperous — but it is almost impossible for it to catch up technologically or economically with the North. To return once more to the example of Bangladesh: its national income was the equivalent of US$5,307 per capita in 2020. In Germany, by comparison, that figure was $54,076, making Germans ten times more prosperous than Bangladeshis.[14]

It is a widely believed fallacy that the Global South simply needs more investment in education for broad-based industrialisation to then set in. Education is a human right, but knowledge alone is not enough for a country to develop an industrial economy on its own. Economic development must be approached as it is in China, where the state is in control and protects the domestic market so that its facto-ries are not crushed by international competition. But that option is only open to very large countries, because the latest technology requires huge factories and a large customer base. Even Bangladesh, with a current population of 166 million, is too small to rely on protectionism.[15]

Capitalism is thus a double-edged sword. Consumer goods spread across the world; cars, mobile phones, the internet, and sneakers are available around the globe. But that does not mean that such products are manufactured everywhere. A small number of countries supply the entire world. As the historian Jürgen Osterhammel once put it, 'It cannot be said that industrialisation is an "all-inclusive" global process analogous to the spread of television.'[16]

Europe and the US cannot help having been the first to industrialise, or that those lagging now find it so difficult to catch up. The very emergence of capitalism was a historical accident. However, the rich North is not completely blame-less in the fact that the Global South continues to remain so poor. There are strategies that could help developing countries. Two immediate measures would be particularly helpful.

The first measure is the introduction of a global mini-mum wage for export goods.[17] So far, the workers of the Global South have been mercilessly exploited, resulting in a situation where a T-shirt can cost as little as 2.70 euros in Germany. A price of at least ten euros would not be too much to expect German consumers to pay. That extra money would be enough to ensure that textile workers around the world earn enough to cover their basic living needs. The minimum wage would have to apply to all countries equally, so that Bangladesh could not be played off against Cambodia or Laos, for example. The necessary legislative instrument for this already exists. In June 2021, the German parliament passed the 'Supply Chain Due Diligence Act'. Under that law, German companies must ensure that any suppliers they use from the Global South maintain human rights and environmental standards. However, the law does not yet include the provision that a living wage must also be paid to workers.

The second measure would be to close down tax havens. It is still possible for those in power in the Global South to plunder their own countries and hide the stolen money away in the North. Malta, Cyprus, Switzerland, and Great Britain are just a few examples of rich countries that are glad to offer their services to help potentates steal from their subjects. This is compounded by the fact that international companies make huge sales in the Global South, but transfer the profits to their home countries in the North, rather than paying tax where the money is made.[18] This results in a shocking situation: the poor South is financing the rich North, although it should be the other way around. Some US$150–200 billion are given by the North in development aid per year, but a far greater amount of money flows out of poor countries to the prosperous nations because tax avoidance and tax planning are still allowed.[19]

Incidentally, the rich North would also benefit from an improvement in the situation of the Global South. When purchasing power increases around the world, even more goods can be exported.[20] Also in the North, technological progress is only profitable when there are customers everywhere who are in a position to buy many goods. Capitalism relies on mass consumption, and so the masses must be able to earn a proper wage.

Critics of capitalism are not convinced by this. They also believe that history is important, evoking slavery and colonial imperialism. They claim the industrialised nations are prosperous only because they have been able to reduce the rest of the world to nothing but suppliers of cheap raw materials. That sounds plausible, and is quite understandable from a moral point of view. But as an economic analysis it is irrelevant here.

CHAPTER SIX

Exploitation and war are not necessary – they are detrimental to capitalism

The belief that capitalism must categorically be based on exploitation might seem an obvious truth. The Industrial Revolution began in England at the same time as millions of slaves were being shipped from West Africa to North and South America. In addition, the southern states in the US were growing the very cotton that was being processed into textiles in Manchester and Cromford. So it seems logical to assume that the cruel practice of slavery was necessary for the Global North to grow rich.[1]

That chain of causality may appear straightforward, but the historical reality was more complex. Slavery is not a modern invention that arose along with capitalism. It is age-old. Slaves have existed since humans first adopted a sedentary lifestyle. Slavery was a pronounced feature of the Ancient Greek and Roman societies,[2] but there were also slaves in Hawaii, India, China, Korea, and among the Aztecs in Mexico and the Maori of New Zealand. Whoever happened to be dominant capitalised on their stronger position:

European Christians enslaved pagans, the Vikings raided continental Europeans, Russian nobles captured other Slavs and oppressed their own serfs.[3] North African pirates seized European fishermen, while, for their part, European seamen captured North African people.[4]

However, no other part of the world was as affected by human trafficking and slave trading as Africa. From the Middle Ages onwards, some ten million people from that continent were enslaved—long before the first Europeans arrived.[5] This trade in human beings was organised by Arabs, and there were several important slave-trading routes: across the Sahara from what is now Senegal to Morocco, as well as from today's Nigeria, Niger, and Chad to Libya and Egypt. Around four million people were forced across the desert this way. There were also slave-trading routes along the River Nile, with around two million slaves forced north that way. Approximately four million people from Egypt, Sudan, and Ethiopia were transported to the Arabian Peninsula or across the Indian Ocean to India.[6]

That slave trade was only possible because the people of sub-Saharan Africa were considered under Islam to be 'heathens' with no rights. The actual captures were not carried out by Arabs or Berbers themselves, but by members of the local population who sold the captives to caravan traders.[7] Africans hunted other Africans to sell them to foreign buyers—a system that Europeans later joined in with.[8]

So Africa was no paradise before the Portuguese, British, and others arrived.[9] Nonetheless, European slavery was scarcely comparable to traditional forms of the practice. In North and South America, trafficked people were mainly utilised for commercial gain on colonial plantations. From an economic point of view, this kind of slavery was structurally completely new. An estimated 11 million people were transported to the 'New World' between the 15th and 19th centuries. That's not counting the approximately 1.5 million who died during sea crossings.[10] The main slave-trading destination was Brazil, where 5.53 million abducted people went ashore. Some 1.2 million Africans were sold into slavery in Jamaica, 911,000 in Saint-Domingue (now Haiti), 890,000 in Cuba, and 608,000 in Barbados.[11]

North America, on the other hand, was not a particularly key destination for slave traders. Around 472,000 Africans were abducted to the US,[12] initially to be put to work mainly on tobacco and rice plantations.[13] Cotton farming was not significant at first, only increasing in importance in the 19th century, when the textile factories of England began producing more and more fabric.[14] Thus, it was not slavery that made industrialisation in England possible, but rather the opposite: it was the rise of capitalism in England that created a market for cotton fabrics.

Most enslaved people were exploited and denied their human rights for the sake of producing luxury goods that were in great demand but whose production was not industrialised. For example, five million slaves worked on the sugar plantations of South America and the Caribbean, and another two million laboured on coffee plantations. Two million were in domestic service, and around one million toiled in mines, mostly extracting silver.[15]

Slaves were not cheap. In fact, as Adam Smith had already pointed out, they were costly: 'The experience of all ages and nations, I believe, demonstrates that the work done by slaves, though it appears to cost only their maintenance, is in the end the dearest of any.' As Smith goes on to explain, slaves, understandably, have no incentive to work more than is absolutely necessary, or to treat tools with care. 'A person who can acquire no property, can have no other interest but to eat as much, and to labour as little as possible,' he wrote in 1776, in his book *The Wealth of Nations*.[16]

The plantations generated great profits; however, those revenues were achieved not because of, but in spite of slavery. Cotton, tobacco, and sugar were so lucrative as products that the expensive forced labour paid off.[17] Grain cropping was far less profitable—which is why there were so few slaves in the northern states of the US.[18] In that region, it made more sense to use paid labour, although those free workers were also very expensive, as they always had the alternative of becoming independent farming settlers themselves. However, the high wages were still economically sustainable, as slave labour would have been even more expensive.[19]

As paradoxical as it may seem, exploitation does not lead to prosperity. The experience was the same in all colonies that used slave labour. Brazil, Jamaica, and the US state of Mississippi all remained as backward as each other. Individual plantation owners were extremely wealthy, but in general, those economies as a whole did not develop. Since the enslaved people had neither rights nor money, there was no mass purchasing power to make technology profitable. It is no accident that only the northern states of the US, where slavery was rare, underwent industrialisation.

Capitalism was associated with brutal violence, but it would be completely wrong to describe it as 'war capitalism'.[20] Modern slavery was a murderous crime, but it was not economically necessary. It was not a driving force of industrialisation, but rather a hindrance to it. Russia's history also shows that exploitation does not create prosperity. The tsars ruled over vast territories stretching from Warsaw to Alaska, but the state remained desperately poor because it was dominated by the nobility, and Russian serfs were stripped of their rights just like slaves.[21]

England's industrialisation was not, then, built directly on slavery—but perhaps there were indirect chains of causality. Karl Marx developed the theory of the primitive accumulation of capital, which still has many supporters today. It holds that it was not until the advent of global trading and colonialism that there was enough capital in England to finance the construction of new factories. With eloquence and irony, Marx explains:

> The discovery of gold and silver in America, the extirpation, enslavement and entombment in mines of the indigenous population of that continent, the beginnings of the conquest and plunder of India, and the conversion of Africa into a preserve for the commercial hunting of blackskins, are all things that characterise the dawn of the era of capitalist production. These idyllic proceedings are the chief moments of primitive accumulation.[22]

He goes on:

> The colonial system ripened trade and navigation as in a hothouse ... The colonies provided a market for the budding manufactures, and a vast increase in accumulation which was guaranteed by the mother country's monopoly of the market. The treasures captured outside Europe by undisguised looting, enslavement and murder flowed back to the mother country and were turned into capital there.[23]

Marx believed that entire cities owed their existence to the exploitation of foreign peoples: 'Liverpool grew fat on the basis of the slave trade. This was its method of primitive accumulation.'[24]

It seems plausible at first glance that slavery could indirectly have enabled the development of a vast military-commercial complex: slave ships were, after all, insured and often financed through bank loans, and sailors were paid their wages. The products from the colonies were sold and traded. Considerable amounts of public money were also spent on conquering and then defending the 'New World'.[25]

But a closer inspection shows that the financial effects in England of slavery were not particularly great. The traders of 18th-century Bristol and Liverpool received a return of almost 10 per cent on their investments,[26] but they had to bear the risk of their ships being lost at sea, along with slaves and crew. Many of the wealthy in Britain therefore preferred to invest their money in safe government bonds, which still yielded hefty returns of 5 per cent. Most significantly, however, there were very few slave ships in operation. In the late 18th century, Britain had a fleet of more than 14,000 ocean-going ships, of which no more than 204 were ever used for the transportation of slaves.[27]

Thus, economically, the slave trade was rather a fringe phenomenon, as cynical as that sounds, and it cannot explain why capitalism developed. European imperialism did not stop at employing slave labour. Colonies were also conquered, the gold and silver reserves of South America were plundered, and raw materials around the world were exploited. It is for this reason that it is often assumed that capitalism could only develop by appropriating foreign treasures with maximum brutality.[28]

It is true that Europeans did not shrink from using violence of all kinds to subjugate other peoples and set up new empires. Only a small proportion of South America's indigenous people survived. Up to 90 per cent were killed by war, forced labour, and sickness. However, that unfathomable brutality benefited almost no one — not even the Spanish and Portuguese.

On discovering large gold and silver deposits, the conquerors hoped those precious metals would bring them huge wealth, but they soon proved to be more of a curse than a blessing. Spain and Portugal grew poorer rather than richer, and those two countries still lag behind the rest of western Europe today. The Spanish soon became aware of their own demise. As early as 1631, the Spanish king's chief minister, the Count-Duke of Olivares, doubted whether the country's South American colonies were a blessing for Spain: 'If its great conquests have reduced this Monarchy to such a miserable condition, one can reasonably say that it would have been more powerful without that New World.'[29]

An estimated 130,000 to 150,000 tonnes of silver were mined in North and South America up to the year 1800.[30] As enormous as that amount sounds, it did not trigger any growth in Europe, because so much of the silver was transported to East Asia to pay for luxury goods. People in China and India had little interest in the European goods, considering them primitive and crude. Asians were only willing to sell silk, spices, or chinaware if enough silver was offered in exchange.[31]

A comparison shows how little significance the South American silver had for Europe's overall economy: the amount of silver reaching Europe per person rose to between 3 and 4.5 grams per year. That is a negligible amount, in view of the fact that an unskilled labourer in London earned the equivalent of 11.5 grams of silver per day.[32] The silver from the New World did not advance Europe's economy, and indeed proved very damaging to Spain and Portugal. The constant influx of fresh money caused persistent inflation in both countries, making Spanish and Portuguese goods significantly more expensive. This caused the rich upper class to start buying cheaper foreign goods—which especially benefited France, the Netherlands, and England. Local markets lost their customers, and the economy fell back. The effects of that demise can still be felt in those countries today.

There were, however, colonies that were not built on slavery and that did not produce silver. The products they were forced to generate were agricultural commodities. Such colonies included Indonesia, which was brutally plundered by the Netherlands for more than 300 years. From 1600 to 1942, the archipelago was forced to surrender a far greater proportion of its economic output than was demanded of India by Britain, for instance. Taking population size into account, colonial trade was more important for the Dutch than for any other nation. Still, even the Dutch did not become permanently prosperous. Per-capita economic performance in the Netherlands stagnated from the 18th century onwards,[33] and the country was late to undergo industrialisation. The Dutch were left behind economically, despite their lucrative colonies. One side effect of this was that the longtime lack of a need for new premises meant the baroque centres of cities like Amsterdam and Haarlem were preserved—making them popular tourist destinations today.

The British were also brutal colonial rulers, but barely needed those possessions. The British East India Company was largely to blame for the Great Famine that started in Bengal in 1770 and killed millions of people.[34] Some colonial officials profited from such crimes,[35] but India was of no significance to the overall British economy. In the 18th century, exports to non-European countries made up only around 2 to 3 per cent of England's economic output.[36]

Conversely, the example of Switzerland shows that nations

can do exceedingly well without colonies. A small, famously landlocked country, Switzerland never had any overseas possessions. Nonetheless, the Swiss began to imitate Britain and build an industry of their own earlier than the Dutch.[37]

The colonies did not supply any essential raw materials for industry; they mainly produced luxury goods such as sugar, coffee, cocoa, tea, spices, and silk. Europe was able to meet its own demand for essential goods and was broadly self-sufficient until the start of the 20th century. Coal was abundant, and there was an ample supply of grain.[38] Cotton was more comfortable than linen or wool, but Europe would have been able to manage without textile fibres from oversees if necessary.

On an intuitive level it seems plausible to think that it is only possible to get rich if others are poor. But that is based on a fallacy that was exposed as early as 1776 by Adam Smith. Attempting to calm his compatriots' fears that continental Europe might develop its own industry and become a powerful competitor, he explained that an exporting nation can only export goods if other countries are wealthy:

> A nation that would enrich itself by foreign trade, is certainly most likely to do so, when its neighbours are all rich, industrious and commercial nations. A great nation, surrounded on all sides by wandering savages and poor barbarians, might, no doubt, acquire riches by the cultivation of its own lands, and by its own interior commerce, but not by foreign trade.[39]

Capitalism is not a zero-sum game that can only be won by oppressing and exploiting all others. The richer each individual is, the richer everyone gets. Everyone grows together. 'Those who believe today that Europe could not have developed as it did without having colonies are making the same mistake as the colonial rulers.[40] Those critics unwittingly dignify exploitation when they hold that violence was necessary for capitalism to arise. The reality is far more bitter: from an economic point of view, the brutal subjugation of other nations was completely pointless, and nations could easily have rejected violence without hurting their own development.

It is not the case that Europe held colonies because its economies would otherwise have collapsed. In fact, the opposite is true: the colonies only came about because Europeans could afford to expand economically around the world. This strange dynamic became particularly evident in the late 19th century, when there was a new surge of colonial subjugation and the European powers divided up Africa and parts of Asia among themselves. In 1880, the colonial powers controlled a territory of 25 million square kilometres; by 1913, that figure was 54 million.[41] Germany did not start acquiring colonies on a large scale until 1884.[42] They included, among others, what is now Namibia, Cameroon, Togo, Rwanda, Burundi, large parts of Tanzania, and a few islands in the South Pacific.

The Germans were extremely brutal, not even stopping at systematic genocide. From 1904 to 1907, they waged war on the Herero and Nama peoples in present-day Namibia with the aim of exterminating them completely. They shot women and children, set up concentration camps to hold their prisoners, and mercilessly drove insurgents into the desert of Omaheke. Before the massacre, the Herero numbered around 800,000; by 1911, only 15,000 remained. The population of the Nama people of 20,000 was more or less halved.[43] The Germans were equally murderous in East Africa. Almost 300,000 local people died in the Maji Maji War from 1905 to

1908, most of them due to starvation because the Germans had destroyed their villages and crops.[44]

That brutality was unparalleled, but, economically speaking, its colonies never became anything more than a permanent loss-making venture for the German Empire. The military costs were substantial, while trade with the oppressed regions never flourished at all. Imports from the colonies made up only 0.5 per cent of German foreign trade, and exports accounted for only 1 per cent.[45]

Chancellor Otto von Bismarck knew that colonies would only be a financial drain on the Empire, and he hesitated for a long time before establishing Germany's 'overseas protectorates'. His motives for doing so were ultimately political rather than economic. Bismarck wanted to distract people from the social conflicts at home in Germany by rallying support among the poor and the working class for the aim of achieving national greatness.[46]

That strategy was not only cynical; it was also expensive. Germany was able to afford global expansion only because the process of industrialisation was already well underway, enabling Germany to finance its costly imperialism. Additionally, seafaring had now been revolutionised. Steam power could be used over long sea journeys,[47] making it far easier to transport troops around the world and control even the most remote island territories. It was capitalism that made colonies possible, not the other way around.

This permanent oppression proved fatal for the colonies. To this day, they have not been able to develop properly due to the social hierarchy established by the Europeans, which is a hindrance to any progress. South America is a good example of this: wealth was concentrated in the hands of a small number of plantation owners, their descendants, and a white upper class, while the rest of the population remained poor. Wages remained so low that mechanisation was not profitable and no widespread industrialisation took place.

However, this senseless imperialism also had a devastating effect on Europe. The competition for colonies was one of the major reasons for the outbreak of World War I in 1914. German generals, not entrepreneurs, were responsible for that catastrophe.[48] Most business owners did not believe that it would really come to war. Europe's economies were extremely interconnected, with all countries closely linked by their import and export flows. Business leaders knew that even the winners of the war would lose out because breaking those supply and credit chains would destroy prosperity. Entrepreneurs trusted their monetary logic: war was impossible because it would be too expensive.[49]

While the diplomats exchanged threatening dispatches, the stock markets remained calm and trading continued as normal. Even a week before the outbreak of war, investors could not believe that a military confrontation was imminent. It was not until 27 July 1914 that investors grew so nervous that the Vienna Stock Exchange had to halt trading. By 30 July, all other stock exchanges in continental Europe had followed suit, and London and New York closed a day later. Within 24 hours, on 1 August, the war that most businesspeople had not seen coming began.

War is always bad for business, despite the claims of many of those on the political left, who say capitalism relies on military expansion to generate profits. The prominent, populist, far-left politician Sahra Wagenknecht, for example, writes: 'Capitalism and war are two sides of the same coin ... The use of military means to improve one's own economic position, secure access to resources and enable their exploitation is a consequence of capitalist logic. The French socialist Jean Jaurès put it perfectly when he said, "Capitalism carries war within it, just like clouds carry rain."[50]

However, Wagenknecht is wrong when she claims that resources can only be acquired by military means. There are much cheaper ways to get hold of them: by simply buying them. Wars are by far the most expensive way of securing the supply of oil, for example. The winner of the Nobel Prize for Economics, Joseph Stiglitz, has calculated the cost to the United States of the Iraq War. The US invasion of the oil-rich country began in 2003 and had already swallowed up $3 trillion within five years[51]—enough to pay for America's oil imports for 27 years.[52]

Capitalism requires peace, not war. But when conflict arises, then under capitalism it is fought with capitalist means. Technology becomes a weapon, and killing takes on an industrial scale. That can lead to huge developmental advances, as was particularly evident in World War I. In 1914, the Germans were still using horses when they invaded Belgium; by 1918, all sides in the war had submarines, aircraft, and poison gas.[53]

War can speed up technological development, but it does not follow conversely that most inventions have military origins. The steel industry, for example, which is so central to arms manufacturing, made its greatest advances during peacetime.[54] During World War I, on the other hand, no new steelmaking procedures developed, which surprised the industry itself. A self-critical German memorandum from the year 1918 reads, 'From a scientific point of view, Germany's iron industry has had almost no successful developments in either quality improvement or the use of byproducts in the past 15 years.'[55]

Many on the political left might be perplexed to hear that capitalism does not require low wages, exploitation, colonies, or war to exist. In fact, this is good news for all those who hope for more justice and equality in the world. If capitalism could really only be conceived as a brutal system of oppression, it would take a violent revolution to bring about improvements. Luckily, such a coup is not necessary; political reforms are enough. Capitalism made democracy possible—and it can be democratically controlled.

That is not to say that capitalism is an automatically just system, or that it always results in prosperity for all. Reforms must be fought for and won—not least of all because many capitalists have no understanding of the way capitalism actually works. Most entrepreneurs see wages as nothing but costs. They ignore the fact that it is precisely those wages that fuel the demand necessary for growth, and that companies can only expand if the purchasing power of the masses expands at the same time. Entrepreneurs must be forced to do what is good for them, and should be grateful for the existence of trades unions and their constant demands for higher wages. It is no exaggeration to say that unions are the saviours of capitalism.

Capitalism is fascinating because it can generate growth and prosperity. Unfortunately, it also requires that expansion to remain stable and avoid sliding into crisis. That imperative for growth is at odds with the fact that planet Earth's resources are not endless: infinite growth is not possible in a finite world.

CHAPTER SEVEN

Expansion or collapse: why capitalism has to grow

In recent years, the global economy has seen average annual growth of 2.8 per cent.[1] That sounds like a harmless figure, but in fact it is rather frightening. Such a rate represents a doubling of the world's economic output every 26 years. That would mean a 16-fold increase in the flood of goods by the year 2100, compared to the turn of the millennium.[2] It doesn't take an economist to realise that such growth cannot continue forever. The Earth is simply too small to sustain it. Or, as the US writer Edward Abbey once put it, 'Growth for the sake of growth is the ideology of the cancer cell.'[3]

People in Germany, Austria, and Switzerland already consume as if they had three planet Earths available. Other citizens of the world treat nature even more recklessly: Americans, Canadians, and Australians squander the equivalent of five planets.[4] The only reason the natural environment has not collapsed completely is that poorer countries produce barely any greenhouse gases. An average Malawian is responsible for emissions of just 0.1 tonnes of carbon dioxide a year; an average German produces 11.3 tonnes.[5]

People in rich countries must change the way they live. But doing without growth is not at all easy, as the financial crisis that began in 2008 made clear. No sooner had production begun to fall than extensive stimulus packages were introduced to save jobs. Even crimes against the environment were suddenly allowed in order to boost the economy. Anyone in Germany who bought a new car received a state 'scrappage bonus' of 2,500 euros for their old vehicle. One-and-three-quarter million people took advantage of the bargain and got rid of their old automobiles, most of which were still in good condition. Waste was deliberately created for the sake of continued economic growth. A similar scheme in Austria that incentivised the scrapping of a car by offering a subsidy of 1,500 euros persuaded 30,000 owners to buy a new vehicle.

Even critics of capitalism accepted this environmental sacrilege: 'This made a lot of sense from a short-term economic perspective, as it allowed companies to maintain both their personnel without layoffs and their production capacity that otherwise would have had to be cut back.'[6]

The European debt crisis that began in 2010 showed once again how quickly poverty sets in when growth fails. In Greece, the economy shrank by 18.7 per cent—a sorry peacetime record.[7] One-third of the country's companies disappeared forever, and unemployment reached 27 per cent at times. Many were plunged into abject poverty, since Greece lacks welfare infrastructures, and unemployment benefit is only paid for a maximum of one year. The Greek economy has still not fully recovered, prompting an exodus of young people. Four hundred thousand young Greeks, 69 per cent of whom are higher-education graduates, now work in other European countries.[8]

The Covid-19 crisis was also a reminder of how tough economic contraction can be. When the virus began to spread across the globe in January 2020, the unthinkable became a reality. Suddenly, there were no planes in the sky, global supply chains broke down, greenhouse gas emissions fell rapidly, and oil became a junk commodity. Globalisation and unbridled capitalism both came to a temporary halt.

But the Covid-19 crisis did not show us the way out of capitalism.[9] Instead, it proved the opposite: that our economic system is doomed to grow. In most countries, lockdowns lasted just a few weeks, but they caused trillions of dollars' worth of damage. Many businesses would have gone under, and almost all employees would have lost their jobs, if the industrialised nations had not introduced huge stimulus packages to stabilise their economies.

The trick was for states to simply 'print' money by taking on more borrowing. The EU mobilised more than a trillion euros. On top of that, Germany spent around 500 billion euros, Austria 70 billion euros,[10] and in Switzerland it was 40 billion francs.[11] Servicing and repaying such gigantic debts is impossible, so growth is seen as the way out. As soon as economic performance rises, debts gradually become less relevant—until they are eventually forgotten.

Capitalism is only stable when it is growing. It is often compared to a bicycle that falls over when it stops moving.[12] But how, exactly, does this growth imperative come about? It seems obvious that a shrinking economy is not a good thing because it leads to companies going bankrupt and people losing their jobs. But why can't capitalism at least stagnate? Why does it always have to keep on expanding, and causing more and more damage to the environment?

One answer is that growth can only occur when loans are taken out—but those debts can then only be repaid if there is further growth. It is no coincidence that capitalism is a monetary economic system. It is fuelled by credit.

This permanent spiral of credit and growth was vividly illustrated by the Swiss economist Mathias Binswanger using the example of a fictional fishermen's island.[13] Initially, the fishermen only own small wooden boats. They sell their catch to the rest of the island's inhabitants—and use the money to buy the food they need, or they spend it at the local pub. This is a circular economy that does not grow. However, when a new government takes power, an international management consultancy firm is hired to explore the island's opportunities for growth. The economists recommend that the fishermen invest in motorboats so they can greatly expand their fishing grounds. This would have the added effect of considerably increasing productivity, because it would allow the fishermen to catch far more fish in the same amount of time. The fishermen take the economists' advice and borrow money to finance their new motorboats. That provides extra income for the boatbuilders, who can now afford to go to the pub more often, among other things. All the extra money indirectly benefits the whole island. However, that new income is also necessary so that the fishermen have buyers for their extra fish and are able to repay their loans. Suddenly, there is growth in the island's economy. More boats are being built, more beer sold, and more fish caught—all thanks to credit.

This little story raises several questions. The first is whether the loans are necessary in the first place. Couldn't the fishermen save up until they had enough to pay for a motorboat? No. As astonishing as it may seem, it would not be a good idea for them to start saving their money. Saving makes an economy poor, not rich. Imagine the fishermen managed to scrape together enough money by no longer going to the pub. That would lead to an immediate drop in the pub owners' income, meaning they in turn would no longer be able to afford to buy fish. And as the fishermen's income dropped as a result, they would no longer be able to buy the new boats anyway. Their income would become so meagre that they would start repairing their own wooden boats because they couldn't afford to pay a craftsman to do it. Now the boatbuilders would no longer be able to afford to buy any fish, making the fishermen even poorer. Thus, saving is extremely dangerous because it causes a sudden drop in demand.

It may be surprising that saving is so damaging, since individuals feel richer when they save money and watch their bank balance growing. But it is important not to confuse business economics with national economics. It is not a problem if some families or businesses save—but it is a problem if they all do it at once. Money held in an account only retains its value if others take out loans in order to invest.

Growth can only be financed through credit, not through savings. But where does that new money come from? The answer is as simple as it is complex. It emerges 'out of nothing' when loans are granted. A short historical excursion will help explain this mechanism.[14]

It is not known how long people have been using money. But we do know that the first loan contracts stem from Ancient Mesopotamia and are more than 4,000 years old. Accounts were recorded in units called silver shekels, which did not yet circulate in the form of coins but had to be weighed out each time, with one shekel equalling about 8.5 grams of silver.[15]

Although the Babylonians and Assyrians did not yet have coinage, they knew precisely how to organise loans and how to calculate compound interest. Loans were granted for various purposes. Some were to facilitate long-distance trade with Anatolia, for example. Others exploited the plight of peasants after droughts, when they had to borrow grain to keep their families fed until the next harvest. Those loan contracts and promissory notes are among the oldest preserved documents in human history. Writing was not invented to pass down literature, but to record commercial agreements.

The Assyrians came upon an idea that seems incredibly modern to us now: they used promissory notes as a means of payment. Merchants did not wait until a loan became due to collect their money. That would have tied up their meagre finances for far too long. Instead, they passed the promissory notes on to other merchants to pay off their own debts.[16] When the loan became due, the last owner of the promissory note took the document to the person who originally received the loan, who then had to repay it. This cycle of promissory notes was the birth of so-called credit money, which is created by the granting of loans.[17] When the loan is repaid, that money disappears again.

Promissory notes have gone out of fashion, and banks now use current accounts to create money, but the principle is the same. New money is created when a loan is granted. This process can be easily understood using the example of a bank overdraft facility. Imagine that a bank customer—let's call her Jane Bloggs—has precisely zero euros in her current account, but she urgently needs a new bicycle. She can easily afford the new bike because her bank has granted her an overdraft facility. So Ms Bloggs transfers 1,000 euros to the bike shop, and at that precise moment, the bank enters a minus of 1,000 euros on her account. Ms Bloggs is now 1,000 euros in debt. That means there are suddenly 1,000 new euros in the world—created by the new bank loan. Money and debt are always created together.

Without credit money, no growth would be possible. Conversely, however, it does not follow that money alone is enough to make an economy expand. The Assyrians already had modern money, but they lived in a stagnating agrarian economy. As we have seen, growth arises only when labour is so expensive that mechanisation makes economic sense.

To return to the fishermen: why does the carousel of growth have to keep turning on their island? It is theoretically conceivable that the fishermen remain satisfied with just a few motorboats and eventually retire rather than continuing to toil out at sea. Why isn't it possible to enjoy a little growth and then get off the carousel?

Binswanger also played out that scenario. If the fishermen suddenly stopped ordering new vessels, the boatbuilders would lose that source of income and have to lay off the workers they had taken on. That would mean lower sales of beer in the pubs, and of fish at the market—and the economy would shrink.

Capitalism is a dynamic system. It needs to grow, or else it will collapse. Crises occur, but they also eventually pass, because the state and industry put their hopes in fresh growth—and invest to achieve it.

But businesses only invest when they can expect it to increase their profits. Everyone knows what profit is: it results when the yield is greater than the cost. That sounds harmless enough, but it is not, because in a national economy, the overall income can only exceed overall expenses when money flows into the economy from outside. Thus, profits are financed out of the same loans that make growth possible.[18]

Profits are also necessary because businesses would

otherwise be unable to get credit. Banks want to be sure that their loans will be repaid—which is not possible if businesses are making a loss. Loans, investments, profits, and growth are all inextricably interwoven into capitalism. A protracted period with no growth will bring the system to collapse. The economy then shrinks until only miserable subsistence remains.

To be clear once again: the growth imperative is triggered by credit because loans have to be repaid. Interest is not the problem, as is believed by many critics of capitalism, who like to cite this horrific calculation: 'At 1 per cent interest compounded annually, any amount of money will double in 72 years; at 3 per cent, in 24 years; at 6 per cent, in 12 years; at 12 per cent, in 6 years; and at 24 per cent, in three years.'[19] This spiral of interest results in a 'pathological growth imperative', believe such people as Margrit Kennedy, who was one of the leading critics of interest. 'The interest that banks demand is the most significant cost borne by our economy. It is the price of money. It establishes the lowest limit for what we consider "profitable". Thus our economy has literally no choice: it must strive for exponential growth.'[20]

That logic appears compelling at first glance. Businesses must generate profits so they can pay the interest on their loans—so interest is the actual driver of growth. But that view fails to go beyond the level of individual companies and to take in the economy as a whole. It once again confuses business economics and national economics.

Interest paid on loans does constitute a cost for businesses, but banks do not simply hoard that money in their vaults. That interest principally serves to cover the bank's costs. They use it to pay their employees or their overheads, such as buying computers or paying rent. The interest becomes the wages of bank workers, who, in turn, spend it on rent, visits to the pub, or trips abroad, for instance. Interest payments constitute costs for the companies that take out loans, but they generate income for other businesses. On a macroeconomic level, interest pays for itself.[21]

There is one more thing that constantly fuels growth: the merciless competition in many branches of industry. Companies must constantly invest in new technology in order to produce more goods with fewer workers, so they don't get swallowed up by their competitors or driven out of business. That technological progress always costs jobs. But it doesn't lead to mass unemployment because the economy grows at the same time, creating new jobs as it does so.

So capitalism does not work in the way suggested by the advertising industry: it is not about satisfying our needs by consuming innovative goods. Those products are just a means to achieving a higher purpose. The ultimate objective is to create jobs. We work in order to work, because only those who work have a disposable income, security, and social recognition.

The American economist John Kenneth Galbraith pointed out a strange phenomenon back in 1958: in times of economic crisis, nobody laments the fact that so many goods are not being produced because the factories are not operating at full capacity. Nobody cares about the falling number of goods. Nobody suffers if cars suddenly stop being made. People only bewail the loss of jobs due to the crisis.[22] We are told we are consuming ourselves to death — but that perception is wrong. We are producing ourselves to death. The collective goal is full employment, not full consumption.

Despite this, some critics of capitalism still believe that the growth imperative is nothing more than an 'ideological construct' or a 'collective myth'.[23] This is partly based on the fact that the term 'economic growth' did not enter parlance until the 1950s.[24] Previously, words such as 'prosperity', 'progress', or 'development' were used. That linguistic observation may be true, but it does not follow from it that the new interest in growth was an arbitrary narrative. It is simply a result of the fact that the political world was late to recognise the economic reality: the severe economic crisis that started in 1929 had plunged millions into the most abject poverty, and the desire was to avoid such crashes in the future. The growth imperative is not a 'myth'; it is real.

However, that growth is not easy to measure. The central indicator is gross domestic product (GDP), which has many flaws. One infamous case in point is the so-called housewife paradox. If a businessman employs someone to look after his house and home, the domestic help's wages are accounted for in the calculation of GDP. If that boss then marries his employed help, overall GDP will shrink, as the domestic work is now unpaid. Conversely, the official figure for GDP would be grossly inflated if previously unpaid labour became commercial. As 'women's work', rearing children, caring for relatives, and putting dinner on the table punctually mostly fell to wives in the past. Nowadays, much of that work is provided by childcare facilities, nursing homes, and food-delivery services—whose revenues all flow into the figure for GDP.

GDP is blind, because it is only interested in payment flows, which often makes the measured values seem cynical. For example, the building of prisons and the treatment of accident victims in hospitals both count as growth. The catastrophic 2021 floods along the River Ahr in western Germany also had a positive impact on Germany's economic output, because the destroyed buildings needed to be rebuilt.

GDP works best for pure consumption goods, but even then there can be strange distortions, as shown by the internet giants. As we know, Facebook is popular and powerful, because users can exchange news and photos on the platform, ranging from pictures of cats to political messages. This social added value is not included in GDP, however. Only Facebook's advertising revenues are counted. 'It is not very clear why advertisements should contribute to the real national product,' notes the Italian-American-British economist Mariana Mazzucato. After all, it is clear that what the users care about is their holiday photos, not the ads.[25]

So GDP has its flaws and is in urgent need of improvement.[26] Despite this, it would still be a mistake to believe that the issue of growth will resolve itself if we just start measuring it differently and including quality of life or environmental damage in the figure.[27] Capital needs growth in order to remain stable. How we record that growth statistically is an entirely different matter. Imagine a patient who has a high fever, but only has a broken thermometer that can't measure beyond 38 degrees Celsius, although the patient's body is well above 40 degrees. The thermometer's measurement error does not alter the fact that the patient is dangerously ill. We must not confuse reality with measurement problems—and the same goes for the issue of growth.

CHAPTER EIGHT

The price of prosperity: the destruction of the world

Humans currently burn about as much coal, oil, and gas every year as was formed over a million years, but large deposits remain to be exploited. At the time of writing, coal deposits will last another 114 years, gas reserves are enough for almost 53 years, and still-unexploited oilfields could fulfil our needs for a little under 51 years.[1]

Those fossil reserves must remain in the ground unexploited if humanity is to survive in any kind of orderly way. Carrying on as we have so far would cause global temperatures to rise by considerably more than four degrees by the end of this century, and to increase by more than six degrees by the year 2200. These figures are estimates; the reality could be significantly worse.[2]

It may sound harmless enough to say the world will warm up by 'only' four or six degrees. But every tenth of a degree makes a huge difference. This can be seen by looking at the past. During the last ice age, 20,000 years ago, the average global temperature was just five degrees colder than it was in the 19th century, but northern Europe was covered by a 500-metre-thick sheet of ice.[3] Humans would find themselves living in a completely different world if temperatures were to rise by four to six degrees due to the unbridled burning of coal, gas, and oil.

Most people in Germany believe climate change is not a natural phenomenon. Eighty-six per cent of respondents in German public TV's monthly political survey said they believed global warming was anthropogenic.[4] However, there are also persistent climate change sceptics who like to point out that the climate has always fluctuated.

It is true that temperatures in Europe have changed significantly many times. The Middle Ages were relatively warm, and even parts of Greenland became ice-free, which explains why the Vikings gave the island that name when they first settled it in the year 982.[5] Temperatures cooled considerably in the early 14th century. That 'Little Ice Age' lasted until around 1850. During that time, it was so cold that the canals of Holland, and even Venice, would regularly freeze over for weeks in winter. The glaciers in the Alps moved deep into the valleys, burying farms and even entire villages.[6] Temperatures did not return to the higher levels of the Middle Ages until the middle of the 20th century.

However, those early climate fluctuations were regional, rather than global phenomena. Global average temperatures did not rise.[7] But modern climate change can be seen everywhere in the world. All the planet's oceans and continents are getting warmer, with a global average rise of 1.2 degrees compared to pre-industrial, pre-19th-century temperatures.[8]

And this is a continuing development. It will not be possible to stop the Earth from heating up further. UN conferences in Paris and Glasgow resulted in agreements to limit the rise in global temperatures to 1.5 degrees, but that aim is illusory and no longer unattainable, as calculated by the Potsdam-based climate researcher Anders Levermann. As he said presciently in 2020, 'The spare budget for reaching 1.5 degrees is so small that the US would have to become completely climate-neutral by 2023. And that isn't possible.'[9]

There are also delayed effects to consider. The Earth system is slow to react: some effects take decades or even centuries to manifest. That means that even if humanity completely stopped emitting carbon dioxide immediately, the global temperature would still rise by at least half a degree in the long term. 'As sad as it is to admit it,' Levermann said, 'the fact is that we have already missed the 1.5 degrees goal.'

One and a half degrees sounds insignificant, but a rise by that amount would put a permanent end to the ideal human world of the Holocene, which began around 12,000 years ago after the end of the last ice age. Not only did the climate get warmer, but the weather also suddenly became more predictable. People now had a much better idea of how much rain would fall and how warm the summer would be. That enabled agriculture to develop, and it is probably no accident that the first farmers adopted a sedentary lifestyle 10,000 years ago.[10]

The Holocene would have lasted another 50,000 years—if capitalism hadn't intervened. The current warming of the Earth is unprecedented, and is occurring up to 100 times faster than any previously recorded change. Humanity has become a geological force by constantly emitting greenhouse gases. That is part of the reason why the climate activist Luise Neubauer calls her fellow campaigners in the Fridays for Future movement the climate generation.[11]

Many young people today barely believe they have a future at all. Neubauer was recently asked by a 13-year-old schoolgirl, 'I just wanted to know if you can ever imagine having children?' It's a question that the climate activist is often asked, and one that gives her pause for thought.[12]

At a demonstration in the US, one girl held a placard reading: 'You'll die of old age, I'll die of climate change'.[13] The Swedish climate activist Greta Thunberg believes the fears of those children must become the fears of adults. She pulled no punches at the 2019 World Economic Forum in Davos, telling the world's most powerful politicians and business leaders, 'I don't want your hope. I want you to panic. I want you to feel the fear I do. Every day. And I want you to act. I want you to behave like our house is on fire. Because it is.' Many adults don't need any persuading. They have long since adopted a pessimistic outlook themselves: on a global level, around half of people surveyed say they believe climate change will lead to the extinction of the human species.[14]

That existential fear is understandable, but it remains difficult to make any precise predictions. The climate crisis is complex, and its impacts are often not felt until decades, centuries, or even millennia later. Its effects are not equally distributed around the globe, or among all populations. 'The truth is that many of us who live in high-income nations with varied landscapes and sophisticated technology will survive our climate suicide,' says the US writer Jonathan Safran Foer. 'But we will suffer permanent injuries.'[15]

Science and the media have often failed to inform the public properly about this creeping catastrophe. Not infrequently, it has been grossly exaggerated. The German news weekly *Der Spiegel* did not dedicate a title page to the climate crisis until August 1985. The front-page image featured a view of Cologne Cathedral half-submerged in a boundless ocean, with only its steeples and roof protruding from the floodwaters, and the rest of the city drowned. The journal's gloomy scenario for the year 2040 described:

Hamburg and Hong Kong, London, Cairo, Copenhagen, and Rome are inundated, swallowed by the sea. The United Kingdom of Great Britain has disintegrated into an archipelago in which England, Scotland and Wales are separate islands ... The sea has swallowed entire countries since the ice at both poles began to melt faster and faster. Denmark, the Netherlands, Belgium, and Bangladesh no longer exist. Large parts of the coastal regions of the US, China, and Northern Europe are all under water.[16]

That prediction was nonsense. Hamburg will definitely still be standing in 2040, and even the Netherlands, a quarter of whose land area is already below sea level, will still exist in 20 years' time. The Dutch are actually rather relaxed about the future of their country in the rest of the 21st century. The Royal Netherlands Meteorological Institute expects sea levels to rise by 1.20 metres in that period—which can be managed by using conventional dykes.[17]

'No one needs to be afraid of the rise in sea levels,' confirms the climate researcher Anders Levermann.[18] He is concerned less with the present than with the far future: since the climate crisis takes time to manifest itself, the decisions we make now will decide whether New Orleans, Hamburg, Kolkata, or Tokyo will still exist in 750 years' time, or if they will have been swallowed up by the sea. Even if humans stopped emitting all greenhouse gases immediately, sea levels would still rise by 2 metres, because carbon dioxide remains in the atmosphere for more than 1,000 years, continuing to warm the Earth.

Every tenth of a degree of warming harbours multiple dangers. The water in the oceans expands when heated, thus taking up more space. So far, the oceans have absorbed 93 per cent of the heat energy related to greenhouse gases.

That's an unimaginable amount of energy, as the Chinese atmospheric physicist Lijing Cheng has calculated: 'The amount of heat we have put in the world's oceans in the past 25 years equals 3.6 billion Hiroshima atom-bomb explosions.'[19] That's equivalent to about four Hiroshima bombs per second.

As the Earth heats up, mountain glaciers and the ice caps in Greenland and parts of the Antarctic are melting. One pivotal 'tipping point' has already almost been reached: if global temperatures rise by two degrees, Greenland's icesheet will be beyond saving. It is currently still around 3,000 metres thick, but the ice cap gets thinner as it melts, lowering its surface to where the air is warmer. And the ice melts away ever more rapidly.[20]

Greenland's ice alone would raise sea levels by seven metres if it melts. But that's not the worst of it by far: if the burning of fossil fuels continues unabated, sea levels could rise by more than ten metres over the long term, because parts of Antarctica's ice would also melt into the sea. In Asia especially, fertile regions that feed billions of people would sink beneath the waves. 'If one of the world's nations were to threaten to seize 10 per cent of another's territory, there would be war,' says Levermann. 'That's what's happening due to global warming, but no countries really believe they are going to have to cede 10 per cent of their territory to the sea.'[21]

While sea levels rise almost unnoticed by around 3.4 millimetres per year, other climate disasters are becoming far more conspicuous.[22] Heatwaves and droughts, especially, are increasing in frequency. By the year 2070, if effective climate-protection measures are not taken, approximately 3.5 billion people will be living in regions where the average temperature exceeds 29 degrees. Currently, only

0.8 per cent of the world's land surface is exposed to such merciless heat, mostly in the Sahara. In just 50 years' time, large parts of Africa and the Amazon would become almost uninhabitable. The Middle East, as well as parts of India, Pakistan, Thailand, Indonesia, and Australia, would also be too hot to support permanent human settlements.[23]

At the moment, however, this worst-case scenario seems unlikely, because states have committed to reducing their greenhouse gas emissions. The current climate models therefore assume that the Earth will heat up by 'only' two degrees by 2050, and by at least three degrees by 2100.[24] But even that prognosis is alarming. Various tipping points would still be reached, and environmental collapse would take on a momentum of its own. To cite just one example: the Amazon rainforest would disappear, replaced by savannah, even if no more trees were cut down. Rising temperatures would cause the local water cycle to break down, which currently ensures that the forest creates its own rain. The Amazon rainforest would no longer be a carbon dioxide sink, but would itself emit huge amounts of greenhouse gases into the atmosphere.[25]

The warmer the climate gets, the greater the chance of simultaneous droughts in regions where the important crops of corn, rice, soybeans, and wheat are grown. The events of 2010 and 2011 give an idea of the consequences. During that period, Russia experienced a heatwave. Drought and wildfires destroyed around 30 per cent of the wheat harvest, prompting Moscow to ban grain exports. Since Russia is one of the world's biggest grain producers, the price of wheat skyrocketed around the world. Soon after, political unrest broke out in Africa and the Middle East because people there could no longer afford to buy their daily bread.[26]

However, the greatest danger is the possibility of as yet

unknown dangers. There have already been several occasions when reality has turned out to be worse than the predictions.[27] For example, in the summer of 2019, researchers made the shocking discovery that the permafrost in some parts of the Canadian Arctic is already thawing at a rate predicted for the year 2090 by the models. Seventy years earlier than expected, we are approaching another important tipping point. The Arctic permafrost stores around twice as much carbon as is currently present in the entire atmosphere. When that ground thaws, billions of tonnes of carbon dioxide and methane will escape into the atmosphere.[28]

Methane is sneaky. Although it remains in the atmosphere for only 21.4 years on average before being destroyed, compared to more than 1,000 years in the case of carbon dioxide, methane causes enormous damage in its short lifetime, and has 25 times the greenhouse effect of carbon dioxide. Unfortunately, it is too late to stop the permafrost regions from thawing. With an air of resignation, the Potsdam-based climate researcher Stefan Rahmstorf predicts, 'Methane is likely to be a growing and uncontrollable source of the greenhouse effect for centuries to come.'[29]

Another unpleasant surprise was the 'heat dome' that formed over the western coast of North America in the summer of 2021. The Canadian village of Lytton registered a record-high temperature of 49.6 degrees Celsius. The far north was suddenly reaching temperatures otherwise only registered in desert regions. Soon after, fires destroyed the area's forests, and Lytton was reduced to ashes. For a long time, people living in cooler zones believed they were safe from the effects of the global temperature rise—precisely because they live so far from the equator. However, the assumptions that the climate develops in a linear fashion and that small changes have only small consequences turn out to be wrong. The climate is a complex system. Tiny deviations can have enormously damaging effects. The heat shock in Canada made it clear to climate researchers how incomplete their models still are.[30]

It is also far from clear how reliable the basic data are. As we know, climate change depends on the amount of greenhouse gases emitted. But those amounts cannot be measured precisely, so scientists must rely on estimates. Official figures state that humanity is responsible for emitting 50 billion tonnes of greenhouse gases per year—but the real figure could easily be eight to 13 billion tonnes more, which would mean the time left to prevent climate breakdown is even shorter than assumed.[31]

All this means that predictions are difficult to make. Current estimates are that by the year 2050, temperatures in Hamburg will reach the level currently seen in San Marino; Berlin and Hanover's climate will be comparable to that of present-day Toulouse; Dusseldorf will be as hot as Rijeka; Cologne and Bern will be like San Marino is now; and Munich will be like Milan, Wiesbaden like Lugano, and Saarbrücken like Montélimar in the south of France. Vienna could be as hot as Skopje, the capital of North Macedonia, is today.[32]

The new record-high temperatures may not seem dramatic at first—indeed, they sound more like good news than bad. After all, millions of German tourists travel south every year to enjoy the sun on the French Riviera or the beaches of Croatia. In future, they will be able to save themselves the long journey and enjoy Adriatic conditions on the Baltic coast instead. But the news is not, in fact, good. Those temperatures in 2050 would just be a momentary snapshot of a world in which temperatures continue to rise relentlessly—unless we protect the climate now.

Even if we do manage to curb climate change, Germany will still be considerably different from the present. Lack of rain will dry out the soil. The Federal Republic is not destined to become a desert, but eastern Germany especially could resemble a steppe.[33] Precipitation is always difficult to predict with certainty, but there is no doubt that our summers will be drier and winters will be wetter.[34] Overall yearly rainfall may not change, but that is of little use when plants require the most water in summer.[35] This water deficit is compounded by the fact that more moisture evaporates when the temperature rises.

Droughts will become more frequent. Central Europe saw almost no rainfall for several months in the summer of 2018, and the temperature was three degrees higher than average.[36] Such a severe dry spell used to be considered almost impossible, but it is likely to become the norm every second year by 2050. Currently, only around 3 per cent of Germany's arable land is artificially watered. That is likely to rise to one-third over the next 20 years. But groundwater levels are already too low in drier areas. 'We will run into conflicts over water use, the likes of which we have never seen,' predicts the hydrologist Dietrich Borchardt.[37]

The type of rainfall will also change. Until now, Germans and Austrians have been used to gentle, steady precipitation, but rains are likely to become far more torrential in future, because warm air can carry more water. The author Wolfgang Büscher described how violent such heavy rain can feel. 'The roaring sound was the rain, now it was on top of me. A hard kind of rain, nothing like the normal type. The first drops started to pummel the parched earth, between the beeches, some hitting me like stones from the kind of catapults we used to shoot each other with as kids.'[38]

In July 2021, some parts of North Rhine-Westphalia and Rhineland-Palatinate received up to 150 litres of rain per square metre within 24 hours. Small rivers such as the Ahr and the Erft, for example, swelled to several metres higher than their normal levels, devastating settlements along their valleys. One hundred and eighty-four people died in the floods, and the cost of the damage to property was estimated at 30 billion euros. Such disasters used to be once-in-a-millennium events, at most. Now, they can be expected to happen at any time.

The future of the forests is also uncertain. The summer drought in 2018, the heatwaves of 2019, and the dry weather of 2020 destroyed 2.5 per cent of Germany's trees—an area of forest greater than the federal state of Saarland. The latest official forestry report estimates that only 21 per cent of the country's trees are healthy. Spruce trees suffer the most as they require a cool, damp climate to thrive. This 'forestry staple' was particularly popular with forest owners due to its rapid growth and straight trunks. However, little now remains of former monoculture spruce forests. The trees have been toppled by storms, burned by wildfires, or—most commonly—eaten by bark beetles. This pest has always lived in our part of the world, but spruce trees have also always been able to defend themselves by pumping the beetles' breeding tunnels full of sap. But they can only do this if they are healthy. If they are weakened by heat and drought, they can no longer defend themselves against this enemy—one single female of which can produce up to 100,000 young in a breeding season—and so the death of the affected tree is sealed.[39]

Spruce have often been planted in the wrong places, but

'drought stress' is also killing trees living in more species-appropriate locations. The German government's forest report estimates all but 11 per cent of the country's beech trees show signs of 'crown defoliation'. Almost all tree species have their own specific pests to contend with, against which they are barely able to defend themselves. Beech can be befallen by 'beech tree slime flux', which causes a reddish mucus to ooze from their trunks; ash dieback is caused by a fungus called *Hymenoscyphus fraxineus*; sycamores are vulnerable to sooty bark disease; and oaks are susceptible to a new kind of mildew. Horse chestnut trees can be struck by a *Pseudomonas* bacterium; wild fruit trees are threatened by bacterial fire blight; and alders face attack by *Phycomyces* fungi.[40] Birch and larch trees are also dying, although they have no such enemies — conditions are simply getting too hot for them.

One-third of Germany and Switzerland is covered by woodland, and in Austria that proportion is as high as 47 per cent. Most forest experts remain optimistic that the woods will survive, and even rejuvenate, as species that are better adapted to a drier climate assert themselves naturally. 'For example, when beech trees die off, they are replaced by hornbeams and linden trees,' observes the biologist Pierre Ibisch. 'Nature often makes better decisions than humans.'[41] But climate change still needs to be halted so that the forests can regenerate. As temperatures continue to rise, every tree will become stressed. 'If the stress becomes too much, annual, herbaceous, and shrub species will have an advantage,' says Ibisch. 'In the worst case, this will result in a forest steppe landscape with a high proportion of grassland.'

Not only forest trees are under threat; fruit farmers should also fear climate change. Pests that were once relatively harmless are becoming rampant, because more of their larvae now survive the warmer winters. Apple trees fall prey to the codling moth, and cherry trees are afflicted by the cherry fruit fly. We currently have no alternative crop-tree species to replace them. Mediterranean fruit species are not viable candidates, because Germany will continue to see subzero temperatures in springtime—despite global warming.

Climate collapse will fundamentally change central Europe, but it won't wipe out all life. The climate will become hot and dry, the old forests will disappear, and agriculture will become much more difficult. Nobody will starve, but this could lead to a kind of bunker mentality taking hold in Europe: closed borders, an everyone-for-themselves society, and a head-in-the-sand response as the climate catastrophe renders other continents uninhabitable.

Such a selfish approach would not only be morally wrong; it would also be dangerous. Germany and Austria getting off relatively lightly is only one prognosis among many. The climate is unpredictable, and can tip at very short notice. We should take a warning from events in central Europe around 12,700 years ago. In a period of just 20 years, temperatures dropped so sharply that the temperate landscape was transformed into frozen tundra.[42] That was a drop in temperature, rather than a rise like today, but the mechanism is identical. It takes just a few tipping points to be reached for the world to be catapulted into a completely different climate. Animals and plants would not have sufficient time to adapt to such rapid change. Humans are the last link in a long food chain, and we cannot survive if everything else dies.

It's a dilemma: permanent growth destroys nature and the environment, but that very growth is necessary for capitalism to remain stable. In an attempt to square this circle, and to reconcile economy and ecology, the concept of 'green growth' has emerged as a possible solution. This concept does not involve changing our economic system, but rather our technology. Instead of relying on burning more and more fossil fuels, it relies principally on wind and solar power.

The idea of 'green growth' can be found in environmental action plans around the world—including those of the UN, the World Bank, the EU, and various political parties. In June 2021, the German parliament decided the country had to become climate-neutral by 2045. There is no lack of ideas about what a sustainable economy might look like. Solar panels, wind turbines, electric vehicles, and heat pumps have all been in practical use for some time. Carbon dioxide capture, green hydrogen, green steel, green cement, and synthetic aviation fuel are all in the test phase. And some advocate for a return to nuclear power.

Unfortunately, this long list of technological possibilities does not represent a real solution. In the next section of this book, I will analyse each suggestion individually, but I can already tell you the results of that analysis: 'green growth' does not exist. It is an illusion.

PART II

'Green Growth' Does Not Exist

CHAPTER NINE

The carbon dioxide will not go away

'Green growth' is a little like the dream of being able to eat as much cake as you want without putting on weight. We have already found a pretty savage solution for removing those dangerous excess kilos of body weight: sucking the fat out. An analogous idea for dealing with climate change is to simply suck the greenhouse gases out of the atmosphere.

The technical term for this is 'carbon capture and sequestration', known popularly as 'carbon capture and storage', as it involves capturing carbon dioxide and permanently storing it underground. This would have the unbeatable advantage of providing humanity with a kind of reinsurance. When it becomes too difficult or too expensive to avoid carbon dioxide emissions, we would simply remove them from the air. Unfortunately, this idea is too good to be true. If capture and storage can be achieved at all, it will only be possible for small quantities, since the filtering technology consumes huge amounts of energy and is still far from reaching technological maturity.

Carbon dioxide is a sneaky gas. Although it is hugely damaging to the climate, it is only present in the tiniest amounts in the atmosphere. There are around 420 carbon dioxide molecules in every million air particles in our present atmosphere.[1] That means a huge amount of air must be filtered for each carbon dioxide molecule captured, and that requires a lot of energy.

Still, various technologies for recapturing carbon dioxide are currently under investigation by scientists. Of course, the idea of simply keeping fossil-fuelled power plants running and capturing the carbon dioxide for storage before it even leaves the chimney is extremely appealing. Greenhouse gases make up 14 per cent of the fumes released by coal-fired power stations, which is a high level of concentration.[2] But even under those very favourable conditions, the energy requirements would still be exorbitant. Power stations would have to burn around 30 per cent more coal to provide the energy to capture the greenhouse gas. The carbon dioxide would then have to be piped to a final storage facility and pumped underground, further increasing the energy required by 10 per cent.[3] Current filters are also not particularly efficient, capturing only 60 to 70 per cent of the carbon dioxide.[4]

So, carbon capture and storage is not a viable technology for keeping fossil-fuelled power plants online. It would result in an expensive zero-sum game in which almost as much carbon dioxide was created as was filtered out of the fumes.[5] This is a painful truth, since billions have been readily pumped into this research.[6] Governments and oil companies alike have invested vast sums in the hope that carbon dioxide will be able to be treated like any normal waste that can be separated out and safely disposed of. However, those hopes are in vain, as the German government established in 2018 when it admitted that the development of carbon capture and storage technology was making 'considerably slower progress recently than was envisaged in the 2000s'.[7]

Germany can only become climate-neutral if it switches from coal, gas, and oil to green-energy sources. However, the issue of capture and storage will remain an important one in the long term, since humanity is highly unlikely to meet the target of limiting global warming to 1.5 degrees. Beyond that threshold, dangerous tipping points loom, so anything that eventually manages to reduce carbon dioxide levels will be a help. The Intergovernmental Panel on Climate Change (IPCC) is counting on improvements in filtering technology to make it viable to suck the carbon dioxide straight out of the air.[8]

One variation on this idea is known as 'direct air capture' (DAC), and involves filtering carbon dioxide directly out of the ambient air. It is a targeted hunt for those 420 carbon dioxide molecules present in every million air particles. This technology follows the vacuum cleaner principle, using huge fans to force the air through membranes or solvents. The Swiss company Climeworks AG already sells technology that can do this. Its first pilot plant was built in Hinwil, near Zurich, in 2017. However, the decentralised filter technology it relies on is very energy-intensive, precisely because carbon dioxide is present in such small amounts in ambient air.[9]

It is not only the filter technology that has its pitfalls. So far, there has been no solution to the problem of what to do with the captured carbon dioxide. One obvious idea would be liquify the greenhouse gas and pump it into spent oil and gas reservoirs and coalmines. That would return the carbon to the place it was originally extracted from, closing the circle perfectly. But, as charming as that notion sounds, it would fail due to the fact that carbon dioxide takes up far more space than oil, gas, or coal. The volume of the carbon dioxide released when coal is burnt is up to 5.4 times greater than that of the fuel; for lignite, it is 1.9 times, and for crude oil, 4.6 times.[10]

This means that spent reservoirs would be too few by far to contain all the captured greenhouse gas. Many former mines are not airtight, and so would be unsuitable as carbon dioxide stores. Lignite is usually extracted using open-cut mining anyway, and many coalmines are like Swiss cheeses due to the many galleries blasted out of the rock to exploit as many of the deposits as possible.

The IPCC calculates that former oil, gas, and coal reservoirs could contain a maximum of 1,100 gigatonnes—that's 1,100 billion tonnes—of carbon dioxide.[11] Humanity currently emits around 50 gigatonnes of carbon dioxide per year, only around half of which is reabsorbed by the oceans, plants, soil, and marshlands.[12] That underground storage capacity would therefore be forever used up within just 44 years—and that is without even taking into account the constant increase in our thirst for energy.

This has provoked a desperate search for other rock formations that might serve as carbon dioxide stores. Geologists are particularly inspired by the possibilities of 'saline aquifers'. These are deep underground layers filled with saltwater.[13] Pumping out the water would leave them free to store the greenhouse gas. However, this solution would also be more difficult to implement than it sounds. The water in the aquifers is, of course, highly saline—raising the problem of how to dispose of it. It certainly could not be discharged straight into our rivers.[14]

Permanently preventing the carbon dioxide from leaking also poses a problem. The option of dissolving the carbon dioxide in water, and pumping the resulting 'fizzy' water into the aquifers, would be safest because the greenhouse gas would be in a bound state. The snag with this otherwise reliable method is that the water would take up too much space. Germany's government therefore concluded, 'Only relatively small amounts of carbon dioxide [could] be stored with the existing storage capacities.'[15]

As promising as such storage solutions look on paper, finding suitable saline aquifers may prove problematic. Germany provides a good example of this. In theory, 9.3 billion tonnes of carbon dioxide could be stored in its saline aquifers.[16] Based on Germany's 2021 emissions of 762 million tonnes of carbon dioxide, that capacity would be enough for more than 12 years.[17] Germany's suitable aquifers are mostly located in the north of the country, as well as beneath the North Sea, in Upper Bavaria, and in south-eastern Baden-Württemberg. Residents in those localities are not keen on having the ground beneath them pumped full of carbon dioxide. Injecting the aquifers with carbon dioxide would increase the pressure within them, increasing the stress on the rock layers above. Many are already 'weakened' and therefore potentially full of holes.[18] If the carbon dioxide is able to escape back into the atmosphere, it makes no sense to expend the large amounts of energy necessary to capture it and pump it into the aquifers. Over the long term, even small leaks can render sequestration pointless.

Such leaks can also pose a potentially lethal threat. Carbon dioxide is not toxic per se — indeed, it is produced by our own bodies when we metabolise our food, and we are constantly exhaling it. But it becomes dangerous in high concentrations when it displaces oxygen. Since carbon dioxide is heavier than oxygen, under calm conditions it collects in low-lying areas of the Earth's surface. The results of an aquifer leaking carbon dioxide could be catastrophic.

A layer of the greenhouse gas several metres thick could form, which would wipe out all life.[19] German environmental organisations fought for a law that would place very tight constraints on sequestration, which was passed back in 2012. It only allows research facilities such as the one in the Brandenburg town of Ketzin. Large-scale storage remains forbidden by law.[20]

Other potential storage sites are available in Europe. Norway, in particular, has set its hopes on the new business model of storing the carbon dioxide emissions of its neighbours beneath the sea. If the world goes climate-neutral, Norway will no longer have a market for its oil and gas, and is now searching for alternative sources of income.

Since 1996, the Norwegians have been pumping almost a million tonnes of carbon dioxide a year into a saline aquifer called Sleipner, located around 800 to 1,000 metres beneath the seabed.[21] However, some doubt remains as to whether the store is leaking or not. Seismic measurements have revealed that the volume of carbon dioxide that Sleipner contains is less than the amount injected into it.[22]

Despite this, the Norwegians remain undeterred and are developing more storage sites. They are currently working on a project to the north of Bergen called 'Northern Lights'. Theoretically, at least, the storage capacity off the Norwegian coast is gigantic. It is estimated at 80 billion tonnes of carbon dioxide—about as much as the entire EU emits in 20 years.[23]

Aquifers are not the only option. Iceland is pursuing the idea of transforming carbon dioxide into rock. A pilot system by the name of Orca began operating in September 2021.[24] It is a fascinating approach: being volcanic, 90 per cent of Iceland is made up of basalt, which contains large amounts of magnesium, calcium, and iron. When the carbon dioxide is dissolved in water and pumped into the basalt rock, it comes into contact with those minerals and reacts with them to form carbonates, which are like a kind of chalk. The chemical process takes about two years, after which the greenhouse gas is permanently petrified and bound in the rock.

With this method, 80 to 200 times the annual amount of carbon dioxide emitted by the entire world could be stored in Iceland alone. And basalt is the most common type of rock on Earth. However, it is mainly found on the ocean floor, and Germany only has one major outcrop—the Vogelsberg mountains. Since that also happens to be the area that supplies the Frankfurt metropolitan area with its drinking water, it is unsuitable as a storage site.[25]

On a global level, there would be enough possibilities to transform carbon dioxide into rock. Unfortunately, the technology is not yet mature. It is extremely expensive, and only small test facilities have been built so far. Iceland's Orca project has already cost an estimated 15 million euros, but is able to extract only 4,000 tonnes of carbon dioxide from the air per year.[26]

Humans are currently responsible for 50 billion tonnes of carbon dioxide emissions per year. That would take 12.5 million Orca plants to remove from the air. If such machines continue to be as expensive as the one in Iceland, the filters alone would cost 187.5 billion euros. That's a sum so astronomical that no one could pay it.

The industry therefore hopes that capitalist history will repeat itself—and that the technology will get cheaper the more often it is employed. However, that comparison is flawed. The steam engine was profitable immediately, which is why the technology sold so well and why its efficiency constantly improved. Carbon dioxide filters, by contrast, are so expensive that they are not commercially viable, so this technology will not develop further without massive state funding. It also remains doubtful how quickly the technology will progress. Researchers at the University of Oxford are not particularly optimistic that carbon dioxide capture will get cheaper in the near future: 'It has exhibited no promising cost improvements so far in its 50-year history.'[27]

The 'get rid of it' method is not going to work, because carbon dioxide cannot easily be gathered up and disposed of. This means that humanity will be forced to move away from fossil fuels and towards green energy. However, there is still no general agreement about what counts as climate-neutral and what does not. A considerable number of countries have decided that nuclear power is environmentally friendly and will provide a worry-free source of energy for the future.

CHAPTER TEN

Nuclear power is still a mistake

Many people in Germany now doubt whether the decision to close all the country's nuclear reactors was a good one. Forty-two per cent of survey respondents said that ending nuclear power was a mistake.[1] That shows a clear reversal of public opinion. The final end of nuclear power in Germany was decided by parliament in June 2011 after the reactors in Fukushima, Japan, were destroyed by a tsunami.[2] At that time, 80 per cent of people in Germany were in favour of closing down all the country's nuclear power plants by 2022.[3]

The climate crisis has set new priorities, however. Nuclear power has the advantage of emitting almost no greenhouse gases[4] and being a reliable source of electricity, unlike wind turbines and solar panels, which cannot operate when the wind is not blowing or the sun is not shining.[5] Barring accidents, nuclear reactors also have a lower impact on the environment than the extraction of coal, gas, and oil because the energy density of uranium is 10,000 to 16,000 times higher than that of fossil fuels. One hundred and twenty-five tonnes of uranium are enough to run a large nuclear power plant for a year.

This newly awakened enthusiasm for nuclear power is

almost reminiscent of the post-war period, when atomic energy fuelled unbounded expectations among the West German public and politicians alike. In 1955, the government even set up a specific nuclear ministry, which was initially run by a conservative Bavarian politician, Franz Josef Strauss.[6] The social-democrat opposition at the time also gushed that a new epoch had dawned 'that will be the age of peace and freedom for all'.[7]

The reality turned out to be less impressive than hoped. Even on their best days, the 19 commercially run reactors in Germany only produced about 13 per cent of the total energy consumed in the country.[8] Nuclear power alone would never have been able to meet Germany's energy needs. Also, those old reactors would not have had much of a useful life left by now, even without the official decision to scrap nuclear power. Most were built to last 40 to 60 years, and simply keeping them running would be highly risky. Material fatigue alone would make a nuclear accident increasingly more likely.

Any country that plans to continue using nuclear power must be prepared to build new reactors. Energy companies are only willing to embark on such a risky venture if they receive state subsidies, because nuclear power plants have so far always incurred losses in the billions.[9] And the amount of loss generated per reactor could be even greater in the future because building new ones is taking longer and longer. An infamous example is the construction of the Olkiluoto 3 reactor in Finland, which began in 2005. It was originally planned to go online in 2009, and to cost only three billion euros. It eventually started operating in 2022, at almost four times the cost. This prompted people in Finland to change their minds about nuclear power: there are no plans to build any more new reactors.[10]

Olkiluoto 3 was supposed to be a great success story. It was the first 'third-generation European pressurised water reactor'. This is the same type as the new reactor in Flamanville, France, which was supposed to go online in 2012 and cost 3.3 billion euros. That bill has now risen to 19 billion euros, and the reactor only started to operate in 2024.[11]

America also learned that new nuclear power plants can turn out to be far more expensive than planned. The two reactors called Vogtle 3 and 4 have been under construction in Georgia since 2012 at a planned cost of $14 billion. Those costs are now estimated to have risen to $32 billion, and the two reactors are not even ready to go into operation yet.

The nuclear energy sector is the only branch of industry in which costs consistently rise. Normally, the more often a technology is employed, the cheaper it gets. But nuclear power plants continue to get more expensive, without even counting the costs they generate after the end of their working lives.[12] Dismantling a nuclear power plant can take decades, and leaves behind many thousands of tonnes of radioactive waste that must be disposed of safely. In Germany, most of the costs for that end up being covered by the taxpayer because the energy companies have bought their way out of the responsibility by making a one-off payment of 24 billion euros into a state fund—although storing spent fuel rods safely could cost 170 billion euros.[13] Even that enormous sum is a conservative estimate. No final storage site for nuclear waste has yet been built; in fact, no potential location for such a facility has even been identified.

The complexity and cost of building new power plants means nuclear energy is stagnating on a global level,[14] with the technology covering only 5 per cent of the world's energy consumption.[15] That is almost nothing. Or, to put it another way: some 15,000 new reactors will need to be built around the world if they are to replace fossil fuels. The number of reactors is constantly dwindling; right now, there are 416 in operation.[16]

It is unlikely that many new plants will be built, since global investment in nuclear power is very small—around $44 billion annually.[17] That might seem like quite a handsome sum at first glance, but not when compared to the total investment in electricity production, which stood at $820 billion in 2021. Of that, $367 billion was invested in expanding renewable energies, and the rest was earmarked for fossil-fuel power plants.[18] Today's investments are tomorrow's energy supplies, and the figures show clearly that neither states nor companies believe in a renaissance of nuclear power. It is simply not profitable.

The constant danger of catastrophic accidents also cannot be ignored. The risks connected with nuclear power are so huge that not a single insurance company in the world is willing to offer policies covering all the possible consequences. The Fukushima nuclear disaster caused damage to the tune of around 100 billion euros, and a worst-case accident in Germany could cost as much as $6 trillion.[19]

Advocates of nuclear power don't let that put them off. They place their hopes in technological advances. One particularly popular idea for the future is to build small nuclear power plants around the world and to decentralise energy production.[20] This seems like a compelling idea at first glance, since such mini reactors are only about the size of two football fields, potentially with modular components, making them suitable for assembly-line manufacture. Mass production would then finally have reached the nuclear power industry, causing prices to fall dramatically. The software billionaire Bill Gates has set up a company specifically to develop mini nuclear power plants. His plan is to install them underground to protect them against terrorist attacks.[21]

A mini nuclear reactor underground: the idea sounds hypermodern and futuristic — but in fact it is very old. People dreamt of tiny nuclear power plants even back in the post-war period. The social-democrat thinker Leo Brandt predicted to his party colleagues in 1956 that reactors would soon be able to fit into a crate, cost just $1 million, and be able to supply an entire city with electricity. They would just need to be 'buried in the ground and covered with half a metre of gravel, with a cable coming out at the back'.[22] The reasoning was the same then as it is today: since the energy density of uranium is so high, only small amounts of the fuel are necessary, making mini reactors possible. There was much talk of such 'power plants in a box', of nuclear-powered planes, and even of 'baby reactors' used as heaters.[23]

As we know, that is not what happened. Mini reactors were never built. Instead, huge nuclear power stations were constructed with output capacities of up to 1,450 megawatts.[24] Big power plants are simply more cost-effective due to the specific problems posed by nuclear technology. It is well known that every reactor produces highly toxic radioactive waste. If mini power plants were scattered all over the world, the question of who must dispose of the fuel residues would crop up everywhere, as would the issue of how to prevent potentially weapons-grade uranium from falling into the wrong hands. Faults in mini reactors can also contaminate the environment. No nuclear power plant can ever guarantee complete safety. Large plants generate enough revenue to cover the huge cost of safety monitoring, but those costs are too large to make mini reactors viable.

They cannot run at a profit if precautions are to be taken for all eventualities.

Initial experience proves that this scepticism is well-founded. The American company NuScale plans to build 12 mini reactors to supply communities in Utah with nuclear-generated electricity. However, some of the local energy companies have already withdrawn from the project due to the exploding costs — the original budget of $4.2 billion has so far swollen to $6.1 billion. Construction has also proven to be much slower than planned, with the first mini reactors expected to go online in 2030 at the earliest.[25]

There are currently only three mini reactors in the world, two of which are in Russia and one in China. Russia's are part of a floating nuclear power station called the *Akademik Lomonosov*, which resembles a normal ship and has been producing power since December 2019. It lies at anchor in the Arctic Ocean, and supplies the remote town of Pevek with heat and electricity. The project seemed simple at first, as it merely involved adapting the technology used in Russia's nuclear submarines. Nonetheless, these mini reactors also turned out to be a money pit when the construction period had to be extended from five years to 12. It remains a matter of debate whether the floating nuclear power plant is safe. Environmental campaigners have called it 'the floating Chernobyl' and 'the nuclear *Titanic*'.[26]

But costs are not the only problem. Global uranium deposits are not enough to replace fossil fuels and supply the entire world with climate-neutral energy. Reserves would last for about 13 years if current reactor types were used.[27] Theoretically, it would be possible to build fast breeder reactors to make better use of the uranium. Other elements such as thorium could serve as an additional type of fuel, or the dissolved uranium could be extracted from seawater. But those technologies are not yet mature. Some have never been tested, others are at the experimental stage, and yet more have been tried and abandoned. What is certain is that none of them will reach market readiness within the next few decades—if ever. In any case, they will be too late to avert the collapse of the climate.

They would also certainly cost even more than current reactors. The fact that nuclear energy is becoming ever more costly should really be food for thought for those who place their hopes for the future in atomic energy. It inevitably follows from this that 'green growth' based on nuclear power will not be possible. Since building reactors is so complex and expensive, electricity would remain a scarce commodity. But capitalism needs an abundance of energy in order to expand.

Nuclear power is not the solution, and it is also dangerous. Those who advocate for 'green growth' must place their hopes in wind turbines and solar panels. Such green power does have great potential—but it will not be enough.

CHAPTER ELEVEN

Unfortunately unreliable: solar and wind power

The sun keeps on shining. Five thousand times more energy reaches the Earth from the sun than would be required by the almost eight billion inhabitants of the planet to enjoy a European-level standard of living. So there is no lack of physical energy, which is why many scientists dream of the world ending its dependence on oil sheikhs cheaply. 'Renewable energy is free—fossil fuels cost a lot of money,' enthuses the prominent German meteorologist Mojib Latif.[1] His fellow meteorologist, TV weatherman Sven Plöger, calculates that Germany 'burned' an enormous 1.17 trillion euros on imported oil, natural gas, and coal between 1990 and 2015.[2] It seems obvious for Germany to save that money by switching to wind turbines and solar panels. Some enthusiasts even believe such a transformation is possible 'at no additional cost' if the billions spent on oil are redirected. 'The energy revolution will be a walk in the park,' claims the social-democrat politician Andreas Berg.[3]

This enthusiasm has a long tradition. As early as the 19th century, scientists and politicians believed we would soon be able to capture as much solar energy as we wanted.

The Swedish American inventor John Ericsson spent years working on a 'solar engine' to concentrate enough heat from the sun to replace steam power. The English economist William Stanley Jevons was so convinced of this idea that he worried about Manchester's future as a great industrial centre—because the city received so little sunshine. 'We shall be replaced,' predicted Jevons. 'The seats of industry will be removed to the sunny parts of the Earth.'[4]

The idea of replacing coal with solar power also fascinated people in Germany. In 1879, the founder of the Social Democratic Party, August Bebel, published a bestselling book with the title *Woman Under Socialism*, in which, among other things, he developed a vision of the future where 'a few square miles of North Africa' would be wholly sufficient to supply the entire German Empire with solar power. Bebel based his prediction on there being no problem transporting that desert power north. He believed accumulator batteries were on the horizon that could store 'large volumes of power … for use at any given place and any given time'.[5] Even the US inventor Thomas Edison was willing to bet on the power of the sun: 'I'd put my money on the sun and solar energy. What a source of power! I hope we don't have to wait 'til oil and coal run out before we tackle that.'[6]

All those ecstatic expectations have so far gone unfulfilled. In 2020, solar panels provided only 2.3 per cent of Germany's final energy consumption. Wind power accounted for 5.4 per cent.[7] Solar and wind power have been subsidised in Germany for more than 20 years, but no real energy transition has yet taken place.

This cannot be due alone to costs holding back the energy revolution, since solar and wind power are constantly getting cheaper. Solar technology is now almost 70 years old—and the price of solar panels has fallen by more than

99 per cent in that time. That's a sensational figure.

The modern solar cell was invented in 1953, when a physician at Bell Laboratories accidentally discovered that silicon is far more efficient at turning the sun's energy into electricity than selenium, which had been used until then. However, the technology was extremely expensive, with the power it produced costing a whopping $300 per watt, compared to only 50 cents for electricity from conventional coal-fired power stations. The commercial future did not look bright, and Bell Labs assumed its new miracle technology would only be put to trivial use. For example, the company considered installing silicon cells in portable radios so youngsters could listen to rock 'n' roll on the beach.

In the end, solar technology was saved by military interests. During the Cold War, the United States and the Soviet Union were engaged in a space race, and both superpowers wanted to put satellites into orbit as quickly as possible. One of the crucial questions was how to power the space probes, since conventional batteries only lasted a matter of days. So they turned to solar power. The US satellite *Vanguard 1* was launched in 1958 with solar cells on board. The tiny spacecraft weighed just 1.5 kilos and was small and light enough to carry in one hand, which prompted the Soviet leader at the time, Nikita Khrushchev, to describe it mockingly as 'the grapefruit satellite'. But thanks to solar power, *Vanguard 1* continued to transmit radio signals until 1964, and provided proof that our planet is not perfectly spherical in shape.[8]

The immense cost of solar energy was not important in spaceflight, as any price would have been paid. Solar technology provided the electricity to power all the expensive measuring instruments that cost millions of dollars. Soon, every satellite would be equipped with solar cells, including the Soviet ones.[9] The increasing demand from the spaceflight industry pushed prices down. In 1976, each watt cost just $100 to produce.[10] But even then, solar power remained far too expensive to make it economically viable back on Earth.

The next turning point came with the oil crises starting in 1973, when 'black gold' suddenly went from being dirt cheap to costing five times as much as before in real terms. Initially, the most obvious solution was to further expand nuclear power, but the charm of the reactor was heavily tarnished by the partial meltdown at Three Mile Island in the US in March 1979, and then the nuclear disaster at Chernobyl in April 1986. Nuclear power was now seen as too great a risk, leaving solar and wind power as the only hopes of kicking the world's oil addiction. As early as 1979, US president Jimmy Carter made a statement by installing solar collectors on the roof of the White House.[11]

However, solar power still remained too expensive for commercial purposes. That gap was closed in 2000 by Germany's Renewable Energy Source Act (EEG), which has since been copied by around 100 countries. The approach was as bold as it was simple: solar and wind power were prioritised by the granting of a 20-year guarantee that the tariff paid for electricity produced in that way when it was fed into the grid would always cover the production costs. Another crucial aspect of the legislation was that it foresaw a 5 per cent decrease per year in that support for new power plants, which incentivised solar panel and wind turbine manufacturers to constantly strive to improve the efficiency of their technology, rather than passively cashing in on their prior success. The results exceeded all expectations. In 1998, the Prognos economic research centre was still predicting that solar power would provide a tiny 0.44 terawatt hours of electricity in 2020.[12] In fact, that figure was 51 terawatt hours—116 times the predicted amount.

That government support has not been cheap, however, costing about 20 billion euros per year.[13] That financial burden was unavoidable, but it was distributed in a highly unfair way. The additional costs generated by the EEG were financed by a so-called EEG levy on electricity consumption, which existed until the middle of 2022. Like all consumption taxes, it was particularly tough on the poorest in society, who spend their entire income simply on making ends meet.[14] The wealthy, on the other hand, are less impacted by taxes on consumption, as they are able to save a large part of their income. A snapshot from the year 2015 shows just how much low earners were burdened in this way: for the poorest 10 per cent, the EEG levy was a substantial portion of their net income, at 1.5 per cent; for the richest tenth of society, it was just 0.2 per cent.[15]

Conversely, it was mainly wealthy people who could afford to install solar panels on the homes they owned, allowing them to claim the guaranteed feed-in payments. Since the subsidies were designed to make investing in photovoltaic systems economically worthwhile, the average return per annum was 'attractive'.[16] That meant the poor were made to pay up so that the wealthy could make a profit. This injustice is so embarrassing to many advocates of the energy transition that they simply deny there is a social imbalance at all. They like to argue that many solar power modules are financed by investment funds, 'in which tenants can, of course, also participate'.[17] This creates the impression that the only problem for poor people in this respect is that they don't own a roof. It seems that highly paid engineers are unable to imagine that the poorer sections of society simply don't have the necessary money. So let me explain it for them: the lower 50 per cent of German citizens own less than 21,500 euros' worth of assets, and often have only debts.[18] They have no extra cash to invest in solar power.

It is dangerous for the success of the energy transition that its social impact has been ignored. It was not lost on those who bear the brunt of the reality that the poor have been funding the rich. A representative survey for the Federal Environment Agency in 2018 showed that 72 per cent of people in Germany believed the costs of the energy transition are 'not fairly distributed'.[19]

Returning to solar power: the price of panels has now fallen so far that even small photovoltaic modules installed on private people's roofs can supply electricity as cheaply as huge coal-fired power stations.[20] Large, ground-mounted solar power plants are even more efficient. In sunny southern Germany, they generate a kilowatt hour of electricity for 3.12 to 4.16 euro cents, and in the cloudier north of the country, a kilowatt hour costs 4.27 to 5.70 euro cents.[21]

However, although solar power is now cheap to produce, it still plays hardly any role in Germany's energy mix. Why? There is a structural problem posed by the fact that solar power systems need to take up a lot of space, because the energy density of light is not very high. On average, three kilowatt hours of solar energy reaches Germany per day and per square metre[22] — only around 16 to 18 per cent of which is captured by a newly installed solar module.[23] Since so little energy can be harvested per square metre, many square metres of solar panels are needed.

Germany is densely populated, so space is scarce. The only easily utilised surfaces are roofs, as long as they are not north-facing. Otherwise, inventive ways are needed to minimise the surface area required. Floating solar power plants in pit lakes are currently being trialled,[24] and panels for vertical walls and windows are under development.[25] Photovoltaics could also be installed over motorways or car parks. Another interesting idea is known as 'agrophotovoltaics', in which fields are put to dual use. Solar panels are installed on high frames so they can generate power while food is grown beneath them. Of course, the most suitable crops are those that are liable to be damaged by too much exposure to the sun anyway. Initial field trials have shown that the shade offered by the mounted panels can even increase crop yields. Celery was the crop that benefited most in the trial, with an increased yield of 12 per cent. Potato yields also increased by 3 per cent.[26] The high-mounted solar panels also protect the crops from heavy rains, hail, and even frost, and trials are now being held to ascertain whether they could also offer protection to orchards. This means, theoretically at least, that the area available for harvesting solar energy would be greater than the space required.

Photovoltaics is a fascinating technology, but it has one serious drawback: the sun obviously does not shine all the time. It disappears overnight anyway, but seasonal fluctuations in day length and light intensity are also enormous. In the summer months of June and July, Germany receives about eight times more energy from the sun than in the winter months of December and January.[27] This means that solar power is only a viable source of energy in the summer, when the days are long and the nights are short. In winter, the panels generate almost nothing.

However, the winter in Germany is particularly windy, somewhat compensating for the lack of sunlight. Wind power has also exceeded all expectations. The lobbyists for nuclear power, who could not imagine there would soon be a green alternative to their reactors, were especially pessimistic. The Information Group for Nuclear Energy wrote in 1990 that wind power would never be able to cover even 1 per cent of

Germany's energy needs due to 'climate conditions'. Three years later, an advertisement read: 'Regenerative energies such as solar, wind, and waterpower can only cover up to 4 per cent of energy needs over the long term. Can we justify such an approach? No.'[28] The conventional electricity providers were completely wrong in their predictions. In 2021, wind power alone generated 21.5 per cent of the country's electricity.[29] Together with solar panels, waterpower, and biomass, renewable energy sources accounted for no less than 42.4 per cent of Germany's electricity production.[30]

However, that clear progress is no reason to lapse into eco-euphoria in the belief that the energy transition is almost done. Although nearly half of Germany's electricity is now generated from renewable sources, power generation is not the only way energy sources are consumed; for the rest, Germany relies on combusting gas, oil, and coal. Most cars still run on petrol or diesel, aircraft rely on kerosene fuel, and many households are still heated with gas. If Germany is to become climate-neutral, industries, transportation systems, and buildings will need to be converted to green energy. In terms of Germany's total demand for energy, renewables still account for a modest proportion. As mentioned above, wind power covers only 5.4 per cent of final energy consumption, and solar power accounts for even less, at just 2.3 per cent.[31]

The biggest renewable energy source is currently biomass, which contributes 10 per cent to the mix.[32] But it has almost reached its full potential because there is no extra land available on which to grow more energy crops such as rapeseed and maize. After all, farmland should really be used to grow our food. Also, designating such monocultures as sustainable is pure window dressing. Rapeseed and maize require large amounts of pesticides, fertiliser, and water. They also have a negative impact on biodiversity, as bees and birds find no food in such industrial agricultural deserts.

So Germany can only become climate-neutral if many more wind turbines are installed, which does not appeal to all local residents. When the current economics minister, Robert Habeck of the Green Party, took office, he had no illusions about the size and strength of that resistance, saying, 'I know anger and altercations lurk behind every bush.'[33] Public abhorrence at the 'blighting' of the landscape with wind turbines is now far less vehement than many people believe. Eighty per cent of survey respondents said they would welcome a further expansion of wind power. Even in communities where the rotors are already turning, public resentment remains surprisingly small: only 16 per cent of residents say they are dissatisfied with the wind parks, although the respondents themselves judged the proportion of their neighbours who are unhappy with the turbines to be 40 per cent. Most in fact said they could even imagine accepting more turbines. Only 26 per cent were against installing new turbines, but believed that 58 per cent of their peers were against expanding the wind parks.[34] Resistance is quite contained, and is likely to crumble further since new legislation has increased the financial incentive for communities that accept wind parks, with payments of around 25,000 euros per year for each newly installed wind turbine.[35]

There are currently around 30,000 onshore wind generators in Germany, occupying about 0.5 per cent of the country's land area. However, the amount of cover required would be 2 per cent—four times as much.[36] That's almost three times the size of the federal state of Saarland, or a third of the size of the state of Hesse. Even then, wind power systems would still take up less space than roads, for example. Two and a half per cent of the country is currently buried beneath tarmac. However, the land occupied by wind farms can also be used as arable land, for instance, or as woodland. The turbines' foundations and access routes account for a tiny fraction of the area occupied by wind farms.[37]

But where is the best place to install the turbines? One obvious idea would be to place them primarily in coastal areas, where the wind is famously strongest. Islands such Borkum or Sylt in the North Sea, or Hiddensee in the Baltic, receive winds with an average speed of almost eight metres per second, compared to just four metres per second in relatively wind-still areas of Germany such as the rift valley of the Upper Rhine, where Germany, France, and Switzerland meet, or the municipality of Halle in Saxony-Anhalt. Mountains are also famously windswept, whether it be the Alps, the Black Forest, or lower ranges such as the Rothaar Mountains in Westphalia.[38] However, if wind parks were located only in coastal and mountainous areas, the power they produced would need to be transported across the entire country. That would make it too expensive, despite the high wind yields. It makes more economic sense to use local winds, even if they are less powerful. Turbines could be located throughout the country, creating a decentralised energy-production network.[39]

This message has not yet reached all the federal states in Germany, however. So far, only Schleswig-Holstein, Hesse, Saarland, and Brandenburg have given over around 2 per cent of their land area to wind parks. Saxony, by contrast, has approved only 0.2 per cent of its area for wind farms, and in Bavaria that figure is just 0.1 per cent.[40]

A common reason for not approving the construction of wind turbines is a concern about bird protection. The

German Nature and Biodiversity Conservation Union (NABU) estimates that around 100,000 birds die every year in Germany as a result of collisions with wind turbines. However, around 100 million birds also die every year colliding with glass-fronted buildings, 70 million are killed by motor and railway vehicles, and more than 20 million fall prey to domestic cats. Even more deadly for birds is intensive farming, with its monocultures, pesticides, and spreading of liquid manure, which robs birds of their natural habitats.[41]

Overall planning is also difficult because there is no consensus on how many more wind turbines are needed. Some studies assume that only 7,000 more onshore units are required for Germany to become climate-neutral. Since 30,000 already exist, that would make a total of 37,000 wind turbines. Other experts believe that at least 67,000 are required—almost twice as many as there are today. This astonishing discrepancy stems from the completely different conclusions reached by researchers into how much green electricity Germany will need to be able to produce annually by the year 2050. Some research institutes believe that just 620 terawatt hours will be enough, while others put the total at 1,000 terawatt hours.[42] That's a huge difference.

Contradictory results are inevitable because all forecasts are based on assumptions. They include estimating how much green energy will be able to be imported from other countries, how efficient electric vehicles are likely to become, and how willing people in Germany are to reduce their consumption. Naturally, every study comes up with different results.[43]

One thing is certain: Germany will not be able to do without wind power in the future. It is cheaper here than solar-generated electricity,[44] and, most significantly, the wind is more reliable than sunlight. There are 8,760 hours in a year, and, in that time, onshore wind turbines achieve 1,960 full-load hours, while photovoltaics have only 910 to 980 full-load hours.[45] Offshore wind parks are even more productive, achieving 3,820 full-load hours.[46]

But, as those rather meagre full-load hours also show, wind turbines and solar panels are often unable to run at capacity due to lack of wind or sunshine. Fossil-fuelled power plants, on the other hand, are perfectly predictable. Gas- and coal-fired facilities supply energy around the clock, and can be fired up to top capacity whenever required.

The strength of the wind does not only vary by the hour, day, or season—it also varies year on year. There may be great differences in the amount of electricity generated in the same calendar month of different years. An example: in January 2017, Germany's wind turbines generated only half as much power as they did in January 2018.[47] Yields in spring 2021 were also catastrophically low due to an unusually wind-still period from January to March that year. Since private households and industry require energy all the time, such fluctuations in electricity generation are difficult to manage.

A particularly feared phenomenon is known by the German coinage *dunkelflaute*, meaning literally 'dark doldrums'. A cold *dunkelflaute* is a time in the middle of winter when the sun doesn't shine and there is also no wind—but everyone wants to switch the heating on. That's the acid test for the energy transition.[48] *Dunkelflaute* events are rare, but they can last for several days, and the electricity supply cannot just be switched off until the wind picks up again. An outage lasting just one hour would currently cause damage to the tune of an estimated 0.6 to 1.3 billion euros nationwide.[49]

But do we have to produce green energy in Germany, and risk the dreaded *dunkelflaute*? One conceivable, if radical, alternative was dreamed of by August Bebel. Solar panels could be installed in the uninhabited Sahara Desert, where the sunshine is far more intense and there is no local population to object to solar power farms.[50] And there would no longer be any need to convince the people of Bavaria to accept wind turbines. The green power would come straight from the desert to Germany through cables. It's a nice idea, but it is not financially viable. The solar power expert Volker Quaschning recently showed in detail why electricity from the desert would be too complicated and too expensive.[51]

It is often forgotten that the Sahara also has night and day, as well as summer and winter. The seasonal fluctuations are less pronounced than they are in Germany, but even in North Africa, the days are significantly shorter in January than in July. So expensive storage technology would still be needed to cover those periods of darkness, even if the power was produced in the desert.

The yields from solar panels would, indeed, be 80 per cent higher in Morocco than in Berlin. But that energy would then need to be transported to Germany, which is no easy undertaking. The first option would be to use high-voltage transmission lines, but that would mean losing nearly 10 per cent of the power along the way, because electricity cannot be transported without energy being lost.

It would also take around 100 transmission lines to transport enough energy from the Sahara to central Europe, which would in turn mean building 750,000 electricity pylons between Morocco and Germany.[52] One hundred electricity pylons would need to be built every 300 to 500 metres across the transit countries of Spain and France. It is highly unlikely that those countries would be willing to blight their landscapes just to transport energy to Germany. The construction costs for the cables and pylons would be considerable—reaching around one trillion euros. And that's not even counting the cost of installing the solar panels in North Africa.

Theoretically, the electricity cables could be laid underground, but that would be prohibitively expensive. Germany is currently constructing an underground cable connection called 'SuedLink' to transport wind-generated power from Schleswig-Holstein in the north to the south of the country. SuedLink will cost ten billion euros—and it is 'only' 700 kilometres long. A connection to Morocco would stretch for 3,000 kilometres, and would have to consist of 100 cables, costing a total of several hundred billion euros.

Since transporting electricity from North Africa to Germany overland is out of the question, ships or pipelines are the only remaining options. Before it can be transported as freight, electricity must be converted to hydrogen—by electrolysis. Many people will remember the principle from experiments in the school science lab. Two electrodes are submerged in a container of water (H_2O). Oxygen (O_2) collects at the positively charged anode, and hydrogen (H_2) gathers at the negative cathode. Since the necessary electricity would come from solar power, the resulting hydrogen would be absolutely climate-neutral, or 'green'. However, electrolysis is a very energy-intensive process, and around 30 per cent of the electricity would be lost. Additionally, this technology only works with fresh water, which is hard to come by in the desert. Desalinated seawater would have to be used, which consumes yet more energy.

Hydrogen would at least have the advantage that it can be employed universally, like natural gas. It can be used to heat our houses, run our cars, generate electricity, produce extreme heat for industry, and store energy, or it can be converted into other base chemicals. It is also burns without any harmful emissions, because it simply recombines with oxygen to produce pure water.

The disadvantage is that hydrogen takes up a lot of space. To make it suitable for transport, it must be compressed under high pressure, or liquefied at a temperature of minus 253 degrees, which consumes yet more energy. There are currently no loading terminals for hydrogen in North Africa. There is also a lack of suitable tankers; there is currently only one ship in the entire world that can transport liquid hydrogen.[53]

Pipelines do not offer an attractive alternative. There are already some pipes transporting natural gas from North Africa to Europe,[54] but that small network would not be enough to pump green hydrogen to Germany. Building new pipelines would be both complex and expensive.

After making it to Germany, the hydrogen would have to be converted back into electric power.[55] In gas-fired power stations, that would mean a further energy loss of approximately 40 per cent. The final balance is disappointing: only 30 per cent of the original energy from the desert could be used, at most. Even if solar panels produce 80 per cent more electricity in the Sahara, only half as much energy would finally arrive than can be produced by photovoltaics in Germany. Electricity from the desert is not viable because of the complex and expensive infrastructure it requires.

All this means that Germany can only become climate-neutral if it generates its own green power at home. That is an inconvenient truth, because wind and solar energy are so unreliable and susceptible to the *dunkelflaute*. Environmentally friendly electricity will need to be stored to cover such periods of low availability. This is a new problem. Energy from fossil fuels does not need to be stored as such, because the fuels themselves are the stores — the energy from dead organic material converted over millions of years into oil, gas, and coal.

Conserving such power is also problematic because it cannot be stored directly as electricity. It is not like a kilo of plums, which can be boiled down and conserved in a jar. Electricity must be chemically converted so that the energy can be stored in batteries or as hydrogen. That process always consumes energy. Green power is expensive, not cheap. It is a mistake to believe that 'the sun doesn't send out any bills'.[56] Sunlight and wind may be free, but otherwise the energy revolution is one gigantic war of attrition.

CHAPTER TWELVE

The storage problem

For the energy transition, it is unfortunate that the sun does not shine at night, as it is not easy to bridge those dark hours. Batteries can store surplus energy from the daytime to be used in the evening, but that immediately adds to the price of solar energy: the cost per kilowatt hour doubles when batteries are charged at the same time.[1]

Batteries are also of limited usefulness. They can be used as a stopgap for a few hours at most. Because they are still so expensive, they only make economic sense if they are charged and emptied as often as possible, as that reduces the overall cost of storage per kilowatt hour. Imagine the opposite scenario: if someone decided to fully charge a battery with solar power in summer, in order to tap into the energy in winter. That would mean the battery would be out of use for six months—making the electricity correspondingly expensive.

Batteries are flexible in their use, however. There are plans to feed the energy stored in the rechargeable batteries in electric cars into the grid at times of high demand. After all, private cars are used for just one hour a day on average, so they could be emptied and recharged while they are standing idle. The disadvantage, of course, is that owners would no longer be free to drive their electric vehicles whenever they please — they would become mostly stationary cars. For this reason, realistic scenarios assume that only around 10 per cent of electric cars would be available to top up the grid at times of high demand.[2]

Batteries are of no help during protracted periods of *dunkelflaute*, however. Bill Gates recently calculated how much storage capacity would be needed to supply Tokyo with energy for just three days: 'The answer is more than 14 million batteries. That's more storage capacity than the world produces in seven years. Purchase price: $400 billion … And that's just the capital cost of the batteries; it doesn't include other expenses like installation and maintenance.'[3]

However, batteries are not the only technology that can be used to bridge temporary gaps in the electricity supply. Another option is to use pumped-storage plants. The basic idea behind this technology is so simple that the first such plants were built as far back as a century ago. When there is a surplus of electricity, it is used to pump water uphill. When there is a power shortage, the water is released, driving a turbine attached to a generator. Pumped storage is quite efficient, releasing around three-quarters of the energy put in. However, Germany has relatively few suitable locations, and even they often go unused because pumped-storage stations take the form of huge concrete blocks in the midst of the mountains, and are considered a blot on the landscape.[4] For these reasons, pumped-storage capacity would only be enough to stabilise Germany's electricity grid for a few hours.[5]

An additional option recently became available with the opening in May 2021 of the 'NordLink' undersea cable connecting the hydroelectric power stations in the Norwegian mountains to Schleswig-Holstein in northern Germany. The bidirectional approach is a brilliant one: whenever there is a surplus of wind-generated electricity in

Germany, the extra power is sent north so Norway can replenish the reservoirs that feed its hydroelectric power plants. When Germany has insufficient wind power, it can make use of the hydroelectric power from Norway.

This 'electricity highway' is a two-way road that can deliver power equivalent to the needs of 3.6 million German households.[6] That's quite impressive, but would be of limited help during a *dunkelflaute*, since Germany has 40.5 million households. Also, other states want to tap into Norway's hydropower. The Netherlands has been connected to Norway via the 'NorNed' undersea cable since 2008, and the 'North Sea Link' between Norway and the United Kingdom opened in autumn 2021.[7] So the availability of Norway's hydropower is limited, and mainly serves as a buffer to keep the electricity grid stable.

Consumers can also act like a buffer by adapting their demand for electricity to its availability. Popular examples of this are washing machines and dishwashers. They don't need to run at a set time, and could be switched on at times when electricity is abundant. Households would save money by doing this, since of course the abundant power would be very cheap. But such 'load management' requires appliances to recognise when power is cheap. They need to be able to receive pricing data, which requires a so-called smart grid.[8]

From a technological point of view, such smart grids have been feasible for a long time. They would also allow homes to act as intermediate storage facilities, as long as they are well insulated and fitted with electric heat pumps. When electricity is abundant, the room temperature would be increased, but by such a small amount that residents would barely notice the difference. When there is more demand for electricity than supply, the heating is switched off for a time, allowing the temperature to lower again by a degree or two. Completely normal buildings would thus become energy-storage batteries.[9]

There are also ways that industry could potentially vary its demand for electricity. Well-insulated cold-storage facilities can do without energy for a long time, and aluminium smelting plants could ramp up production when electricity is particularly abundant.[10] But, as creative as all these ideas are, load management alone will never be enough to bridge longer periods of *dunkelflaute*.

The fear of blackouts is not new, and has occasionally been abused to further particular interests. For example, in 1975, the premier of the German federal state of Baden-Württemberg, Hans Filbinger, warned that 'without the Wyhl nuclear power plant, the lights will start going out in Baden-Württemberg by 1980'.[11] Wyhl was never built, and south-western Germany was not plunged into darkness. Still, it would be a mistake to think that such anecdotes prove it is okay to ignore the risk of power outages. If a completely green electricity supply is to work, it must be able to cope with times of *dunkelflaute*, as the solar power expert Harry Wirth underlines: 'The storage capacity of the system must be designed for the worst case of a primary energy failure (sun and wind) lasting several weeks, i.e., a prolonged lull in winter, possibly exacerbated by a closed snow cover.'[12]

Germany's national weather service has predicted the frequency of *dunkelflaute* periods lasting more than 48 hours, during which time wind turbines and solar panels would be able to deliver at most 10 per cent of their nominal capacity. Their forecast sounds reassuring at first: such a period can be expected only twice a year in Germany, and is likely to remain regional in scope, rather than affecting the whole of Europe. A continent-wide *dunkelflaute* occurs on average only once every five years.[13]

Despite this, it is still impossible for Germany to rely completely on its neighbours for power during a nationwide *dunkelflaute*, when elsewhere in Europe the sun is shining or the wind is blowing. The necessary network of cables simply does not exist. Although a European 'energy union' exists, which aims to provide new power connections between EU member states, they are only intended to compensate for minor fluctuations. The energy union does not aim to balance out a longer-lasting *dunkelflaute* because the necessary high-voltage lines would be far too expensive. The problem of installing cables right across the continent is familiar from our earlier considerations of using solar power from the Sahara.

All this means that Germany needs to be able to help itself whenever the wind and sun are too weak to generate electricity. And true *dunkelflaute* periods, when 90 per cent of the system's nominal capacity is missing, are not the only threat. The energy-supply system approaches its limits when less than half the installed capacity is available—which is the case for 362 hours per year. That's the equivalent of approximately two weeks.[14]

From a purely technological point of view, a solution is already on the horizon: 'green hydrogen'. Although it would be far too expensive to import all our green energy from the Sahara, small emergency reserves could be financed. Also, some of the 'green hydrogen' could be produced in Germany, since there is occasionally too much power in the grid when the sun shines intensively in summer or the wind is particularly strong in winter. That surplus could be fed into devices that turn it into hydrogen for storage (electrolysers). They would once again be rather inefficient, however, as only around 35 per cent of the green energy put in would remain for use after storage.[15]

So far, these are all still projects for the future. There are currently no efficient electrolysers with which to produce the green hydrogen. Optimistic predictions say the technology could be mature enough to go into regular operation by the year 2030.[16]

It is already clear that green hydrogen will be expensive. The costs can be predicted relatively reliably because a climate-damaging version is already produced. Hydrogen is an important base substance for the chemical industry, and is currently extracted from natural gas, generating a lot of carbon dioxide emissions. This fossil hydrogen is around three times more expensive than normal natural gas, and the green version may generate much higher costs, making it ten times more expensive.[17]

There are also insufficient gas power stations to supply the whole of industry with electricity. There are widely varying estimates of how many additional gas turbines would be required if Germany were to rely entirely on green power and still be able to bridge periods of *dunkelflaute*. However, most studies agree that the capacity of Germany's gas power stations would have to double at least, if not triple. That would mean Germany had more power stations than it does at present, even including the capacities of currently active coal-fired power plants in the calculation.[18] But unlike today, those many power stations would mostly lie idle, running only when there is a shortage of electricity. They would be in operation for a grand total of 362 hours a year, and for the remaining 8,398 hours of the year they would be nothing but dead capital.[19] That is another factor driving costs up.

The energy transition will be complex and expensive. It will require many new wind turbines, solar power systems, batteries, power cables, electrolysers, and gas turbines.[20] Nonetheless, most climate-protection activists are convinced that future electricity prices 'will be lower than they are today'.[21] Green energy is not only supposed to save humanity—but to be a good business proposition, too. Unfortunately, that is not the case.

CHAPTER THIRTEEN

The energy transformation will be expensive, not cheap

No one knows how much batteries or electrolysers will cost in 30 years' time. No one can see into the future, so there can be no exact predictions. The Austrian British philosopher Karl Popper summed up the problem in one apt sentence: 'If we could predict what we will know, we would already know it.'[1] Since detailed forecasts are impossible, it is usual in the debate about the climate to develop scenarios with various degrees of probability.

This is a legitimate approach, and there is no alternative to it anyway, but intrinsic within it is an opportunity for authors to give free rein to their own particular hopes, so most of the resulting scenarios are extremely optimistic in nature. Authors need not fear being contradicted, because their assumptions cannot be disproven. Some researchers from Oxford are particularly upbeat, predicting an unprecedented financial bonanza for humanity: 'A rapid green energy transition will likely result in trillions of net savings.'[2] Climate policies apparently cost nothing at all, but generate enormous profits.

The Fraunhofer Society, a renowned German research

organisation, also comes to a reassuring conclusion, although it does not deny certain costs. It predicts that the energy transition in Germany is likely to require around 50 billion euros a year—which is significantly less than is spent on Christmas presents. Its gratifying conclusion is that, 'The annual amounts ... are compared to the business turnover during Christmas time, which for 2019 in Germany was just under 102 billion euros, i.e. about twice the average net annual expenditure for the energy system transformation.'[3]

The scenarios are so optimistic because they rely on the principle of 'the trend is your friend'. The cost of solar units and wind turbines has fallen sharply—so it is assumed that this pattern will be repeated for storage technologies and green hydrogen. It can already be seen happening with batteries, which have fallen significantly in price. In 1992, each kilowatt of storage capacity cost no less than $6,035. By 2016, the price had fallen to just $244.[4]

Even the experts are surprised by how rapidly environmental technologies have become cheaper. Very few predicted such a development, as can be seen by a historical analysis: most forecasts for the period from 2010 to 2020 assumed that the cost of solar panels would fall by only 2.5 per cent a year. In fact, the price fell by an annual 15 per cent.[5]

However, solar panels, batteries, and wind turbines are rare exceptions; the cost of most other industrial products does not fall that quickly. Bicycles, refrigerators, or automobiles—none these has seen its price plummet in that way.[6] A modern mid-range VW car is not 99.6 per cent cheaper today than a Ford Model T was when it rolled off the assembly line in 1914 Detroit. On the contrary, cars are now more expensive than they were 100 years ago.[7] Of course, they are more powerful and comfortable now, but the fact remains that the price has gone up, not down.

We can be glad that solar panels, wind turbines, and batteries follow an unusual trend in falling rapidly in price. Otherwise, the energy transformation would be so costly that humanity would remain forever shackled to the climate-killing fossil fuels of coal, oil, and gas. But it is no cause for boundless optimism. Although batteries are now much cheaper than they were 30 years ago, they are still expensive. As already mentioned, the cost of solar power systems doubles when batteries are included. Electrolysers are also not yet cost-effective. The price of environmental technology would have to fall further for the energy transition to be cheap. Unfortunately, there is no guarantee that this trend will continue in the future. Important raw materials might become so scarce that they push prices up sharply.

Solar panels and wind turbines are currently a niche phenomenon. Solar power delivers 0.4 per cent of global primary energy, while wind power accounts for 0.8 per cent.[8] Electric cars have a global market share of a measly 1 per cent.[9] And, although there is barely any environmental technology around the world, there are already concerns that the necessary raw materials will not be sufficient for the energy transition.

Green technology not only gobbles up steel, concrete, and aluminium—which have so far been in plentiful supply. It also devours scarce mineral resources. They include lithium, nickel, copper, cobalt, manganese, graphite, and rare earths such as neodymium. It takes 35 kilos of those raw materials to manufacture a traditional car, whereas an electric car requires around 210 kilos—six times as much. Wind turbines also do not produce power out of thin air. More than 10,000 kilos of those mineral resources are consumed for every megawatt of installed capacity. That rises to no less than 15,000 kilos for offshore turbines. Solar panels do not require quite so many raw materials to make, but the corresponding figure is still 7,000 kilos. Conventional power plants are far more economical: burning coal uses 2,500 kilos of mineral resources per megawatt, and for gas the figure is as little as 1,200 kilos.[10]

The demand for mineral resources is therefore likely to explode if the entire world's economy wants to become climate-neutral. The International Energy Agency predicts that, by 2040, the demand for lithium will increase by 42 times; for graphite, by 25 times; for cobalt, by a factor of 21; for nickel, by a factor of 19; and for rare earths, by a factor of seven. Demand for copper could more than double.[11]

The danger is not that these resources will become depleted and that no more deposits can be found. The Earth's crust has enough to offer. But it is becoming more difficult to extract these resources. By 2030, the demand for lithium is expected to have grown so much that all currently existing and planned mining operations will only be able to cover half the world's needs. However, it takes 16 years on average to open up new mines.[12] So it is already clear that lithium will become scarcer—although it is essential for the manufacture of electric cars, batteries, smartphones, laptops, and tablet computers.[13]

The more the quality of deposits decreases, the more they are exploited. This is simple economic logic: the first sites to be mined are those that generate the biggest profits, because they are easiest to access and to guarantee high-quality minerals. Less attractive deposits only come into play when the best sites are largely depleted or are no longer sufficient to meet demand. A much-cited example of this is copper. Chile is the world's biggest exporter, but the metal content of Chile's copper ores has fallen by 30 per cent in just 15 years. The lower the copper content, the more energy and ore are required to extract it, which in turn drives up production costs, greenhouse gas emissions, and the amount of waste. The International Energy Agency therefore concludes, 'These risks to the … mineral supply are manageable, but they are real.'[14]

Technology optimists are not put off by these gloomy predictions. They believe in the bountiful realm of solar energy, in which raw material reserves are endless. The Silicon Valley entrepreneur Tony Seba has a particularly curious take on this vision of the future:

> The Stone Age did not end because humankind ran out of stones. It ended because rocks were disrupted by a superior technology: bronze. Stones didn't just disappear. They just became obsolete for tool-making purposes in the Bronze Age. The horse and carriage era did not end because we ran out of horses. It ended because horse transportation was disrupted by a superior technology, the internal combustion engine … The age of film photography did not end because we ran out of film … The web did not disrupt the newspaper industry because we ran out of paper … The cell phone did not disrupt the old landline telephone industry because we ran out of copper. Enough copper is underground to last one hundred years.[15]

Thus, the optimists' message is that humanity's creativity is inexhaustible. Our intelligence is the raw material that matters. The planet will provide what we need.

It cannot be denied that raw materials which appeared to be scarce in the past have often turned out to be abundant.

The famous 1972 bestseller *The Limits to Growth* included the assumption that gold reserves would be exhausted by the end of the 20th century.[16] But the year 2000 came and went, and gold is still available because the known reserves of the precious metal have quintupled in the meantime. Known silver deposits have tripled over the same period, and known aluminium deposits have increased by almost 25 times.[17]

There are two effects that can turn scarcity into abundance. First: when prices rise, it pays to use raw materials more sparingly. This phenomenon can be observed in the case of solar power systems. Today's panels require 40 to 50 per cent less silver and silicon than the first models, which is what made the boom in photovoltaics possible at all.[18] Second: when raw materials become more expensive, it becomes profitable to seek out new deposits. Copper is once again a good example here. The known reserves in 1970 amounted to 280 million tonnes, but some 600 million tonnes of the metal have been consumed since then — and available copper reserves are currently around 870 million tonnes. As paradoxical as it may seem, consumption increases the amount of known reserves.[19]

Technology optimists also point to the fact that rare earths are not actually all that rare.[20] That is true. Global reserves of rare earths are estimated at 120 million tonnes, of which only around 280,000 tonnes a year are currently used.[21] So reserves are likely to last a long time. However, these elements never occur in their pure form in nature. They are combined with other minerals, which can often be radioactive. Acids and salts are used to extract the rare earths, leaving behind highly toxic, radioactive mud as waste.[22]

Nonetheless, it has long been apparent that the era of cheap minerals is coming to an end. To return to copper once again: a tonne of the metal cost $1,850 at the beginning of the year 2000; by May 2022, that had risen to $9,392; and prices could continue to rise.[23] The cost of raw materials rises so relentlessly because the global economy cannot grow without consuming a constantly increasing volume of mineral resources. Our planet is being ransacked. A historical survey illustrates the extent of the plundering: in 1900, one-twelfth of the resources were consumed compared to 2015. Most importantly, consumption is increasing at an increasing rate. Around one-third of all raw material consumption since 1900 took place in the short time between 2002 and 2015.[24]

Companies have now begun searching for ways to replace scarce raw materials. Research is underway into cobalt batteries and electrolysers that require as little iridium as possible, for example.[25] This may be enough to cover individual temporary shortages, but the real vicious circle remains: since the global demand for raw materials is constantly rising, the best deposits have already been exhausted. The metal content of available ore keeps dropping, so more and more of it must be mined to extract the same amount of minerals. That means that more dead material must be moved, which drives up prices.

Recycling is also of no help here. Batteries and electrolysers do have the massive advantage that their raw materials can be reused, while petrol or diesel go up in smoke, leaving nothing but volatile waste in the air in the form of carbon dioxide.[26] But as good as the idea of using old batteries as a 'quarry' appears, even the best circular economy would never be able to solve our current raw materials problem.

There are several reasons for this. First, most batteries are newly manufactured and have not yet reached the end of their useful life. Their parts are not available to be cannibalised for the production of new batteries. Second, recycled materials are not of the same quality as fresh raw materials—they are worn-out scrap metal;[27] at best, some can be reused for their old purpose, but the rest is 'down-cycled' and may be good for nothing more than surfacing roads. Third, recycling is not free: it consumes energy, meaning there is often no real financial saving involved. Fourth, 'green growth' in essence means expanding the economy, which will create a demand for more mineral reserves to be extracted than before.[28] The International Energy Agency calculates that even by 2040, only around 10 per cent of the materials needed to make batteries might come from recycling.[29] That is far too little to satisfy our hunger for lithium, copper, cobalt, and so on.

When the cost of raw materials goes up, so does the price of the end product. In the case of batteries, minerals now account for up to 70 per cent of the overall cost. Manufacturers are victims of their own success. Since production costs have fallen so rapidly over the past ten years, raw materials are the only high-cost part of the production. They dictate how expensive batteries are.[30]

Raw materials are not the only thing that is becoming scarcer and more expensive—the necessary workforce could also soon be lacking. The energy transition requires a huge amount of construction to install all the necessary solar power systems, wind turbines, heat pumps, and gas power stations. A calculation carried out for the Green Party in the German Bundestag predicts that around 767,000 skilled workers and engineers will be needed by 2035, and there is already a shortage of labour in those professions.[31] Homeowners are aware of the problem, as it is already difficult to find heating engineers, for example. Of course, government promotion of vocational training could tempt more people to take up technology-based jobs in the climate-protection sector. But those who are recruited will be well aware of the fact that they are in short supply and high demand, which is likely to drive wages up.

All this means that the energy transition will be expensive, not cheap. This conclusion may sound surprising, as climate-protection activists make out that the calculation is simple: in two years at most, solar power systems generate enough power to make up for the energy required to manufacture and dispose of them.[32] Since their average working life is 20 years, this would mean that these modules would generate free electricity for 18 years.[33] Wind turbines come out even better. They are said to make up for the energy they use within 11 months at most, and can continue to turn and provide free energy for many years.[34] How can that be anything but a good deal?

This convenient calculation falters due to its failure to take system costs into account. There is an incessant, round-the-clock demand for energy. But wind turbines and solar plants can only provide power when the conditions are right. That means batteries and hydrogen are required to balance out the gaps in supply. It may seem obvious, but a fact that is often overlooked is that those stores do not produce any new energy. They only conserve it—and themselves consume large amounts of energy in the process. Thus the net energy yield of the system as a whole is much reduced.

The energy transition is imperative, but it will not allow us to live a life of overabundance in the future. Green electricity will remain scarce and expensive. Most studies admit implicitly that energy will be in short supply in the future, since all the scenarios revolve around the question of how to increase efficiency. The basic idea is that we need to make better use of power, since it is limited. That plan is correct, but it is associated with illusory hopes for the future.

CHAPTER FOURTEEN

The dream of 'decoupling' will not work

Germany currently consumes a huge 12,779 petajoules of energy per year.[1] That figure sounds very abstract, so consider this: the same amount of energy would be released by 13 asteroids the size of the largest Egyptian pyramid hitting the country per year.[2] This may be a strange-sounding comparison, but it gives an idea of how dependent Germany is on energy.

Any attempts to protect the climate are bound to fail if this enormous consumption is not reduced, since green electricity can provide only a fraction of that amount. For this reason, all the scenarios are based on the necessity of drastically lowering energy use, with most studies assuming it must be halved at least.[3] That means radical energy-saving measures are required.

The logical consequence would be to shrink industry, since all the technology it relies on must constantly be fed with energy. But most climate-protection activists steadfastly insist that 'green growth' is possible. The Climate Neutrality Foundation is particularly confident, even promising an 'economic miracle' comparable to Germany's post-war economic boom.[4]

What results is a kind of minimax principle — producing an ever-increasing amount of goods and services with little energy. The idea is to 'decouple' eco-economic input from the return it brings. The concept is reminiscent of lazy teenagers who like to fool themselves into believing they can get top grades while studying as little as possible.

Nonetheless, the idea of 'decoupling' is not completely far-fetched, because energy can easily be saved in some branches of industry. For example, green electricity has the advantage of being fed directly into the grid from the wind turbines and solar panels that produce it. Conventional coal- and gas-fired power stations, on the other hand, first have to use the energy to drive turbines to produce electricity, and that is very inefficient. There are no such costly intermediate steps with green electricity, which means huge savings of up to 23 per cent could be made in primary energy consumption.[5]

It is not just energy production that would become more efficient. Energy consumption could sometimes also be reduced easily by switching to electric power. Electric heat pumps for domestic heating are a prime example of how this works.[6] Heat pumps work like refrigerators, only the other way around and with far more power. Fridges cool our food by conducting heat from the inside to the outside. Heat pumps, on the other hand, remove heat from the ambient air or the ground and transport it inside a building. In this way, three to four kilowatt hours of warmth can be generated from one kilowatt hour of electricity — if the building in question has underfloor heating and is very well insulated.[7] Today's heat pumps are suitable not only for detached and terrace housing, but also for apartment blocks.[8] If all suitable buildings were equipped with this new technology, private households would save a third to a half of their overall energy consumption.[9]

To take stock briefly: Germany's energy consumption could fall by 31 to 36 per cent overall if fossil-fuelled power plants were decommissioned and heat pumps were used instead.[10] That's an impressive saving, but, unfortunately, it is still not enough, in light of the fact that most scenarios say we must halve our energy consumption at least. But that is the end of the list of simple solutions. Electric cars are still often touted as miracles of efficiency, but closer inspection shows that battery-driven vehicles do not have much of a future—at least not as a private means of transport.

This vision of the future may seem surprising at first, since, in their daily operation, electric cars save a lot of energy thanks to their 64 to 70 per cent efficiency.[11] Petrol engines, on the other hand, are extremely inefficient, utilising only around 20 per cent of the energy put in. That's a loss of 80 per cent—when the motor is running normally. When cars are stuck in traffic, or have to stop at almost every set of traffic lights, their efficiency can fall to a dismal 5 per cent.[12] Diesel motors make better use of energy, but their efficiency is nowhere near as high as that of electric vehicles.

While electric cars initially seem to perform brilliantly, conventional combustion cars are often mocked as 'radiators on wheels' because they produce so much waste heat. Despite countless millions being invested in research and development, there is no hope of significantly improving the efficiency of conventional cars, due simply to their basic engineering design.[13]

Electric vehicles do have their supporters. Bill Gates drives one, and has written euphorically that he 'loves it'.[14] But, as pleasant as it might be to glide almost silently through city traffic, it is anything but climate protection on wheels.

Manufacturing the batteries for large electric vehicles gene-rates 15 to 20 tonnes of carbon dioxide emissions. A car with a fuel-efficient combustion engine would have to have more than 200,000 kilometres on the clock before it had emitted such a huge amount of greenhouse gas.[15] Petrol cars may be radiators on wheels, but the environmental credentials of large electric vehicles are little better. Smaller electric cars are, of course, more efficient, but even their improved impact on the environment does not kick in until they have 40,000 kilometres on the clock.[16]

Comparisons between electric cars and combustion engines are popular, but such tunnel-vision concentration on the type of drive technology ignores the fact that cars are a fundamentally inefficient way to get around. Even electric cars weigh one to two tonnes and carry only 1.3 people, on average, per trip.[17] Such wasteful behaviour will no longer be possible when only half as much energy as we currently use is available to us.

All studies agree that the number of cars must go down. There are currently almost 50 million private cars on Germany's roads. That will need to fall to a maximum of 30 million.[18] But Germans need not fear being left stranded on the roadside. Private car use could be made more efficient. Currently, most cars stand around unused for an average of 23 hours a day. Computer technology will make it possible for cars to be directed to where they are needed at any given time.[19] An especially popular idea is that of self-driving cars, which move and steer themselves autonomously. Stressed-out drivers could sit back in future and enjoy a cup of coffee or check their emails. After dropping passengers off at their destination, cars would drive themselves off to pick up their next passenger somewhere else.

Such future scenarios aim to stress the fun factor in

saving energy and giving up on private car ownership. There is nothing wrong with that. You don't have to own a car to be happy. But these sophisticated models overlook the fact that using fewer cars would not generate 'green growth'. It would be 'green shrinkage'.

One and three quarter million people are currently employed directly or indirectly in Germany's automobile industry.[20] A 40 per cent reduction of the country's fleet of private cars would leave many of those workers unemployed. Some auto workers could, of course, become bus drivers or railway workers, since all scenarios of the future include an expansion of local and national public transport systems. But the demand for train drivers would not be enough to provide a job for every VW employee made redundant in the future.

Increasing exports would not be a viable way to secure German automotive industry jobs.[21] Exports are already so high that there is hardly any headroom for them to grow further: German auto companies made 64.2 per cent of their overall sales abroad in 2020. In addition, there would be far less demand abroad for German cars if they were all small, light electric models. Any country can produce such cars itself. (And China is already dominating that market.) The success of Germany's automotive giants is based on their perfecting of dinosaur technology. They specialise in luxury cars with combustion engines that unfortunately have nothing to contribute to climate protection.

The automobile industry is not the only sector that would have to shrink. Aviation also has no future, although many climate studies prefer to leave the issue of air travel aside. It seems they do not want to confront their readers with the fact that there will be no more holidays in Bali or flights to Mallorca in the future. Plane travel is too harmful to the climate for round-the-world and cross-continental flights to be viable.

Officially, air travel accounts for just 3 per cent of German greenhouse gas emissions. That may sound harmless, but it is not the whole truth. It makes a crucial difference whether oil is combusted on the ground or at an altitude of 10,000 metres. When aircraft burn kerosene, the process produces not only carbon dioxide, but also water vapour and soot. These form into condensation trails and cirrus clouds, which enormously increase the greenhouse effect. They prevent heat from radiating from Earth into space, instead reflecting it back down to the ground. This is why flying is responsible for around 10 per cent of the climate damage caused by Germany.[22]

Climate-harming kerosene is mostly burned by the wealthy. Poor families fly on average once every five years, while rich Germans treat themselves to almost three flights a year—and fly much greater distances.[23] The global figures are even more stark. Nearly 90 per cent of the world's population never fly at all, while 1 per cent of humans fly so much that they account for more than half of all the kerosene burned around the world.[24]

Each return flight from Germany to New York generates around 2.6 tonnes of carbon dioxide emissions per person. The figure is 5.8 tonnes for flights to Australia and back.[25] That soon mounts up to huge quantities when the rich are permanently jetting across the skies. Some years ago, the ecologist Stefan Gössling decided to take a closer look at the flying habits of famous people. He was easily able to do so simply by analysing their posts on Facebook and Instagram. His results showed that no one flies more than

Bill Gates, who spent at least 350 hours in his private planes in 2017—emitting more than 1,600 tonnes of carbon dioxide in the process. Second and third place went to the hotel-chain heiress Paris Hilton and the actress and singer Jennifer Lopez, who generated 1,200 tonnes and 1,000 tonnes respectively.[26]

Bill Gates is fully aware that he is a danger to the climate. He contritely admits, 'I own big houses and fly in private planes … It's true that my carbon footprint is absurdly high.' But Gates believes he has found a solution. 'In 2020, I started buying sustainable jet fuel.' He then goes on to show his readers that the biofuel is two and a half times more expensive than normal kerosene.[27] So Gates' message is that money can solve all climate problems.

The multibillionaire is not alone in this belief. The German government also puts its faith in biofuels for aviation; its aim is to raise the proportion of biofuel mixed with normal kerosene to 2 per cent from 2030 onwards. But it is questionable whether such 'biofuels' really are 'bio', because they are mainly produced from monoculture crops such as rapeseed, maize, and palm oil, which also occupy agricultural land that is needed to grow food crops. For a long time, scientists hoped they would find an alternative in algae,[28] which could produce the necessary biomass in the water without occupying land areas. But that enthusiasm has now cooled off. 'The algae hype is over,' according to the German Aerospace Centre.[29]

Biofuels for jets are also far from climate-neutral. They have the advantage of not generating any additional carbon dioxide, because the carbon dioxide they emit is what was previously fixed by the plants used to make the fuel. But they still generate water vapour and soot—and so still cause condensation trails and cirrus clouds.[30] Planes that run on biofuels are half as damaging as traditionally fuelled aircraft, but they are ultimately still harmful. It turns out that money cannot solve all climate problems, and that Bill Gates remains a maximum source of damage to the environment.

Humanity must keep its feet on the ground if it is serious about climate protection. This realisation is so painful to face up to that even the German Greens prefer to suppress it. 'Flying is a great product,' enthuses the Greens' transport spokesman, Toni Hofreiter. 'It connects people, it promotes cultural exchange.' Hofreiter does not believe in biofuel for aviation, however, but instead imagines that the aircraft of the future will run on synthetic fuels.[31]

From a technological point of view, this would be the same process as described for electricity from the desert. Solar power would first be used to produce hydrogen, which would then be added to carbon dioxide to create synthetic kerosene. The snag with this wonderful idea, however, is that it would guzzle enormous amounts of electricity, tripling the cost of aviation fuel, at least [32] Prices could also go through the roof if environmental technology does not continue to get cheaper and raw materials become scarce.

Synthetic kerosene does, at least, produce less soot and water vapour than biofuel, and if flight routes are optimised, climate damage could be reduced by about 90 per cent.[33] That's a lot, but it's not enough. Humanity must achieve net zero to avert a climate catastrophe. Even residual emissions of 10 per cent would be 10 per cent too much.[34]

This is a fact that is ignored even by climate-protection activists, who share well-meaning tips about how to reach distant continents as economically as possible: 'I recommend long overseas trips. It makes no difference to the local population whether tourists fly there once for a long stay or three times for a short trip.'[35] So anyone who goes to the Canaries should stay for at least three weeks.

But jetting around the world at a leisurely pace cannot be the solution. If those who want to fly are fair, they must accept that the entire population of the world should be allowed to take 'long overseas trips'—and not just the wealthy. But if billions of people were to take to the skies, climate collapse would soon come about, even if each individual flight only caused a small amount of damage.

Airlines have already realised that they have to promise to achieve net zero if they are to have a future. They reassure their customers that they are on track to 'achieve a neutral carbon dioxide balance' by 2050. For a time, Lufthansa's website optimistically pointed out that, 'Scientific and technological foundations are already in place', although in the same sentence the airline hedged its enthusiasm, admitting that 'not all of the solutions currently exist'.[36] Those few words, and the fact that this sentence no longer appears on the website, indicate that, in reality, the airlines have no idea how they can ever become completely climate-neutral.[37]

If we are to protect the climate, we must say goodbye to flying. That's not easy. It is true, after all, that the ability to get to know the whole world is one of our freedoms. Also, 850,000 people in Germany depend on the commercial aviation sector either directly or indirectly for their jobs.[38] They would all have to seek new employment if Germany began to take climate protection seriously.

There will be no shortage of new jobs. Organic farming would require more workers than the current agroindustry employs. Forests are also likely to be so damaged by climate change that large areas will need to be reforested. But such rescue measures cannot be called 'green growth'. They are undoubtedly necessary, but they do not create capitalist added value, and the overall economy would shrink despite them.

The end of plane travel would not mean the end of contact between continents—there would still be ships. Fresh-cut flowers from Kenya or fresh fruit air-freighted from Peru would no longer be on Europe's supermarket shelves, but most other goods can be shipped by sea. However, ships are not environmentally harmless either. They are currently responsible for around 3 per cent of global greenhouse gas emissions.

Some of those emissions would be cut automatically if the world switched to green energy. Oil, coal, and gas currently account for around 43 per cent of all sea-going freight.[39] Most other commercial goods would still be needed, however. Ships primarily transport iron, steel, grain, wood, phosphorus, and bauxite—although those commodities don't attract much public attention. Shipping containers have become the symbol of globalisation, but only around 16 per cent of all sea freight is transported in them.[40] Still, it is no accident that shipping containers have come to embody intercontinental trade: they are mainly used to ship processed products, which make up 60 per cent of shipped freight by value.

Shipping companies also vow that their goal is to become climate-neutral by 2050. Research is continuing into how that can be achieved, since there are currently no alternative propulsion systems. Batteries are out of the question, because they are too heavy and would take up the entire ship if they were to be big enough to provide power for a voyage across the oceans. They would leave no room for the actual cargo. So, once again, the only option is green hydrogen generated with solar power, which would then be converted into methanol or ammonia. Prototypes of possible motors are currently being developed by the Fraunhofer Society, among others.[41] The technical problems can probably be solved, but, like all synthetic fuels, biofuel for ships would be very energy-intensive and expensive.[42]

This would not end globalisation, but it would change it. For many cheap products, it would no longer pay to import them from faraway countries if costly biofuel was used to transport them. It is also difficult to imagine a continuation of the boom in cruise travel if ocean voyages were to become significantly more expensive. On a purely economic level, the losses in that industry would be bearable, since there are only 500 cruise ships worldwide.[43]

A green economy would have to shrink because there is not enough green electricity for all cars, planes can never be completely climate-neutral, and biofuels for ships are too expensive. But the problems don't end there. Industry has difficulty weaning itself off oil, gas, and coal. They are not just cheap fuels; they are also necessary for industrial chemical processes. Steel is a good example here. It is made from iron oxide, which first has to be stripped of its oxygen atoms. This is done with coke, which plays a dual role in the process. It heats the blast furnace to more than 1,000 degrees, and bonds chemically with the oxygen present in the iron ore. This results in pure iron—and very large amounts of carbon dioxide. The ThyssenKrupp steelworks in Duisburg alone emits 20 million tonnes of carbon dioxide per year. If it were a country, it would be about half the size of Switzerland, at least in terms of its greenhouse gas emissions.

Green hydrogen could replace coke in the process. Then the factory stacks would no longer belch out carbon dioxide, but pure water. That green hydrogen would be so energy-intensive, however, that the steelmaking industry would require 12,000 additional wind turbines to be built. As a reminder: Germany currently has around 30,000 working wind turbines.

The costs would be considerable, pushing up the price of a tonne of steel from 400 to 600 euros.[44] However, keen motorists still need not fear being unable to afford a car of their own—according to the Wuppertal Institute, at least. Its climate economists believe the cost of a mid-range car would barely increase, predicting 'a price rise of significantly less than 1 per cent'.[45]

Until now it has been the case that the price of raw materials has had little impact on the cost of cars or mobile phones, etc. However, that pattern cannot be mapped onto a climate-neutral future, because there is unlikely to be enough green electricity to power the production of all the industrial goods that we take for granted today. An estimate for the chemical industry places the total amount of energy required if all its production were environmentally friendly at a huge 685 terawatt hours per year.[46] That is more than Germany's entire annual consumption today.

Some of that energy could be imported, but it would not be cheap, as shown by the case of electricity from the desert. This has led to a kind of competition in climate policy, when calculating the energy requirements of the chemical industry, to massage the numbers to make them appear as small as possible—until only 372 terawatt hours remain.[47] This is almost a halving of the permissible energy amount, which can only be achieved if production shrinks.

Some production processes would automatically become obsolete if the industry went green. For example, there would be little need to synthesise ammonia, because organic farming uses almost no synthetic fertilisers. Some basic chemical processes could be outsourced to sunnier counties where green electricity is cheaper.[48] However, the greatest hopes are placed on the circular economy; in other words, on 'mechanical and chemical recycling'. But it remains unclear how this comprehensive recycling system will work, since the quality of most materials degrades when they are reused several times. This recycling plan has 'not yet been reliably analysed', the Wuppertal Institute admits.[49] There is a good possibility that energy requirements would remain immense—while production has to shrink even further.

Furthermore, the chemical industry cannot possibly become completely climate-neutral. Some 2 per cent of current greenhouse gas emissions would still enter the atmosphere.[50] To be climate-neutral, chemical companies would have to extract carbon dioxide from the air and store it underground, which again drives up costs. Research is still going on in the industry into what its climate-neutral future might look like, but it is already clear that the industry must shrink significantly. In any case, 'green growth' is definitely impossible, because the chemical industry's energy consumption is so high.

The construction industry is also a difficult case due to its unavoidable, heavy reliance on concrete, which is cheap, durable, fireproof, and rustproof. Reinforced concrete can bear extremely large loads, making bold skyscrapers possible.[51] Unfortunately, it creates large carbon dioxide emissions that cannot be avoided. Concrete is made with cement, which in turn is made from lime—by removing the carbon dioxide from it. That means there can never be 'green cement', because its production will always involve the release of carbon dioxide gas.[52]

Some 7 per cent of worldwide greenhouse gas emissions come from the cement industry. Among the alternatives, wood is particularly attractive, because it binds carbon dioxide.[53] There is already a wooden skyscraper in Vienna, called the HoHo Tower, which is an impressive 84 metres high, with 24 storeys. However, even this flagship project could not be built using wood entirely. Its core structure was made of concrete in order to give the tower the required stability.

Anyway, there is simply not enough wood in the world to replace the 4.6 billion tonnes of cement used in construction around the globe every year. It is already such a scarce resource that prices have skyrocketed.[54] And it is likely to become scarcer. Forested areas are shrinking at an alarming rate, because they are being cleared to create farmland in many countries.[55]

A more interesting alternative to cement is clay. Every culture around the world has used this construction material for millennia, because it is virtually ubiquitous and easy to work with, it can be completely recycled, and it is warming in winter and cooling in summer. However, clay is not suitable for constructing high-rise buildings.[56]

Another approach focuses on reducing the amount of cement used by mixing it with bamboo, wood fibre, or sugarcane.[57] This is a good idea, but it won't be enough. The world has to achieve net-zero greenhouse gas emissions. Each tonne of cement produced makes that impossible — unless the carbon dioxide can be collected and stored underground. The carbon dioxide would be relatively easy to capture in cement works, because it is present in high concentrations. But this is not a cheap solution, and it would not capture all greenhouse gases by far.[58]

The construction industry must also contend with the fact that it can never be totally climate-neutral, because it requires ground space. Every day in Germany, 60 hectares of unsealed land are lost as they are asphalted over or built on.[59] Unsealed areas are necessary for groundwater to accumulate and to bind carbon dioxide. Globally, around 1.5 trillion tonnes of carbon are stored in soil and humus — three times more than is absorbed by all the world's forests put together. When construction seals the ground, it is lost forever: it takes at least 100 years for one centimetre of new humus to build up.

Germany has pledged to reduce such ground loss to zero by 2030. This is agreed in the UN's Sustainability Goals.[60] However, the voracious consumption of land continues unabated, and it is considered almost a civil right that every family should be able to dream of owning its own home. The political debate immediately descends into hysteria when home ownership is criticised. This is borne out by the experience of the German Greens during the 2021 election campaign, when their parliamentary party leader, Anton Hofreiter, stated in an interview: 'Single-family houses consume a lot of space, a lot of construction materials, and a lot of energy; they also create urban sprawl, in turn causing more traffic.'[61] Those are undisputed facts, but they must not be expressed in public. As soon as they are, a hail of accusations that the Greens are 'the party of prohibitions' and that they have a 'dysfunctional relationship with ownership' descends on them. An exasperated Robert Habeck, as party co-leader, was forced to give the reassurance that detached houses are part of the palette of housing options in Germany. 'It is part of many people's lives, their life plans and their wishes. This will not change.'[62]

As popular as the idea of home ownership is in Germany, it cannot be seen as a civil right for every family to build its own house. The consumption of land would be gigantic. If everyone in Berlin lived in a separate house, the German capital would reach all the way to the Baltic coast.[63]

Every new build is a crime against the environment. Even supposedly ecological buildings are not ecological. A passive house may use very little power, but building such supposedly green houses consumes a great deal of 'grey energy' in the first place. 'New builds are never energy-saving,' the construction critic Danial Fuhrhop says.[64] Rather than creating new 'energy-efficient houses', it is more efficient to renovate and modernise existing buildings. Post-war housing in Bremerhaven was modernised—consuming far less energy than building new passive houses.[65]

But could Germany manage with absolutely no new construction? There is an apparent housing shortage. Rents are skyrocketing in all Germany's major cities because so little housing is available. But appearances are deceptive. There is in fact no shortage. Space is simply badly distri-buted. There were 42.8 million dwellings in Germany in 2020,[66] but only 40.5 million households.[67] Simple arithme-tic shows that 2.3 million dwellings stood empty. However, no one really knows where that unused accommodation is, since most local authorities do not keep track of the vacancy rate in their jurisdiction.[68]

One thing seems clear: most unused housing is located in rural areas, while metropolitan centres continue to attract an influx of residents. But there is also a lot of vacant housing in the cities that does not necessarily appear in the statistics. Real estate properties have become a popular way to invest speculatively, and the rich especially like to put their money in 'concrete gold'. It is no rarity for well-heeled dentists or lawyers who live in, say, Bonn, to buy themselves a second home in Berlin as a place to stay when they fly in for the occasional visit to a concert at the Philharmonie. Although it is mostly unused, owning such an apartment is good business for them, since they can usually sell it

later for a higher price.[69] This targeted gain materialises
almost automatically: rents and house prices rise because
the unused housing creates a scarcity. This is why Daniel
Fuhrhop calls for privately owned accommodation to be
either owner-occupied or rented out to tenants. 'Currently,
the only people with such a legal residence requirement
are asylum-seekers. How about introducing a residence
requirement for the rich instead, to stop our local
neighbourhoods from becoming deserted?'[70]

The average living space for people in Germany is 47.4
square metres.[71] That is a lot, but not everyone can afford so
much space. Well-off pensioners tend to live in large spaces,
while poor or young families often live in very cramped
conditions.[72] This problem has long been known, but it has
never been solved despite the constant construction of new
housing. New builds alone do not seem to help — but they
are ruinous for the environment.

This means that the right course would be to construct
no new buildings, to refurbish existing stock to make it
energy-efficient, and to redistribute living space more fairly.
(See chapter 19 for more.) This is a radical proposal, because
it would mean an end to people's civil right to continuously
expand their living space. But there is no other way to end
our voracious consumption of land. To reiterate: we need
unsealed land so that groundwater can accumulate and
carbon dioxide can be bound.

The construction industry currently employs 1 million
people in Germany.[73] They would not be in danger of losing
their jobs if all new construction were stopped. Almost every
existing building still needs to be insulated and equipped
with heat pumps.[74] Construction workers are also desperately needed for the energy transition itself: thousands more
wind turbines, solar power systems, gas-fired power stations,

and electrolysers are needed. There is currently a lack of skilled labour to manufacture and install them, so additional workers would be welcome.

Employment is not the same as growth or rising income, however. Germany's economic output would shrink in a climate-neutral world, because fewer goods would be produced. Among other things, there would be fewer cars, no flights, fewer chemicals, smaller dwellings, and no new office blocks or logistics centres. Nobody would starve, and life would still be good—but it would not be 'green growth'. It would be 'green shrinkage'.

There is only one branch of industry that could and should expand: green energy. However, that would not be growth in the familiar sense, because it creates a product out of something that was always free in the past—humans' survival on Earth. So far, it has not cost money to spend time outdoors, engage in agriculture, or use fresh water. In future, preventing potentially fatal global warming will cost billions every year.

So new costs will arise, while economic output shrinks in order to avert a climate catastrophe. This balancing act is completely unprecedented. Until now, all social spending has been financed through economic growth. No one has had to suffer a lack of anything so that the healthcare or education system could be built. Now those days are over. The challenges will grow, and the funds will shrink. Consumption must fall, which immediately begs the question of who should cut back and by how much. Distribution conflicts will be inevitable. (See chapter 19.)

Many climate economists reject this pessimistic analysis, spreading optimism instead. They promise a green economic miracle, and give the impression that climate protection could even trigger a boom. Agora Energiewende predicts annual growth of 1.3 per cent for Germany,[75] and the Potsdam Institute for Climate Impact Research forecasts annual growth of 2.14 per cent for the global economy.[76]

However, those cheerful forecasts are plucked out of thin air. As the authors themselves admit, they were not made on the basis of economic research. For example, Agora Energiewende says that, 'The economic effects of climate-protection measures were not explicitly investigated.'[77] And the Fraunhofer Institute also admits that, 'No macro-economic analysis was carried out that took value added and employment issues into account.'[78] However, such self-imposed blind spots in their knowledge have not prevented such experts from blithely claiming that climate protection will be cheap. Allegedly, as already mentioned, it will cost less than annual spending on Christmas gifts.

It is not good scientific practice to make claims that are completely unsupported by research. Unfortunately, however, it is standard practice among climate economists. They postulate 'green growth' because the end of economic growth is such a disagreeable thought. One green thinker who falls prey to this sham logic is Ralf Fücks: 'The logical consequence of the belief that environmental crisis can only be overcome by radically reducing human activity on Earth—less production, less consumption, less travel, less data generation—is an environmental state of emergency.'[79] That analysis is completely correct. Restrictions are unpleasant. However, it does not necessarily lead to 'smart growth', as Fücks hopes.

The German state funds a very large number of climate scientists and institutes. Despite that investment, none has so far come up with any credible proof that 'green growth' is feasible. The Federal Environment Agency states, for example, 'The authors of this study are not aware of any explicit consideration of the possibility of compliance with several, or all, planetary boundaries while economic output is growing.'[80] The issue of growth is usually excluded, as the Wuppertal Institute reports in one of its meta-studies: 'Essentially no expansion of production takes place in the scenarios, but nor is there a large decline in production.'[81]

Most studies seem to assume that 'green growth' will somehow materialise by itself. This is another case of relying on the principle of 'the trend is your friend'. Capitalism has survived every crisis it has faced so far, so it is simply assumed that it will also survive the climate crisis. Glib reference is made to the fact that the prophets of doom have always been wrong in the past. The fall of capitalism has been forecast many times, but so far it has continued to flourish because technological solutions have been found in time to overcome existential difficulties.

A new technological miracle is touted as its saviour this time: digitisation. It is seen as the way to avert climate collapse and to enable 'green growth'. Unfortunately, however, the hope that technological innovation will save our current way of life is misplaced. Past doomsday scenarios were indeed wrong—but this time, capitalism really will come to an end.

CHAPTER FIFTEEN

Why technological innovation and digitisation cannot save the climate

There is nothing original about predicting the end of capitalism. Its dynamics seemed uncanny from the start, leading to the death of the new economic world order being foreseen even in its infancy. Adam Smith ridiculed the constant economic doomsaying as early as 1776:

> The annual produce of the land and labour of England, for example, is certainly much greater than it was, a little more than a century ago, at the restoration of Charles II. Though at present, few people, I believe, doubt of this, yet during this period, five years have seldom passed away in which some book or pamphlet has not been published ... pretending to demonstrate that the wealth of the nation was fast declining, that the country was depopulated, agriculture neglected, manufactures decaying, and trade undone.[1]

The English economist John Stuart Mill also noted and was annoyed by the permanent pessimism of his contemporaries, accusing them of self-importance. In 1828, Mill remarked, 'I have observed that not the man who hopes when others despair, but the man who despairs when others hope, is admired by a large class of persons as a sage.'[2]

Marx was the first economist to devise an entire system to justify the inevitable end of capitalism.[3] But even convinced socialists soon doubted that a revolution was necessary. The social-democrat theoretician Eduard Bernstein coolly remarked in 1899 that the situation of workers was far from hopeless. Rather, many proletarians were able to better themselves, as was shown by figures from the tax office: 'The fact that ownership figures are rising rather than falling is not an invention of bourgeois harmony economists, but a fact discovered by the tax authorities, often to the annoyance of those concerned.'[4] Bernstein's 'revision' carried weight among the comrades, because he was not only a close friend of Friedrich Engels, but also the executor of his will.

While the workers reconciled themselves to capitalism, entrepreneurs had other worries. They were soon troubled by the same question that still concerns us today: will there be enough raw materials to feed voracious capitalism forever? Even in the 19th century, the industrial barons of the Ruhr Valley feared they might run out of fuel. The steel manufacturer Leopold Hoesch mentions discussions about 'whether there was enough coal and coke in the world to make all the pig iron the world needs'.[5]

Those concerns over raw materials never completely went away, but they became increasingly focused on oil. In 1970, the American ecologist Kenneth Watt predicted that 'by the year 2000, if present trends continue … there won't be any more crude oil'.[6] That forecast was, of course, also wrong.

The destruction of nature also began to be seen as increasingly threatening. US researchers expected that 'between

75 and 80 per cent of all living species will be extinct' by the turn of the millennium. *Life* magazine reported that 'scientists have solid experimental and theoretical evidence that ... in a decade, urban dwellers will have to wear gas masks to survive air pollution ... By 1985 air pollution will have reduced the amount of sunlight reaching the Earth by one half.'[7]

Feeding the entire population of the world also seemed to be impossible. The bestseller *The Population Bomb* by the US biologist Paul Ehrlich appeared in 1968. It predicted mass starvation in the Global South: 'In the 1970s and 1980s hundreds of millions of people will starve to death.' It particularly pinpointed India as unable to feed its growing population: 'India couldn't possibly feed 200 million more people by 1980.'[8] Once again, the opposite turned out to be true. Instead of food becoming scarcer, harvests became more plentiful. Since those warnings were written, India's wheat and rice harvests have tripled, while its population has only slightly more than doubled. India's economic output increased by no less than a factor of 50.[9]

The 'population bomb' never exploded, because new, more productive crop varieties were cultivated, with shorter stems and bigger grains. Or, to look at it from the opposite point of view, if the grains common in 1960 were still cultivated today, additional agricultural land the size of the US, Canada, and China combined would be required to feed the growing population. That extra land does not exist — but it was not needed, thanks to the spectacular success of biologists' selective-breeding efforts.[10]

Ehrlich underestimated the extent of scientific progress, which is also a charge levied at the 1972 bestseller *The Limits to Growth*. The Club of Rome commissioned that study, which was the first to use computer simulations to model future developments.[11] Its predictions were bleak: 'If the present growth trends in world population, industrialisation, pollution, food production, and resource depletion continue unchanged, the limits to growth on this planet will be reached sometime within the next one hundred years. The most probable result will be a rather sudden and uncontrollable decline in both population and industrial capacity.'[12]

It is still less than 100 years since that prediction was made, but at the 50-year point in 2022, many newspaper articles appeared, cheerfully proclaiming that the classic work 'no longer has any contribution to make to the social debate', and that it should be 'put back on the bookshelf': 'The authors' conclusions have turned out to be wrong.'[13]

Indeed, several of their predictions have not come true. As previously mentioned, they assumed gold reserves would last only 29 more years at most. They also predicted that silver reserves would be depleted in 42 years, while copper would last 48 years, oil 50 years, and aluminium 55 years.[14] The end of those reserves is still not in sight today. However, the authors never denied that some of the details of their analysis could be wrong. 'We shall emphasize just one more time that none of these computer outputs is a prediction. We would not expect the real world to behave like the world model.'[15]

Some of their forecasts were astonishingly accurate. For example, they correctly predicted the rise in greenhouse gases in the atmosphere,[16] although in 1972 it was still impossible to assess in detail the risk those emissions posed: 'It is not known how much carbon dioxide ... can be released without causing irreversible changes in the Earth's climate.'[17]

But even back in 1972, the authors were certain that scientific progress alone would not be enough to save the planet, as their model calculations showed that 'even the most optimistic estimates of the benefits of technology in the model did not prevent ... the collapse beyond the year 2100.'[18]

Technology optimists do not accept such a fatalistic view. Their main counterargument is based on the observation that scientific progress has always been underestimated in the past because of our tendency as humans to think of the future in terms of the present. They can fill pages citing amusing anecdotes of completely false predictions of technology's potential. The following are just a few selected examples.

As early as 1870, many German engineers were convinced that the innovative potential of electricity had largely been exhausted.[19] The telephone was also considered to be a technology with little future: in 1876, the president of Western Union, William Orton, adjudged it to have 'too many shortcomings to be seriously considered as a means of communication'.[20] Agricultural economists believed farmers would never employ any technologies at all. In 1893, the Hohenheim Agricultural Academy found that 'the construction of the most customary machines is almost complete'. Tractors and huge mechanical harvesters were inconceivable.[21] The British politician John Douglas-Scott-Montagu remarked, 'I do not believe the introduction of motor-cars will ever affect the riding of horses.'[22] The IBM president, Thomas Watson, was famously wrong when he said in 1943, 'I think there is a world market for maybe five computers.'[23] Almost no one foresaw the advent of small personal computers, as evidenced by the plans forged by Siemens and AEG in the 1970s for a 'mainframe-computer union'.[24] The shipping container revolution was also a surprise: the metal boxes were initially conceived as a means of transporting goods more cheaply along the east coast of the United States.[25] Bill Gates reportedly dismissed the internet as 'hype' in 1993, and in 1985 the management consultancy McKinley predicted that a maximum of one million mobile phones would be sold annually by the year 2000. In fact, 106 million were sold, and the figure is now well above six billion.[26]

The list of false predictions is long. However, this does not imply the converse: that anything is possible with technology. Many problems remain unsolved, despite decades, or even millennia, of trying. For example, humans had the idea of filling cavities in their teeth around 13,000 years ago. They used a mixture of naturally occurring bitumen, hair, and plant fibres to make such fillings. Other materials they sometimes turned to include beeswax, tree resin, powdered rock, and plant seeds. Today, fillings are most commonly ceramic — but the perfect material for treating tooth cavities remains to be found.[27] There is also a lack of ideal sleeping pills, painkillers, and sedatives, although pharmacologists have been searching and researching for more than a century. Nor is there a perfect antidepressant that is reliably effective, free of unpleasant side effects, and non-addictive.[28] Many types of cancer remain undefeated, despite the billions spent annually on the battle to find a cure.

Sometimes, technology is simply too expensive — even for things we often take for granted. The water toilet was invented 2,800 years ago in Mesopotamia, but even today, some 2.5 billion people do not have access to safely managed sanitation.[29] Many of those in extreme poverty now own a mobile phone — but don't have a toilet. Using the phone now costs almost nothing, but the telecommunications revolution has done nothing to lower the cost of installing sewage systems.

Technology cannot always be relied upon to provide solutions — sometimes it fails to find any, or the solutions remain expensive despite being in use for millennia. Thus, it would be reckless to trust blindly in technology's ability to prevent the climate catastrophe.

The main issue, however, is a lack of appreciation of the different timescales involved. Amusing anecdotes like the ones above aim to show that the future of technologies is always better than expected. That may well be the case, but we now no longer have the time to wait for possible technological breakthroughs. We must act immediately if we are to avert climate collapse.

Another, related problem is the fact that it usually takes a long time for technologies to become widespread. Even if game-changing inventions or discoveries are made in the near future, it could take decades for those fantastic eco-ideas to reach market maturity. Progress moves at a snail's pace. The first computers were built towards the end of World War II — but it was not until 55 years later that a widespread computerisation of industry took place. Even today, digital networks are not the standard everywhere. In Germany, the Covid-19 pandemic revealed to the public that many health authorities still relied on fax machines to transfer their data.

We must deal with the climate crisis using the technology that exists now. But that technology will not enable us to produce enough green energy sufficiently cheaply to fuel 'green growth'. So the only remaining option is green shrinkage: fewer new buildings, fewer cars, fewer chemical products.

This purely quantitative view considers only product volumes, which often raises the question of the possibility of 'qualitative growth'. After all, it is the case with many products that they use up fewer materials over time, while increasing in efficiency. Digitisation in particular raises great hopes that new opportunities for expansions in computer technology will be opened up by virtual reality, which would have absolutely no impact on the environment. The Harvard psychologist Steven Pinker enthuses: 'Whereas the first Machine Age that emerged out of the Industrial Revolution was driven by energy, the second is driven by the other anti-entropic resource, information.'[30]

So the knowledge revolution is expected to liberate us from almost all our earthly needs. Even nearly 30 years ago, the renowned environmental economist Herman E. Daly realised the absurdity of this concept: 'The notion that we can save the "growth forever" paradigm by ... substituting information for resources is fantasy. We can surely eat lower on the food chain, but we cannot eat recipes!'[31] The growth critic Niko Paech expressed a similar sentiment: 'To date, no car or aeroplane in the world runs on liquid knowledge instead of petrol or jet fuel.'[32] In addition, knowledge does not spread through thin air; it requires a material infrastructure, as Daly pointed out: 'Information does not exist apart from physical brains, books, and computers, and, further, ... brains require the support of bodies, books require library buildings, computers run on electricity, etc.'[33]

Even Pinker must know that a computer without power is just dead material. Nonetheless, he sees huge potential for freeing us from the curse of raw materials, drawing on the experiences of every consumer: 'The digital revolution, by replacing atoms with bits, is dematerializing the world in front of our eyes. The cubic yards of vinyl that used to be my music collection gave way to cubic inches of compact discs and then to the nothingness of MP3s. The river of newsprint flowing through my apartment has been stanched by an iPad.' The smartphone, in particular, fuels the fantasy of consumption without consuming resources. To quote Pinker once more:

> Just think of all the plastic, metal and paper that no lon-
> ger go into the forty-odd consumer products that can be
> replaced by a single smartphone, including a telephone,
> answering machine, phone book, camera, camcorder,
> tape recorder, radio, alarm clock, calculator, dictionary,
> Rolodex, calendar, street maps, flashlight, fax and com-
> pass — even a metronome, outdoor thermometer, and sprit
> level.[34]

As beguiling as all those examples may be, they are of no use. The end of vinyl records did not reduce greenhouse gas emissions. On the contrary: digital music-streaming guzzles more energy than good old records ever did. In 1977, when vinyl still dominated, US music fans were responsible for 140,000 tonnes of carbon dioxide emissions per year. In 2016, that figure was around 300,000 tonnes.[35]

Watching videos on smartphones is even worse. Phones may replace telephone books, street maps, and the like, but they have also become mobile cinemas, consuming huge amounts of electricity. Video conferencing and cloud computing, web searches, and social media use are also not completely harmless: in 2025, digital technologies are expected to surpass automobiles in terms of global carbon dioxide emissions.[36]

The first mobile phones entered the market in 1983, weighing almost 800 grams and costing so much that they were only seen in the hands of police officers and millionaires — and in Hollywood movies. The unscrupulous broker Gordon Gekko in the blockbuster *Wall Street* had one of those 'bricks' glued to his ear, signifying his status as one of the super-rich.

Today, almost everyone can afford a smartphone, since they are now around 50 times cheaper than in Gekko's day. Technological progress has made it possible to produce mobile phones using far less energy and fewer resources. However, no materials have been saved from consumption, as so many billions of phones have been manufactured. It is precisely because their price has fallen so consistently that they were able to spread exponentially.

This is another instance of the 'rebound effect' observed in the 19th century in the case of steam power. More efficient manufacturing of machinery or goods does not lead to a reduction in the raw materials consumed, but rather to an increase in the volume of goods produced. That, in turn, leads to growth, which would be impossible without it.

The rebound effect can be seen everywhere.[37] Every computer user is familiar with the paradoxical experience that a new computer's memory is initially too big, and soon becomes too small because the new capacity allows more data to accumulate, which, in turn, requires more memory space.[38] Televisions have become cheaper and cheaper, but many now have screens almost as big as movie theatres. Fridges need less and less electricity, but are getting bigger, and many now have integrated wine coolers, freezers, or ice-makers. The amount of energy required to heat one square metre of residential space fell by 15 per cent between 2000 and 2015, but over the same period, the amount of space occupied per person grew by 14 per cent.[39]

The rebound effect also destroys all attempts to save resources in the automobile industry. Car engines are becoming ever more efficient, but the demand for petrol and diesel has not fallen as a result. Instead, the horsepower output of vehicles has grown by 29 per cent over the past 15 years.[40] A similar trend can be observed in aviation. Planes require less and less kerosene per passenger, but, unfortunately, the number of flights continues to increase. It is estimated that global air transport will triple by 2050.[41]

Even environmentally friendly means of transport such as rail are hit by the rebound effect. The high-speed route between Berlin and Munich is a good example. It opened in 2017 at a cost of 17 billion euros, and reduced the travel time between the two cities from six hours to four. In its first year, 2.2 million new passengers travelled on this route. Half of those would previously have driven or flown, which is good, but the other half, accounting for about 3,000 passengers per day, were additional travellers who chose to make the journey because it was now so quick.[42]

In addition, there is no certainty that flights are actually saved just because some passengers now take the train between Munich and Berlin. Some flight connections to the German capital may have been abolished, but that will simply have freed up the slots for other routes. In any case, there is no evidence that the people of Bavaria took fewer flights as a direct result of the new rail service to Berlin. On the contrary, numbers at Munich Airport continued to grow unabated. Over 42 million passengers passed through the airport in 2016. That number had grown to over 46 million by 2018.[43]

Politicians like to make attractive offers to voters to make them choose climate protection of their free will, including fast, frequent trains to tempt citizens to use the railways. But that approach fails because mobility in general is increasing. New trains mean more traffic, not more climate protection.

Since the Covid-19 pandemic, hope has grown that working from home might help lower traffic volumes.

Unfortunately, the hope that traffic will be reduced by workers communicating mainly online is unfounded. Workers do commute less to the office, but that allows them to make journeys they would not previously have made, for example to do shopping that they would otherwise have done on the way home from work. Teleworking also leads to a greater motivation among workers to settle further away from their employer's premises, if they know they will only have to be there occasionally in person. The number of work journeys falls, but the distances become greater.[44]

Even the bicycle is subject to the rebound effect, although it is promoted as the way to free city centres from traffic noise and pollution. Amsterdam and Copenhagen are admired throughout Europe because people imagine that there is hardly any car traffic in these self-styled 'bike cities'.[45] But that attractive image is deceptive. In reality, there are more cars per capita on the roads of both those cities than in Berlin, for example.

In Berlin, only 26 per cent of journeys are made by car; in Amsterdam and Copenhagen, the figures are 31 and 32 per cent, respectively. The bicycle has not in fact replaced cars there; it is simply the case that fewer people walk than in Berlin. Also, considering exclusively inner-city traffic distorts the picture, since car travel is increasing rapidly on a national level. The Dutch travelled around 127 billion kilometres by car in 1994. That had increased to 139 billion in 2017. The number of kilometres travelled by bike rose in the same period from 14.1 billion to only 14.5 billion. In Denmark, there has actually been a decline in cycling in the past 30 years—falling from 680 to 487 kilometres per person per year, while car travel increased significantly.[46]

It is an illusion to believe that technological efficiency will solve everything. It cannot solve the climate problem, because any saved resources are promptly used to produce even more goods and generate growth. A look back over the 20th century affords the opportunity to quantify this rebound effect. Between 1900 and 2005, global economic output increased 23-fold. In the same period, there was an eight-fold increase in the consumption of raw materials.[47] That means there was a certain amount of 'decoupling', since the economy grew three times faster than resource consumption. But that is cold comfort. The environment would only have been helped if far fewer resources were consumed. But that, in turn, would make growth impossible.

Such rebound effects shatter any hope of the possibility of 'green growth'. That is why they are simply ignored in most studies, as the Wuppertal Institute states: 'Rebound effects are implicitly recorded as being only weak or as having been avoided by external conditions.'[48] Once again, economic climate research fails to meet the accepted standards of the academic world. Although new studies are appearing all the time, the crucial problems are left aside.

Thus there is no such thing as purely 'qualitative growth'. Capitalism cannot transform into a knowledge society that flourishes in the virtual worlds of the internet. Indeed, digitisation guzzles enormous amounts of energy, and the fact that smartphones now exist does nothing to change old consumption patterns. Cars are still on the roads — only the drivers now all have phones stuck to their ears.

However, there is another, completely different view of what 'qualitative growth' means. The argument is that a targeted effort should be made to expand activities that are important for society but that generate few emissions.[49] The emphasis is mostly placed on the care industries, education, and art. There is no doubt that many Western countries need more people to staff their hospitals and care homes, and that there is shortage of teachers. But, as sensible as it would be to invest in care and education, it would not result in 'qualitative growth'.

Instead, the result would be a kind of 'consumption swap'. If Germany, for instance, were to decide to employ more care workers or to pay existing ones better, social security contributions would have to rise to cover the additional costs. People would then have less money in their pockets and would not be able, for example, to fly to Mallorca so often. On the other hand, care workers would have more money—and would be able to afford holidays in the Balearics. In the end, there would be just as many Germans flying to Mallorca, but the passengers would be different individuals.

To put it another way: 'qualitative growth' does not exist because nursing staff also want to buy cars or build homes for themselves. Even if a specific activity generates almost no greenhouse gas emissions, the wages paid for it will be spent on goods, most of which are harmful to the climate. 'Qualitative growth' would require extra teachers to make use of the extra education offers they create, and nothing else. Which is a ridiculous idea.[50] The growth critic Niko Paech summed this up rather pithily: 'A carbon dioxide-neutral euro, dollar, or yen is impossible simply because they embody the demand for material values.'[51]

Furthermore, it is not true that care work, education, or art are purely intangible, and do not generate any greenhouse gas emissions. The *Schaubühne* theatre in Berlin recently commissioned an investigation into its climate footprint, and the results were shocking. The theatre is responsible for large emissions because it flies all over the world, making around 100 guest performances a year.[52]

'Qualitative growth' is as illusory as 'green growth'. These terms simply obfuscate reality. There is no miracle technology that can suddenly 'dematerialise' capitalism. So the problem remains that there will not be sufficient green energy to fuel the entire economy. It's time to start thinking about 'green shrinkage'. Very little research has been done on this difficult topic until now, because it touches on the unthinkable: the idea that capitalism breaks down in the absence of growth. It seems that it really is 'easier to imagine the end of the world than the end of capitalism'.

PART III

The End of Capitalism

CHAPTER SIXTEEN

Green shrinkage: when the economy collapses

The word 'shrinkage' has an unpleasant ring to it, putting us in mind of prohibitions and sacrifices. But might it not be liberating to escape the spiral of permanent growth? Many climate-protection activists are convinced that a better future is possible. 'We are talking about a world that will be more beautiful, quieter, greener, healthier, less stressful, more sustainable and more just,' enthuses the solar power engineer Volker Quaschning. 'In cities, we will enjoy a much higher standard of living than today. With the energy transition, we will create countless new, sustainable, secure jobs.'[1]

Happiness research also shows that satisfaction does not increase automatically when the economy grows. Real economic output has roughly doubled in Germany and Austria since 1978,[2] but the level of satisfaction has not grown over the same period. Life was also good in the past. No one suffered because strawberries and asparagus were only available in early summer, or because no kiwi fruits were flown in from New Zealand.

The meaning of life is not to constantly consume more. Or, as the sociologist Harad Welzer ironically put it, 'When people are seriously or terminally ill, they don't want their obituary to read, "He drove an Audi Q7 and went on five cruises." ... When they are dying, they want to be remembered as good, kind, loving people. They want their life to have meant something to others.'[3]

Many people in Germany feel so oppressed by their own possessions that they flock to buy advice books about how to escape the flood of overabundance. The perennial bestseller *Simplify Your Life* is now available in several editions. These books go into detail about how to 'gain control of your kitchen, cellar, and closets in a stress-free way' in order to 'finally have more time'. Time is, in fact, the only truly scarce commodity in our affluent consumer society. Everyone knows that death ultimately awaits us all, so it is senseless for humans to waste their precious and limited time accumulating and protecting possessions they don't even need.

All the more so because those unneeded possessions also have to be earned. No one can afford all the junk in their cupboards without having an income to pay for it. However, many people are highly dissatisfied with their working life because they are stuck in 'bullshit jobs'. This refers to jobs that are considered pointless, even by those who are employed in them.[4] In a survey carried out in the United Kingdom, 37 per cent of employees said they believed their work was unnecessary. The sentiment is shared by as many as 40 per cent of the Dutch. It is most common among office workers, whose jobs may be well paid, but are unsatisfying because they are pointless.[5]

The solution seems obvious: we should consume less, and then we could work less. The many bullshit jobs will not be missed by anyone, and everyone would have more time to enjoy the important things in life. A circular economy would emerge, in which everything consumed can also be recycled.[6] The degrowth movement has now come up with a benign vision of such a climate-neutral existence: we would eat only local and seasonal food, do any necessary repairs ourselves, and make our own garments.[7]

This 'sharing economy' would involve joint ownership of articles of daily use with neighbours—including cars, lawnmowers, drills, toys, books, and kitchen mixers, for example.[8] No one would have to miss out on fun or holidays. People would even have the time to make long-distance trips without flying—hitching a ride on a cargo ship for a leisurely passage to China, for example.

This world of climate-neutral consumption may sound romantic and nostalgic, but the intention is not to go back to the pre-modern age. The dream is not to return to a 'greened' version of a picture-book past. The degrowth movement also values the machines that are the result of capitalist development and that make our lives so much easier today.[9] The degrowth movement does not advocate for abolishing washing machines or computers—especially since the internet is the place where the hoped-for shared economy is already widespread today. Users write reviews and Wikipedia articles for free, post videos online, or meet up virtually to write new code in collaboration. Money is not important in such activities; they generate a sense of appreciation and community.[10]

But as positive as such a world of climate-neutral consumption may sound, capitalism soon catches up with it. The US sociologist Juliet Schor once placed great hope in the sharing of unused residential space through Airbnb, couch-surfing, and home exchange holidays making holidays free for all.[11] As a pioneer of environmental thinking at the time, she never imagined that these ideas could be commercialised and that Airbnb would grow into a multi-billion-dollar concern.

The idea of a sharing economy is also not as new or revolutionary as is often claimed. People have always realised the obvious advantages of sharing or swapping items. Libraries are ancient, but the concept has been rebranded in trendy German by giving it the English name 'book sharing'. Many apartment buildings already have communal laundry rooms with shared washing machines, and farmers have long since set up cooperatives to pool the use of agricultural machinery. Outgrown children's clothes, household utensils, and used camping equipment have always been sold on to new owners at flea markets.

Growth has never been negatively affected when people swap or share things, because it once again triggers a rebound effect. For example, when parents sell their children's old clothes at a flea market, they make money to spend on buying new things. Couch surfing does not necessarily reduce commercial activity, even if it makes accommodation free when it is not organised through Airbnb. The money saved on hotel expenses will simply be spent on taking more flights.[12]

Introducing a shared economy alone would not break the rebound effect. Incomes would also have to fall significantly to create a scarcity of money and in turn stimulate new growth. So the only logical conclusion is that the degrowth movement wants to halve commercial wage labour.

There is just one more problem that critics of growth like to ignore: shrinking economies rapidly descend into chaos. When incomes fall, crisis spreads wildly throughout all sectors of the economy. Imagine if a large number of Germans suddenly decided privately and independently to stop buying cars because they are so harmful to the climate.

Some 1.75 million people whose jobs depend directly or indirectly on Germany's auto industry would suddenly be out of work. Those former car workers would then have no money to spend at the pub or supermarket, or to renovate their homes. The incomes of publicans, shop owners, and craftspeople would sink as a consequence. The economy would be in freefall. (See chapter 7.)

Chaotic shrinkage should not be thought of as a peaceful process. The global economic crisis of 1929 showed the dangers that ensue when people lose their jobs, incomes, hopes, and prospects. They tend to vote for populist leaders. Hitler came to power in Germany in 1933.

Most critics of growth make the mistake of confusing their visionary goal with the path to achieving it. They see a circular economy not only as the final objective, but also as paving the way to a transition from capitalism to a climate-neutral world. Juliet Schor, for example, writes of her variation of the shared economy that it is a 'strategy for surviving during [the] transition' to a perfect circular economy: 'Creating a truly sustainable system will require ecological restoration and technological innovation, over a period of many years.'[13]

There is no doubt that Schor is right when she says the environment needs nursing back to health, and that would be aided by even cheaper and more efficient green techno-logy. But there is a gap in her thinking: she fails to mention the economy at all—although it was the economic system of capitalism that created the huge environmental problems in the first place.

Most people don't give capitalism much thought because its critics portray it as if it were a pie. When half a pie is thrown away, there are still pieces left to go around. By the same token, critics of growth want incomes to be halved and the rest to be distributed fairly. But capitalism is not a pie that can be sliced into pieces whichever way we like. When incomes are falling, they continue to fall until there is almost nothing left. Shrinking capitalism is more like an ice-cream sundae left out in the sun with a crack in the bottom of the glass. The ice-cream not only melts in the heat, but the sticky mess that results trickles out and into the ground to be lost forever. In the end, everything is gone, as if it had never been there in the first place.

Capitalism is neither an object nor a state; it is a dynamic process. If it does not grow, it shrinks. Economic crises occur repeatedly, but they are able to be overcome only because entrepreneurs assume that the economy will return to growth at some point and are therefore willing to keep investing in that future. However, as soon as economic activity is stifled by politics, and permanent shrinkage looms, companies have no incentive to buy new machinery or hire new workers—and the economy continues to shrink in chaos.

Some environmental thinkers try to circumvent this dilemma by advocating a bit-by-bit approach. They suggest that changes could initially be made in tiny stages that no one would notice individually. The environmental law expert Felix Ekardt writes, for example:

> If I put a whole wheel of cheese on the buffet at my birthday party, it will go uneaten. But if I cut it into cubes, all of it will go. Although the cheese is exactly the same … The line between 'getting fat' and 'not getting fat' is blurred by the bite-size morsels … In the same way, the bit-by-bit approach is an appropriate way to introduce reforms to politicians and businesses.[14]

Similarly, the sociologist Harald Welzer suggests sticking to 'the smallest possible changes to the status quo': 'There is a completely different ring to that phrase than terms like the "Great Transformation", the "Great Utopia", or the "Great Revolution."'[15]

It cannot be denied that it would be very convenient if capitalism were a big cheese that could shrink by 'the smallest possible' chunks. But, unfortunately, capitalism is neither a pie nor a wheel of cheese. It cannot be repeated enough: capitalism is a dynamic system. Even small falls in income are too much for it to survive if they are repeated year after year. Capitalism depends on growth. When growth is absent for a period, chaotic collapse is inevitable.

Such an analysis might sound abstract, but it is easier to envision by looking at it from the other direction and imagining what a truly climate-neutral Germany might actually look like. To begin with the obvious: all airports would have to close, since even flights powered with green kerosene are harmful to the environment. They still cause condensation trails, which contribute to global warming. Almost 850,000 people are currently employed directly or indirectly in Germany's aviation industry, and all of those people would need new jobs.

The future would also look dim for private cars. As already described (see chapter 14), buses and trains would have to run far more frequently if people in rural areas were not to be stuck in their villages with no way to leave. It would be bad news for employees in the automobile industry, since the big carmakers are concentrated in very few regions. If fewer private vehicles were manufactured, the question immediately arises of what would happen to regions such as that around Stuttgart, or the area between Wolfsburg and Braunschweig.

Comprehensive climate protection would not only change production industries. Many services would also disappear if the economy shrank. Advertising would become redundant in a situation where goods are so scarce that they are always guaranteed to find a buyer. There would no longer be any work for PR agencies, logistics providers for trade fairs, and graphic designers. It is also unclear how media outlets and Google would be financed if advertising no longer existed.

Life insurance would also become obsolete. Everyone is familiar with the principle of paying a small premium every month so as to receive a sizeable surplus on final payout. However, that gain can only occur if the economy is growing. As soon as it starts to shrink, such surpluses no longer accrue—and the money paid in even loses some of its value.

Banks would also collapse. As we have seen, their core business is granting credit. But loans can only be repaid if the economy is growing. (See chapter 7.) When production falls, no one takes out loans, and the banks lose their economic basis. Some small banks might survive by offering cash-management services—but holding accounts have always been a loss-making business for banks. They have always made their profits from lending.

The same fate would await investment banking, which speculates with shares, interest rates, currencies, and raw materials. Although this financial casino has been largely superfluous in the past, and so no damage would result if it disappeared, hundreds of thousands of people currently make their living directly or indirectly from it.[16] It benefits not only those employed by the big banks, but also finance lawyers and tax consultants. Most of those working in the banking sector in Germany are based in the area around

Frankfurt, again raising the question of the economic future of that region.

When industrial companies, banks, and insurance brokers collapse, shares and savings also lose their value. Little would remain of Germany's stock market index, the DAX. Shares in the aircraft manufacturers Airbus and MTU would immediately become worthless if all flights were cancelled. Shares in financial giants such as Deutsche Börse, Deutsche Bank, Allianz, Hannover Re, and Munich Re would also plummet in value if they were to lose their main areas of business. The carmakers BMW, Porsche, Mercedes-Benz, VW, and their suppliers such as Continental would be a mere shadow of their former selves if most passenger and goods transportation were to move to the railways.

Other businesses would survive, but would lose a large proportion of their sales because there would not be sufficient green energy to manufacture their products in a climate-neutral way. This problem would affect the chemicals giants BASF, Bayer, Linde, Brenntag, Covestro, Henkel, and Symrise, as well as the building-materials group HeidelbergCement, and many others.

The green transformation would cause around half of DAX-listed companies either to go under completely or to survive in a very diminished state. However, some companies are likely to be less impacted by a transformation to climate neutrality because their products meet an existential need. These include the pharmaceutical and healthcare companies Fresenius Medical Care, Fresenius, Merck, Qiagen, Sartorius, and Siemens Healthineers. At least some postal and telecommunications services would also still be in demand.

Large digital and technology companies such as SAP, Siemens, and Infineon could even benefit in individual areas because their expertise is important for the energy transition. Energy giants such as RWE and E.ON could also see their business expanding if the entire economy switches to green energy. But those possible profits at Siemens, RWE, and so on will not make up for the enormous losses faced by shareholders in financial companies, carmakers, chemical giants, and the rest. On aggregate, stock market values would fall rapidly.

Those in the finance industry often rave about the 'green returns' that will supposedly be generated by the energy transition. But profits cannot be made when the economy shrinks. Climate protection is not a 'favourable business case', despite the excited claims of the management consultancy McKinsey.[17] Initially, at least, it will generate huge losses.

Those losses would affect the wealthy first, since only 17.1 per cent of the German population are shareowners.[18] There is no reason to gloat, however, because a green revolution would batter anyone who has a few savings in the bank, since even normal savings accounts would lose some of their value. Germans currently own financial assets worth eight trillion euros, for which there would no longer be sufficient equivalent value if far fewer goods were to be manufactured.[19]

When sales figures and incomes fall, the state naturally takes in less money. Falling tax revenues make it difficult for the state to finance the green transition. It is a catch-22 situation: the economy can only become climate-neutral by shrinking, but that shrinkage makes it almost impossible to finance the green transition. The Green Party politician Ralf Fücks comments caustically, 'Zero growth solves not a single problem, it merely creates new ones.'[20]

'Green growth' would doubtlessly be more convenient;

but, unfortunately, it doesn't exist. The Wuppertal Institute has calculated the amount by which every person in Germany would have to reduce their resource consumption to remove excessive stress on the environment. Currently, around 30 tonnes of resources are used up per person per year in Germany. That would need to fall to just eight tonnes.[21] That means cutting almost 75 per cent of material consumption — and that, once again, would make growth impossible.

Those figures can be shocking, and there are widespread fears that we will have to 'go back to the Stone Age' if capitalism ends. But those worries are groundless. No one need fear having to 'live in caves again'. Critics of growth have demonstrated clearly that living in a climate-neutral way can also be pleasant. The unsolved problem is just finding a way to realise such a green circular economy without triggering a severe economic crisis along the way that would panic the population and put a dictator in charge.

People need and want security, as the prominent German climate-protection activist Luisa Neubauer was forced to find out. She was in the habit of asking people the same question: 'What comes to mind when you think about the future?' The answers she received were not what she expected:

> Many of them spoke about wanting a stable income, an affordable home, a liveable environment in which they didn't have to worry about letting their kids play outside. We were bemused ... While we were concerned with the disaster that global society is hurtling towards, many of the people around us were worried about their incomes, their homes, and their neighbourhoods.[22]

That longed-for security would be threatened by the end of capitalism. Millions of people would lose their jobs and their savings. That's why climate protection can only have a chance if people never, even for a second, lose certainty about what they will live from and how their lives will be shaped in the future.

The degrowth movement does not have a solution to the problem of how to make that transition, because its vision is to create a circular economy, but it also believes the circular economy is the way to achieve that vision.

Some critics of growth recognise that their concept has holes in it. The alternative economist Tim Jackson, for example, writes: 'There is as yet no fully developed macroeconomics for a post-growth society.'[23] That statement may sound harmless, but it is a bombshell, because without economic modelling, it is impossible to leave capitalism behind.

It should really be the job of economists to come up with concepts for the way to move forward towards a climate-neutral world. But economists have so far remained largely silent on the matter. That's unfortunate, but it isn't an accident.

CHAPTER SEVENTEEN

The failure of economists

Most economists believe protecting the climate is absolutely no problem. They are convinced that 'green growth' is possible, because they are completely unable to entertain the idea of a shrinking of the economy. Their theories would all collapse if capitalism were to end, so they spin yarns about the wonderful 'returns' that a climate-neutral world is expected to offer.[1]

Most economists follow one of two schools of thought: Keynesian and neoclassical economics. As their name suggests, Keynesians follow the theories of the British economist John Maynard Keynes, who published his *General Theory* in 1936. It was meant to secure long-term growth after the Wall Street Crash of 1929 made it clear that capitalism had to be controlled politically to prevent serious turbulence. Keynes developed his so-called principle of effective demand, which said that states should take on debt to stimulate the economy in times of crisis.[2] The last time that suggestion was heeded was during the Covid-19 pandemic, when countries such as Germany and the UK mobilised vast sums to pay furloughed workers and support businesses.

Thus the Keynesians deserve great merit for their ability to cope with economic crises. But precisely because growth is at the centre of their theory, Keynesians are completely at a loss when it comes to managing long-term shrinkage. There is no provision in their concepts for a drop in production.[3]

Neoclassicists, for their part, focus on 'the market'. They believe it should regulate the economy, with the state having only a modest role to play. Many people intuitively find it reasonable for an economic theory to concentrate on the market. After all, everyone shops regularly. That is perhaps why they fail to realise that markets are where finished goods are exchanged. If you are only interested in the final product, it is easy to lose sight of the process behind its production. For that reason, neoclassical economics barely considers investments, loans, large banks, technology, and energy, although those aspects are central to real existing capitalism.[4]

Neoclassicists are mostly concerned with 'equilibrium'. They believe that markets are in equilibrium when prices create a situation in which supply and demand are covered. For example, if there are too many potatoes on the market, their price will keep falling until even the surplus spuds find a buyer.

Neoclassicists construct their models as if the only kind of economic activity were bartering, and as though industrialisation never took place. They describe a kind of fictitious Middle Age, in which only apples and pears are traded at small weekly markets. The theory may be lacking, but economists are extremely attracted to it because it can be expressed in mathematical terms.

Since neoclassicists are keen to describe a static equilibrium, they are unable to conceive of capitalism as dynamic, and are unable to develop a solid theory of growth.[5] Nonetheless, neoclassicists also implicitly assume economies will expand, since the optimum markets—those that always tend towards equilibrium — cannot exist if the supply of goods shrinks, because that causes a risk of rapid inflation.

Imagine a situation in which flying were no longer allowed, except for a few flights, in order to protect the climate. Ticket prices would immediately rise because there would be so few seats available. Eventually, only the rich would be able to afford the expensive tickets, while everyone else would have to simply stay on the ground. Such an unjust situation could perhaps be tolerated if it were only flights that became scarce. But in a climate-neutral world, the entire economy would have to shrink, so such distribution conflicts would be constant and ubiquitous. There would no longer be any fair 'equilibrium' to be achieved using 'market mechanisms'.

Keynesians and neoclassicists debate almost all economic issues vehemently, from minimum wages to public debt and export surpluses. Only on the issue of climate policy is there a cosy consensus. Both schools believe in 'green growth', and put their faith in the power of prices to solve environmental problems.

The central idea is that harming the climate should no longer be free. Businesses and consumers should have to pay for the damage caused by carbon dioxide emissions. This puts a price on the environment, and there are various models for levying it. Suggestions include carbon taxes, carbon dioxide emission certificates, and state-controlled price paths for fossil-fuel energy sources. Those subtle differences[6] are of secondary importance in view of the fact that the vast majority of economists see the 'nudging effect of prices' as the appropriate tool to do this.[7]

The claim is that when emissions become expensive enough, climate protection will automatically become economically profitable, since using green technology would then save money. By the same token, wasting fossil energy will become unprofitable when large levies are imposed on carbon dioxide emissions. The idea is that this will provoke businesses into finding creative ways to reduce their greenhouse gas emissions.

At first sight, using 'market forces' seems like an extremely elegant solution, because it means the state does not constantly have to interfere with the economy to ensure the climate is protected. Governments would not have to come up with detailed emissions quotas for different branches of industry, or legislate for the use of certain technologies. The price of emitting carbon dioxide would automatically ensure that emissions were cut in the cheapest and most efficient way.[8]

The price of carbon dioxide emissions would also act like a sieve, filtering out any goods that were too expensive for the modest benefit they bring. Harald Welzer is full of hope that 'smart watches, apple corers and capsule-guzzling coffee machines' would disappear from the market.[9]

But, for all its elegance, relying on putting a price on carbon dioxide emissions has some real pitfalls. The problems begin with the fact that it is impossible to quantify precisely the damage caused by greenhouse gases. For example, more and more wetlands are drying out due to a lack of rain. How much value is placed on the toads that lose their habitat and die? Such things cannot be expressed in monetary terms.

One thing is obvious: the damage caused by greenhouse gases is enormous, so the price of emitting carbon dioxide should be set as high as possible. Germany's Federal Environment Agency calculates that it should be at least 195 euros per tonne. That currently seems like an unattainable goal for Germany. The price of carbon dioxide emissions connected with transport and heating was set to rise to a measly 55 euros in 2025.

Climate-protection activists look to Switzerland or Sweden with envy. Switzerland's 'national incentive tax on fossil fuels' is currently set at a whopping 120 Swiss francs per tonne of carbon dioxide emitted,[10] while the Swedish government receives the equivalent of 114 euros per tonne.[11] This sounds like an environmentalist's paradise, but a surprising phenomenon has arisen in both countries: although the official prices for carbon dioxide emissions are four times higher than in Germany, Switzerland and Sweden fare no better than the federal republic in international environmental rankings.[12] They are also Western, industrialised nations that consume enormous amounts of resources.[13] How can it be that high prices for carbon dioxide emissions fail to have an effect?

The first mistake is to focus only on official carbon dioxide levies. For a true international comparison, all energy taxes must be considered. This reveals that car fuel, at least, is very highly taxed in Germany. Of the price paid for a litre of diesel, 47.04 cents go on energy taxes.[14] Each litre of diesel emits 2.65 kilograms of carbon dioxide when combusted, which works out at a carbon dioxide price of 177.50 euros per tonne. For petrol, 65.45 cents of the litre price goes to the tax office, and it emits 2.37 kilos of carbon dioxide into the atmosphere per litre burned, corresponding to a price of 276.16 euros per tonne of carbon dioxide emitted. That is far more than even the Federal Environment Agency recommends.

Germany is no exception in this; car fuel is also heavily taxed in other European countries.[15] If it were true that high taxes on energy have a strong nudging effect, Europeans would get rid of their cars *en masse* and would all take the bus. But there is no sign of people abandoning their automobiles anywhere in Europe. The hydraulic effect of prices appears not to be as simple as many market-oriented climate-protection activists assume.

Germany also faces the particular problem caused by the fact that taxes are much lower on company cars than on private vehicles, which encourages many employees to seek out oversized vehicles that are paid for by their companies.[16] This crime against the environment, which aims to promote German carmakers, costs the state 3.1 billion euros a year.[17] But the climate disaster playing out on Germany's roads cannot be explained by cheap company cars alone. Ownership of luxury cars is not promoted in other European countries, but drivers remain attached to their beloved vehicles there, too. There are many countries where carbon dioxide emissions per vehicle are somewhat lower than Germany, but there, too, greenhouse gas emissions caused by car traffic have barely fallen.[18]

The nudging effect of environmental taxes is limited, not least of all because, for most people, price is not the only concern. For many car owners, the trivial monetary cost of their vehicle is less important than its function as a sought-after status symbol suggesting success, freedom, and indulgence.

Most important, however, is the fact that most drivers are easily able to afford to pay the high fuel tax. Those levies do not disappear into the abyss, to lie unused. Instead, they continue to circulate through the economy. Car owners have to reach deep into their pockets at the petrol pump, but the taxes they pay flow to the state, which spends those funds immediately, creating jobs and income for people. In the end, the amount of money in circulation remains the same.

Environmental taxes barely decrease energy consumption, because they do not reduce income overall, but at best redistribute it somewhat. This effect is particularly obvious in the case of 'energy repayments', several variations of which are currently under discussion. The idea is that the state would not spend the income from carbon dioxide emission levies directly itself, but would distribute the money to citizens as an equal per-capita payout. Poorer families benefit from this because they tend to consume less energy than the rich, who use more energy, and so would pay more of the tax. As fair as that plan sounds, it would do nothing to change the overall amount of money that households have to spend on travel, to fill up their cars, or to subscribe to internet streaming services.[19]

Individual flights to Mallorca would become more expensive if there were a carbon dioxide emissions levy on kerosene. But, for most people, paying the increased ticket price would not be a problem, as they would be able to use their energy repayment money. Ultimately, there would be just as many Germans sunbathing on the beaches of the Balearics as before—only with a huge tax carousel now also involved.

However, economists disagree: they hope carbon dioxide levies will help cut energy consumption, because such taxes would change the entire price structure in Germany. Not only would flights to Mallorca become more expensive; rail tickets to holiday destinations in Germany would be cheap, because they consume little energy and produce hardly any carbon dioxide emissions. For this reason, economists expect that German beach tourists would opt for Mecklenburg over Mallorca. Keen mountain hikers would no longer head for distant Nepal, but would explore the much closer Alps.

The idea that many tourists would choose the cheapest

offer and dutifully travel to the Baltic states, may not be completely wrong. But it still does not mean to say that those penny-pinchers would end up emitting significantly less carbon dioxide, since the familiar rebound effect would once again make itself felt. If individual rail trips were cheap, people might be inclined to travel far more frequently. This might mean that they would not limit themselves to visiting the Palatinate Forest, but might also take the train to Rome, Copenhagen, or Paris, especially since those price-conscious travellers would also have their energy repayment money to spend on enjoying their penny-pinching lives. Perhaps a little carbon dioxide would be saved overall, but it would never be enough to reach net-zero greenhouse gas emissions.

Economists would even welcome it if Germans continued to consume so much, because the alternative is economic collapse, and the economic mainstream has no models for that. To return to flights to Mallorca: every flight is so harmful to the climate that the carbon dioxide emissions price should be so high as to make air travel extremely expensive, discouraging anyone from flying at all—whether to the Balearics or to Bali. But what would then happen to the 850,000 people whose jobs depend directly or indirectly on the German air travel industry? The economists never even mention that problem.

So it seems a safe bet that the price of carbon dioxide emissions will continue to be set too low in future. It will continue to fail to reflect the danger posed by greenhouse gases—remaining moderate so as not to jeopardise growth. The vast majority of economists fail to notice this contradiction because they are blinded by their faith in 'green growth'.

International comparisons also show the absurdity of trusting in 'the steering power of prices'. As already mentioned, Malawi emits just 0.1 tonnes of carbon dioxide per capita per year. That sustainable way of life is not the result of carbon dioxide emissions costing more in southern Africa than in Germany—indeed, no price is set on emissions there. The simple fact is that Malawians are too poor to own cars and to fly to distant holiday destinations. They don't have enough income to ruin the entire planet.

It is extremely unfair that the whole of humanity must suffer the consequences of climate change caused only by a rich minority. (See chapter 19.) And it is certain that this situation will not be changed by wealthy countries' tinkering with carbon dioxide emissions prices.

Climate-protection activists often fail to understand the fact that economists only operate within their own models. That leads to serious misunderstandings, especially when it comes to the issue of whether fossil energy is 'subsidised' or not.[20] The International Monetary Fund (IMF) believes it is, placing the global amount used to 'subsidise' coal, oil, and gas at a monstrous $5.9 trillion per annum. That corresponds to 6.8 per cent of the world's entire economic output.[21] Many climate-protection activists think that those 'subsidies' are actual money, which could be redirected to environmental protection, immediately solving the problem of how to fund the transition to green energy. But those billions don't exist. The IMF uses an extraordinarily broad definition of 'subsidies', most of which do not take the form of real money.

When damage to the environment and/or human health is not factored into prices, the IMF counts this as a 'subsidy'. Per year, 43,407 people die prematurely in Germany due to bad air quality.[22] But those deaths are not factored into the price of energy in Germany, and the IMF counts this as an indirect subsidy.

Other 'subsidies' arise due to the different taxes paid on different fuels. As already mentioned, 47.04 cents of the price of a litre of diesel is a tax, while the tax on a litre of petrol is 65.45 cents. For the IMF, this means that diesel is subsidised, although in reality it is heavily taxed—just not quite as heavily as petrol.

Whether the IMF's definition makes sense is a matter of debate.[23] But it is clear that the German government does not spend money on persuading citizens to consume oil. On the contrary: in 2021, the German state collected no less than 33 billion euros in energy taxed on diesel and petrol.[24] The state profits substantially from oil.[25] Of course, there is no reason why diesel should not be taxed as highly as petrol, which could generate 8.2 billion euros a year in extra tax revenue for the state.[26] But it would be a mistake to assume from this that the state has always pumped enormous amounts of money into fossil-fuelled traffic.

By contrast, the energy transition *will* cost real money. Solar power systems and wind turbines only make economic sense because owners are paid for feeding energy into the grid.[27] Heat pumps, electric vehicles, and passive houses are also subsidised by the state so that as many people as possible will buy them. Promoting environmental technologies is the right thing to do because it improves the efficiency of those technologies. But it is not cheap.

The central mistake made by market-oriented economists is to treat green energy like a normal product that can be multiplied at will whenever demand increases. They believe that all that is needed to increase the number of wind turbines and solar panels is the right 'price signals'. Their idea is that, if carbon taxes are high enough, fossil energy will become so expensive that every household and business will happily switch to green power. But green power cannot be multiplied at will. It will remain a scarce commodity. (See chapters 13 and 14.) Economists ignore such physical and technological facts, preferring to stick to their world of prices.

The two camps in this debate have become so entrenched that they are apparently irreconcilable. Most politicians, climate researchers, and economists place their hopes in 'green growth', although there is unlikely to be enough green energy to meet our needs. On the other side, critics of growth demand that incomes and consumption must fall, although they do not have a plan for achieving this without triggering a major economic crisis that would catapult millions of people into poverty and desperation.

What is needed is a concept for shrinking the economy while avoiding a descent into chaos. Luckily, history provides us with an example of precisely this. Britain's war economy from 1939 onwards serves as a model for how to move towards a climate-neutral world without descending into chaos. Of course, it would be ludicrous to simply copy the measures introduced at that time — after all, the world has moved on in the intervening 85 years, and we are not at war with the climate. But there are enough parallels to provide a blueprint for a sustainable future.

Just to prevent any misunderstandings right from the outset: I will only describe the British war economy from 1939 onwards here. It was by no means the only war economy in world history. Putin's brutal attack on Ukraine has shown only recently that all military conflicts have dire consequences, including economic ones. Also, there can be several different models for transforming the economy even within a single war. In World War II, it was not only the British and the Americans who introduced a war economy; Hitler and Stalin introduced their own forms of a war economy, too.

Not every war economy provides a suitable analogy for an ecological transformation. The British war economy from 1939 onwards, however, unites several factors that make it an interesting proposal. First, Britain was a democracy—its prime minister, Winston Churchill, led an elected government. Fears of an 'eco-dictatorship' are justified, but, as Britain showed, democracies are also capable of taking decisive action.

Second, the British were not fighting a war of aggression, but defending themselves against Hitler. They were involuntarily thrust into an emergency situation, which they were, however, late to recognise. For a long time, the British hoped to appease Hitler and prevent him from starting a war. The situation is reminiscent of climate change today: the seriousness of the situation was understood late, and is forcing us to act now. Third, Britain had to shut down its normal industry in a very short space of time to free up factory capacity for the production of military equipment. That means we can learn from Britain about how to organise the shrinking of an economy.

Critics of growth are often accused of taking pleasure in tormenting their fellow humans. 'Those who think up prohibitions enjoy patronising people,' complains the *Bild* right-wing tabloid journalist Nena Schink, for example, who is terrified that Germany could 'mutate into a nation of prohibitions'.[28]

Unfortunately, prohibitions will be necessary. Our way of life can only be ecological if we stop consuming everything uncontrollably all the time. That's why World War II analogy is fitting: it makes it clear that sacrifices will be necessary if we are to build an ecological circular economy. Only by making sacrifices can we survive—just as in times of war.

CHAPTER EIGHTEEN

A model: Britain's wartime economy from 1939 onwards

When there is a problem to be solved, it is not unusual to talk in terms of war. Wars have been waged against poverty, drugs, and even cancer. But in those cases, 'war' is meant as a metaphor, intended to highlight the huge effort involved.[1]

Military comparisons were common during the Covid-19 pandemic. US president Donald Trump said at his first press conference on the disease, 'We are at war with an invisible enemy.' The French president, Emmanuel Macron, also saw himself as a war leader, calling for a 'general mobilisation', while Britain's Queen Elizabeth spoke of healthcare workers being 'on the front line'.

Those analogies with World War II were meant literally, and some states even reactivated wartime legal provisions. Trump revived the Defense Production Act, passed in 1950 soon after the start of the Korean War, this time to force the carmaker General Motors to start producing ventilators. Just as tanks were produced for battle in the past, the 'weapons against the virus' were now masks and vaccines.[2]

And, as in times of war, the state assumed responsibility for all important decisions: within a matter of days, schools and restaurants were closed, employees were sent home to work from there, huge financial-rescue packages were put together, and some borders were closed. Money was no object in the pursuit of 'victory' over the virus.

So the state can act if it wants to. That fact has not escaped climate-protection activists. They are also inclined to compare the battle for the climate with World War II. In 2018, the IPCC called for a 'mobilisation',[3] and the winner of the Nobel Prize for Economics, Joseph Stiglitz, also advocated for the idea.[4]

Climate-protection activists are most excited by the speed with which the Allies in World War II were able to produce the arsenal of weapons necessary for victory over Germany and its allies. They want wind turbines, solar panels, and electric cars to be manufactured just as quickly. However, most authors are less interested in Britain than in the US, which was able to erect huge arms factories almost out of nothing after the Japanese attacked Pearl Harbor in December 1941. In only six months, the Americans built, among other things, an aircraft factory in Michigan that produced 24 B-24 bombers a day, even though each plane was made up of 1,225,000 individual parts and 313,237 rivets.[5]

Equally impressive was the US's production of standardised *Liberty* cargo ships to replace the 231 vessels sunk by German submarines in the Atlantic. Initially, each cargo ship, consisting of 250,000 parts, took eight months to build. Eventually, a new ship was produced every five days.[6]

At the same time, existing factories were simply repurposed. Heating-systems manufacturers started producing helmets, underwear makers switched to manufacturing camouflage nets, adding machines were turned into pistols, and vacuum-cleaner bags found their way into gas masks. Car seat covers were turned into parachutes, while automobile manufacturers produced machine guns, cannons, aircraft engines, fighter planes, tanks, and anti-tank weapons.[7]

The US government spent more money between 1942 and 1945 than it had in the entire period from 1789 to 1941. During the war years, the US produced 87,000 naval vessels, 300,000 aircraft, 100,000 armoured vehicles and tanks, and 44 billion rounds of ammunition. Even president Roosevelt was amazed at this 'miracle of production'.[8]

That huge material battle powerfully boosted growth at the time, and many climate-protection activists paint a similarly optimistic picture of the future battle. The American activist Bill McKibben, for example, enthuses: 'Gearing up to stop global warming would provide a host of social and economic benefits, just as World War II did.'[9] The Filipino economist Laurence Delina wants to avoid 'debilitating pessimism', and believes a war economy is the right means to develop 'the most optimistic strategies that frame climate action as one of the greatest opportunity [sic] for social, technical, political, economic and cultural change'.[10]

Climate activists also love the United States' war economy so much because it was largely painless. Americans had to make some sacrifices during the war, as companies stopped producing cars or nylon stockings, and made tanks and parachute silk instead. But, overall, the sacrifices were minimal. There was still more than a kilo of meat per person per week consumed—which is precisely the amount eaten by the average German today.[11]

Arming the country was also financed easily. Although the military devoured up to 42 per cent of economic output, the overall economy expanded more than quickly enough to absorb that.[12] US economic performance grew by a total of 90.5 per cent,[13] while in neighbouring Canada, it doubled, growing by more than 100 per cent. North Americans grew richer during the war.

But precisely because of the incredible growth in the US at the time, copying its war economy cannot be our green future. There could never be enough green energy to produce such a deluge of material. Of course, we must invest as much as we can in wind turbines, solar panels, heat pumps, electrolysers, power grids, railway tracks, and batteries—so, in that respect, there is a comparison with America's mobilisation during World War II. But this must not result in rapid and exorbitant growth.

Britain's war economy is better suited as a model for the future, since the United Kingdom had to cut civil production drastically in order to free up capacity for the military. The war took up around 50 per cent of British economic output—which barely grew during that period.[14] Overall growth between 1939 and 1945 was only 27 per cent.[15] The British could obtain goods and weapons from North America and the Commonwealth, but those imports were far from sufficient to maintain the peacetime standard of living.[16] The war took its toll.

For most people in Britain, World War II came as a surprise. The primatologist Jane Goodall grew up on the south coast of England, where she experienced the start of the war: 'Our defences against the Nazi here on the beach were a couple of rolls of barbed wire. England was not prepared for the war. But we were the only country in Europe that was not defeated, that didn't surrender. Although I was only a small child at the time, that is when I learned that there is always hope.'[17]

The British had underestimated Hitler for a long time

because they wanted to avoid having to fight another war. 'Never again' was their motto after the horrors of World War I. More than 16.5 million people died in the war between 1914 and 1918, of whom 723,000 were British soldiers, and another 230,000 were troops from countries of the British Empire.[18] The British were also wary of the cost of another war: the Wall Street crash and the global economic crisis that followed had caused severe damage to the economy, and by 1934 Britain had reduced its defence spending by a quarter in order to ease pressure on the national budget.[19]

But the truth must also be told that some sections of the British upper class were not so averse to Hitler. Members of the nobility, in particular, liked to travel often to 'the Third Reich' to see for themselves how it had 'created order' and 'banished the threat of communism'. The British elites were terrified of a possible Bolshevik revolution on home soil—although there were only 6,000 registered communists in Britain at the time. The assassination of the Russian tsar and his family in 1918 had struck them with fear, so fascism was seen as a welcome bulwark, in both its Italian and German versions.[20]

The Conservative prime minister, Stanley Baldwin, who is still considered one of Britain's leading political figures, said in 1936, 'We all know the German desire ... to move east, and if he [Hitler] should move east I should not break my heart ... If there is any fighting in Europe to be done, I should like to see the Bolshies and the Nazi doing it.'[21] Although Baldwin was as opposed to Nazism as he was to communism, he could not conceive of Hitler becoming an existential threat to Great Britain.

The Liberal former prime minister David Lloyd George even went so far as to visit Hitler at his Berghof residence in Berchtesgaden in 1936, where he regaled the dictator with praise, calling him 'the greatest German living'. Back at home, Lloyd George continued with his panegyrics, describing Hitler as 'the George Washington of Germany'.[22] In doing so, the former prime minister insinuated that the 'Third Reich' was an emerging young democracy, as the US had once been.

The British secret services were well informed about Hitler's military build-up, but for a long time the government reassured itself with the idea that his aim was simply to restore Germany's 'national unity'. Hitler's forces occupied the demilitarised Rhineland in 1936, an act that had been forbidden by the treaties of Versailles and Locarno, but the British were unconcerned. The secretary of state for war at the time, Duff Cooper, openly told the German ambassador, Leopold von Hoesch, that England 'did not care "two hoots" about the Germans reoccupying their own territory'.[23] There was a similar reaction to Hitler's invasion of Austria in March 1938. That *Anschluss* seemed to most people in Britain like the logical unification of two German nations.[24]

It was not until the 'Sudeten crisis' in 1938, when Hitler issued an ultimatum demanding the German annexation of the Sudetenland area, that the British began to worry. The Sudeten Germans had been subjects of the Habsburg monarchy, and then became Czechoslovakian after World War I. As with Austria, British people could understand why a predominantly German-speaking region would want to be part of Germany[25]—but Czechoslovakia could not survive as a state without the Sudetenland area. It was in this border region that most of the country's industry was located, as well as Czechoslovakia's best agricultural land. In addition, the mountains there served as a natural line of defence, which had been further strengthened with forts and military barracks. Without the Sudetenland area, Czechoslovakia would be defenceless against Germany, which was of course precisely what Hitler intended.

Despite their misgivings, the British signed the 'Munich Agreement' in September 1938. It allowed Germany to occupy the Sudeten area, while Hitler agreed to respect the sovereignty of the rest of Czechoslovakia. The British failed to realise that this was a deception on Hitler's part—until 15 March 1939, when German tanks entered Prague.[26] World War II began on 1 September 1939, when Hitler invaded Poland.

In retrospect, Britain's prime minister, Neville Chamberlain, seems naive to have believed for so long that 'Herr Hitler's objectives [were] strictly limited' and that he was 'telling the truth' when he said that he 'did not want to bring Czechs into the Reich'.[27] But at the time it seemed inconceivable that Hitler would want to start another world war, since it was a foregone conclusion that he would lose such a conflict. The German Reich was simply too poor to subjugate the whole of Europe.

In the period leading up to 1939, Hitler had managed to put together an army of 2.6 million troops. But most of those men had barely any equipment, often having to fight with machine guns from World War I. Of the 54 divisions of the army, only 15 were motorised, while the rest had to go into battle on foot or on horseback. The army had 3,600 tanks, but 'most were too poorly armed for modern warfare', according to the military historian Sönke Neitzel.[28]

By contrast, Britain was a military superpower at that time. It had the biggest naval fleet and the largest aircraft-manufacturing industry in the world. Its army was small, but fully motorised.[29] No British soldier had to go to war on foot—they all rode in armoured vehicles.

However, there were technical problems. At the start of the war, some of Britain's military equipment failed, as highlighted by the British historian of technology David Edgerton:

> The British placed emphasis on modern weapons which simply did not work very well. Britain had a fleet of great bombers, which in 1940–1941 could do little or no damage to Germany; on the other side, expensive night air defences were ineffective until 1941. In other words, the problem was not merely a lack of modern weapons, but overinvestment in them.[30]

There was a need for costly improvements and additions, especially since the war lasted much longer than the British initially assumed. In September 1940, British military leaders believed they would achieve victory by 1942.[31] The war dragged on for five painfully long years.

When World War II began, the British wanted to avoid the mistakes they had made in World War I. The decisions made in 1914 and later had been mostly taken on an *ad hoc* basis, and the British took a long time to realise that a total war requires complete planning.[32] So, in 1939, the British did not waste precious time and immediately organised a kind of 'private planned economy'. The state stipulated what was produced—but businesses remained in private ownership. Companies both large and small, restaurants, and shops were not nationalised, and continued to be run as their owners or managers saw fit.

This British planned economy differed fundamentally from the socialism practised at the time in the Soviet Union under Stalin. In that centrally planned economy, all companies were state-owned, and their production of goods was regulated down to the last screw.

The British government, on the other hand, exercised only indirect control over companies — in the way it distributed raw materials, loans, and labour.[33] Workers, in particular, were so scarce that businesses could only manufacture products when they were allocated employees. This 'manpower budget' became the government's main steering mechanism.[34]

The planning authorities required a lot of manpower themselves. The Ministry of Food had 3,500 employees in 1940; by 1943, that workforce had grown to 39,000. Despite their size, these authorities were not just huge bureaucracies with no connection to real, day-to-day life, as they were full of experts and entrepreneurs. They specifically hired economists, scientists, engineers, and businesspeople.[35]

Initially, they lacked the statistical information they needed to make their plans. National accounting did not exist as such. No one knew how many guns, aircraft, or tanks could be produced without the country having to go hungry. The concept of GDP was invented as a measuring instrument to fill that information gap. It was one of Britain's weapons of war, so to speak. It was such a resounding success that it was later adopted by almost every country in the world. GDP has now become the most important statistical value in the field of economics, because it provides a measure of economic performance and therefore also of economic growth. (See chapter 7.)[36]

GDP enabled economists to determine that precisely 66 per cent of British industrial capacity would be needed to arm the military.[37] That left almost no goods available for the civilian population, although more were actually needed than in peacetime, due to the destruction of more than a million British homes by German air raids.[38] Food supplies also had to be cut, since Britain was not self-sufficient, relying on imports for 70 per cent of its food.[39] Those imports had to be cut because the ships were now needed to transport arms and military raw materials from overseas. Food took up valuable space.[40]

Detailed calculations were made of how many calories could be imported with which foodstuffs. The result was that 1,000 cubic feet of shipping capacity could transport 83,000 calories' worth of sugar, more than 100,000 calories of fat, and 56,000 calories of grain—but only 12,000 calories if fresh eggs were the cargo.[41] So eggs were struck off the import list, and powdered egg was invented.[42]

The British did not starve during World War II, as each person was allocated 2,800 calories a day.[43] That was sufficient: these days, the NHS recommends a maximum daily calorie intake of 2,500 for men and 2,000 for women.[44]

But quantity is not the same as quality. Meat, cheese, fat, sugar, tea, and soap were in such short supply that they had to be rationed. However, there was never a complete shortage even of those rare commodities. There was enough to provide at least 540 grams of meat per person per week; military employees even enjoyed a handsome weekly meat ration of 1.2 kilograms.[45] Healthy adults had to do without milk and eggs most of the time, as they were reserved for children, pregnant women, and nursing mothers.

There was no rationing of potatoes, flour, and bread.[46] There were also no limits on fish, poultry, game, offal, vegetables, or fruit, since those foodstuffs were either quick to spoil or highly seasonal, or they were not sufficiently available to guarantee a regular ration for every individual.

There was, of course, a scarcity of extras such as canned goods, biscuits, chocolate, sweets, and dried fruit. A points system was introduced for such items. Customers could decide for themselves what to 'spend' their points on. The government changed the number of points needed to buy each product according to its availability.[47]

The points system also covered furniture and clothing. In order to save both materials and labour, such goods were standardised, so every chair or dinner plate looked the same. There were also strict regulations on garments, banning unnecessary decorations. Women's dresses, for example, were not allowed to have more than two pockets and five buttons.

These quantity and price controls were tremendously popular in Britain. As the British government noted as early as 1941, the rationing program was 'one of the greatest successes on the home front'. This state-imposed egalitarianism turned out to be a blessing: ironically, the lower strata of society were better supplied during the war than ever before. During peacetime, a third of the population had an insufficient calorie intake, and a further 20 per cent were at least partly undernourished. Now, amid war, the population was healthier than ever, and 'the fitness of babies and school children was particularly striking'.[48]

Rationing was so popular in Britain because everyone had exactly the same entitlement. However, it was only partly true that wealth no longer made a difference. The elite had enough money to buy expensive unrationed goods such as fish and game, and to eat at restaurants.[49] But those injustices were later forgotten. The war was later glorified as a 'time of public spirit, in which class and social differences paled and the nameless are as important as a prince'.[50]

Consumption fell by a third—and in a very short space of time.[51] That huge reduction and restructuring makes Britain's war economy a fascinating model for modern times: consumption in Germany needs to fall equally drastically if the climate is to be saved. However, no one need fear having to eat nothing but potatoes and bread, and make do with two dresses per year. It would not be that bleak. The German economy has grown tenfold in real terms over the past 80 years. Even if only half of that enormous prosperity remained, we would still be as well off as we were in 1978.[52]

Those who were alive at the time remember it well: *Star Wars* was filling the movie theatres, and Argentina won the football world cup. Kids were riding chopper bikes, and playing with slime. Life felt little different from today, but it was slower-paced. Instead of jetting off to Mallorca for a long weekend several times a year, people got into their own cars and drove to Italy for three weeks in the summer. In a climate-neutral world, that journey would be made by train, but such holidays would still be the norm.

A circular economy could be a very agreeable thing. The 'share economy' has opened up enticing visions of a pleasant way to live while consuming only as much as can be recycled. (See chapter 16.) The destination is clear; only the way to get there must be found. As yet there is no plan for ending dynamic, growth-based capitalism without awakening the threat of a severe economic crisis. Britain's wartime economy could provide such a model, demonstrating how a private planned economy can shrink civilian production in an orderly way—and how scarce goods can be rationed in a way that maintains social harmony.

Planned economies and rationing have a bad reputation these days. Anyone who does not put their faith in the 'free market' is immediately accused of wanting to torment their fellow human beings. The Greens politician Anton Hofreiter expressed his exasperation with this when he said in an interview, 'Should people be given a quota for how far they can drive their cars? Will there be coupons for buying meat? That's absurd. We live in a free society and, luckily, such mechanisms don't exist.'[53]

Many people believe 'the free market' and state control are polar opposites and are absolutely mutually exclusive. But that is wrong. Planning has always been a part of capitalism—be it on the part of companies or governments.[54] Britain's wartime economy was able to work so well because it did not introduce anything radically new, but rather radicalised aspects that were already inherent in capitalism. The state plays a leading role even in normal times, and so it should be possible at any time to return to a kind of war economy in order to save the climate.

CHAPTER NINETEEN

Our future lives

The US president Ronald Reagan once summed up the widespread aversion to state involvement with the sentence, 'The nine most terrifying words in the English language are: "I'm from the government, and I'm here to help."' The market is seen as the cradle of freedom and efficiency, while the state apparently just gets in the way.

That view is fundamentally wrong, as we last saw during Covid-19. When the pandemic reached Europe in March 2020, the stock markets panicked. The German share index, the DAX, lost 40 per cent of its value—and would have fallen further if the government had not intervened and pumped billions of euros into the economy. Without the state, there would no longer be a 'market' at all.

However, the state does more than just dealing with crises; it also promotes technological progress. Neoliberals stubbornly believe that only the 'free market' can produce innovations.[1] In fact, almost all today's important inventions came from government laboratories or were subsidised with public money. That's as true of the internet as it is for solar panels. The powerful Covid vaccines would also not have existed if the state hadn't previously sponsored years of bio-tech research into messenger RNA.

Even the icon of the digital age, the smartphone, would never have been invented without the state's help. Apple founder Steve Jobs was undoubtedly a brilliant man, but he was not a researcher. His achievement was to combine existing knowledge to create a new product. The crucial elements of his iPhone—touchscreens, GPS, and lithium-ion batteries, for instance—had already been developed in government laboratories.[2]

Most billionaires know full well what they owe the state. Bill Gates recently admitted, 'The personal computer business—including Microsoft—would never have been the success that it was if the US government hadn't put money into research on smaller, faster microprocessors.'[3] And the godfather of investment, Warren Buffet, has advocated for years for the super-rich to pay more taxes, because 'society is responsible for a very significant percentage of what [he's] earned'.[4]

There's nothing new about the state steering the private economy. Back in the 19th century, the modern global giant Siemens would have faltered early but for the repeated orders for telegraph lines it received from tsarist Russia and the kingdom of Prussia.[5] Efficient aircraft also only exist today because governments have invested continuously in that technology for more than 100 years.[6]

Those who advocate for the 'free market' often forget that private companies only make up part of the economy. It can often be more efficient to avoid commercial companies. Whether it is for schools, roads, railways, health insurance, water, or electricity-supply systems, the provision of public services works better and is cheaper if the state takes control.[7] For an example of how inefficient the 'free market' can be, we need only look at the US healthcare system, which has no statutory insurance system, and which is therefore extremely expensive. The US spends almost twice as much on healthcare per capita than any other industrialised nation. And that huge spending brings no advantage. The average life expectancy in the US is three years lower than in Sweden.[8] Americans themselves are deeply dissatisfied with their healthcare system: they have considerably less confidence in their system's ability to care for their health than the much poorer Cubans, Indians, or Vietnamese, for example.[9]

The climate crisis will also require state intervention, as green electricity will not flow by itself. Photovoltaics, wind turbines, heat pumps, new power networks, charging points, battery-storage systems, green hydrogen, rail network extensions, and additional public transport can only come about if the state is involved in steering, researching, financing, and subsidising.

Most climate-protection activists would immediately admit that comprehensive planning is necessary if we are to transition to an ecological economy.[10] The crucial issue is rationing. Those who believe in 'green growth' consider it completely unnecessary to require people to make sacrifices. Instead, they envision a plentiful supply of green power that can fulfil the wishes of all.

The unpopularity of the idea of rationing often obscures the fact that growth optimists also call for a form of apportionment themselves. They just give it a different name: the carbon budget.[11] This refers to the amount of greenhouse gas each country is allowed to emit. The approach is both correct and fair. First, calculations are made to determine how much greenhouse gas humankind can still emit without pushing global warming beyond 1.5 to 1.75 degrees Celsius. The resulting amount is then divided by the number of people on Earth. For Germany, the result shows that we must become climate-neutral by 2035 at the latest. India, on the other hand, has until 2090 to become sustainable, because it only emits 1.8 tonnes of carbon dioxide per inhabitant per year, so it is not using up its budget allocation as quickly as Germany.[12]

The target has already been defined: countries count as climate-neutral when they emit no more than one tonne of carbon dioxide per inhabitant per year. Emissions do not have to hit absolute zero because nature is capable of absorbing some carbon dioxide.

Many countries already remain within that one-tonne limit, or even fall far below it. They include Afghanistan, Angola, Bangladesh, Benin, Burkina Faso, Burundi, Cambodia, Cameroon, Chad, Ethiopia, the Central African Republic, the Comoros, both Congos, Côte d'Ivoire, Djibouti, El Salvador, Gambia, Ghana, Guinea, Guinea-Bissau, Haiti, Honduras, Kenya, Kiribati, North Korea, Liberia, Madagascar, Malawi, Mali, Mauretania, Mozambique, Myanmar, Nepal, Nicaragua, Niger, Nigeria, Pakistan, Papua New Guinea, Rwanda, Senegal, Sierra Leone, Somalia, South Sudan, Sudan, Sri Lanka, Tajikistan, Tanzania, Togo, Uganda, Vanuatu, Yemen, Zambia, and Zimbabwe.[13]

Only a few countries are major climate sinners. Top of the league is the oil sheikhdom Qatar, which emits 32.4 tonnes of carbon dioxide per inhabitant per year. Bahrein, Brunei, Kuwait, Oman, Saudi Arabia, and the United Arab Emirates also stand out in a negative sense. The US, Canada, and Australia consume enormous amounts of energy, too, emitting about 15 tonnes of carbon dioxide per person and year. The people in the eurozone emit 6.5 tonnes each per year, the Japanese emit 8.7 tonnes, and the Chinese 7.4 tonnes.[14]

Rich countries, not poor ones, are responsible for the climate crisis. Nonetheless, the Global South is often accused of being the cause of environmental problems—because

it is supposedly 'overpopulated'. But even if Africa had no
inhabitants at all, the climate crisis would remain unaf-
fected because those people generate almost no carbon
dioxide emissions.[15] The problem is not too many people,
but rather people consuming too much. The journalist for
the *Zeit* newspaper, Bernd Ulrich, put this in a nutshell
when he wrote, 'It's not about overpopulation but people
overconsuming.'[16]

The figures are shocking: the richest 10 per cent of
humanity are responsible for 48 per cent of overall carbon
dioxide emissions, while the poorest 50 per cent are responsible for just 12 per cent.[17] Although the world's poorest
contribute nothing to climate change, they are particularly
hard-hit by it. Droughts and heatwaves will mainly affect the
Amazon, Africa, India, Pakistan, and Indonesia.

The richest 10 per cent of the global community have an
average annual income of 87,200 euros.[18] Germany is a rich
nation, but not everyone in the country belongs to the top
10 per cent of global high earners. The poorer 50 per cent of
the German population survive on an income of just 15,200
euros a year.[19]

Income is distributed very unequally, which is directly
reflected in the figures for carbon dioxide emissions. The
richest 1 per cent of Germans are responsible for a massive
117.8 tonnes of greenhouse gas emissions per person per
year. The top 10 per cent emit, on average, 34.1 tonnes.
The 'middle class' emits 12.2 tonnes—and the lowest 50
per cent only 5.9 tonnes.[20] That means the rich produce 20
times more carbon dioxide emissions than the poor.

Many of Germany's wealthy are completely unaware of
this gross injustice. On the contrary: high earners especially
tend to consider themselves particularly environmentally
friendly. They buy organic vegetables and energy-saving light

bulbs while failing to notice that they live in luxury flats and take frequent flights. Germany's Federal Environment Agency found that there was a 'widespread belief among the wealthy that they make sparing use of resources'. The agency suspects that these environmentally aware high earners mainly compare themselves to members of their own class—and are completely oblivious to the fact that people from poorer backgrounds are able to consume far less than they do.[21]

Anton Hofreiter sounds very democratic when he praises our 'free society', in which anyone can consume as much as they like. But what Hofreiter is really doing is welcoming the fact that the wealthy are ruining the world at the expense of everyone else. This extreme injustice only goes unrecognised because Hofreiter claims at the same time that 'green growth' is possible. For him, unbridled consumption is permissible because it can supposedly be sustainable.

But when 'green growth' turns out to be nothing but an illusion, the only remaining option is rationing. It must be done just as climate-protection activists calculate: each person on the planet would not be allowed to emit more than one tonne of carbon dioxide per year. That would leave Malawi plenty of room to continue developing, since its inhabitants currently only emit an average of just 100 kilograms of carbon dioxide per year.

The sacrifices would have to be made by the Global North—and, in particular, by the wealthy. Of course, it would be very painful for Germany's richest if they were no longer allowed to emit 117.8 tonnes of carbon dioxide per year. It would mean the end of their jet-set lifestyle.

That is not a pleasant prospect for the well-heeled, which is why some writers propose a kind of middle course: 'Each person would have a private carbon dioxide account.

They would be allowed to emit two tonnes a year for free—but anything after that would be more expensive.'[22] However, that well-meaning suggestion would immediately thwart climate-protection measures. The rich would have no problem simply paying for additional emission rights, and would continue to be responsible for too many greenhouse gas emissions. But, more importantly, it would discredit the whole idea of climate protection if everyone except the rich were forced to make sacrifices.

The British only accepted rationing so willingly during the war because it applied to everyone. The government knew precisely how damaging visible class differences would be. As the English writer George Orwell noted in late 1940, 'The lady in the Rolls-Royce car is more damaging to morale than a fleet of Goering's bombing planes.'[23]

Climate protection will only have a chance of success if everyone's sacrifices are the same. But what would it mean for Germans if they could only emit one tonne of carbon dioxide each? No one can give a definitive answer to that question at present, as it depends on how efficient green technology becomes in the future. The more green power it can provide, the more comfortable life will be. 'Green growth' is not possible, but a large part of today's economic output could be maintained. Germans would still be able to go on holiday, use their smartphones, read books, and eat in restaurants.

However, flying would become a thing of the past, there would be hardly any cars on the roads, and real estate would have to be rationed: if the voracious consumption of land is to end, the constant construction of new first homes, second homes, holiday homes, offices, and industrial estates must also end. Germany's existing stock of buildings would have to be enough for everybody.

Meat consumption would also have to be limited, since livestock is a climate killer. Intensive farming currently causes 21 to 37 per cent of all greenhouse gas emissions globally. Cattle, goats, and sheep, in particular, are extremely harmful for the climate because, as ruminants, they emit methane. There are around a billion cattle trampling the Earth, and each adult cow releases at least 300 litres of methane per day from its front and back ends. Germany's health minister, Karl Lauterbach, came up with the following comparison to give an impression of how large an amount that is: 'The waste gas produced by a single cow in a year would be enough to heat a four-person family home for a month in winter—including hot water.'[24] A molecule of methane typically remains in the atmosphere for only around 12 years, but it causes so much damage in that short time that it is considered 25 times more potent than a molecule of carbon dioxide.

Livestock farming produces not only methane, but also nitrous oxide, which is as much as 300 times as harmful as carbon dioxide, and persists in the atmosphere for some 100 years. This trace gas currently accounts for a minute 0.0000334 per cent of air particles, but that tiny amount is enough to generate around 7 per cent of global warming.[25] The most common source of nitrous oxide is over-fertilisation of farmland with nitrogen. Animals even produce some of that fertiliser themselves with their urine and manure, but that does not mean that such slurry is 'organic'. It also contains nitrogen, which eventually becomes nitrous oxide.

Meat is a luxury product because—depending on which calculation you accept—it takes around ten plant-based calories to produce one calorie's worth of meat. There is no way of changing this energy-intensive way of farming meat. Most of the energy in animal feed is lost, as it is used up just keeping the animal alive, growing, and fattening up. It would be far more efficient for humans to consume the grain themselves that they feed to livestock. However, the reverse is happening: as the Global South gets richer, more people there can afford sumptuous meat-based meals.

More and more forests are being cleared to create pastureland for livestock, or arable land for growing animal feed. The felled trees are no longer available to fix carbon dioxide, which also accelerates the advent of the climate catastrophe. The Amazon, in particular, is being rapidly deforested, and Brazil now has as many bovine inhabitants as human ones.

Intensive farming is not only worsening the climate crisis; it is also wasting fresh water reserves, destroying humus soils, and eradicating countless species. The decline in insect populations is particularly alarming. Many remember having to scrape a layer of dead insects off their windshield after a long car journey. That is now a thing of the past. The biomass of flying insects in Germany has fallen by 75 per cent, and on a global level, one-third of all insect species are threatened with extinction.[26]

A world without insects in inconceivable. They pollenate almost 90 per cent of flowering plants and 75 per cent of the most important crop plants. About a third of our food would not exist without that natural service. The 'labour' performed by insects is estimated to be worth between $235 billion and $577 billion a year. The little hexapods not only make food crops possible, but the production of fibres, medicines, biofuel, and construction materials also depends on insects flying out to crawl into flowers.[27]

Entire ecosystems collapse when insects disappear. Around the world, some 400 to 500 million tonnes of insects are eaten by birds alone annually, but they are also a source of food for amphibians, fish, and small mammals.[28]

'The disappearance of insects is a drama, but not (yet) a tragedy,' says the environmental researcher Josef Settele.[29] Agriculture has to change if the insects are to survive, with less reliance on monocultures and no pesticides.

Environmental farming requires more space. One reason for this is that less fertiliser is used, so the yield per hectare is lower. That additional farmland can only be available if people eat the farmed grain themselves rather than feeding it to animals. And this brings us back to the main point: if we want farming to be ecological, we must ration meat.

Ration it — not abolish it altogether. No one will be forced to become a strict vegetarian and give up their beloved sausage on the barbecue. Poultry, pork, or steak would be allowed occasionally. Livestock would not completely disappear, as two-thirds of the world's land area is unsuitable for arable farming. Those areas can only support grass, which humans are unable to digest, so the circuitous route to the table via animal products would be unavoidable there. Cattle can also help with climate protection if they are widely spread over large areas of pastureland, because they fix more carbon dioxide than they emit methane. Their dung and urine fertilise the grass, improving its growth. They trample plants into the soil with their hooves, which also fixes carbon. Their manure provides a habitat for other animals: the dung of one single cow can support more than 100 kilograms of insect biomass per year.[30]

Rationing has an unpleasant sound to it. But perhaps life could be more pleasant than it is today, because justice and equality make us happy. Societies are more relaxed, healthier, and more tolerant when the gap between rich and poor is small. The poorer sections of society are not the only beneficiaries of such a positive atmosphere. Global surveys show that members of the elite also live longer when they are part of a fair society.[31]

To clear up one last misunderstanding: rationing would mean scarce goods being distributed fairly, but this is not the same as a universal basic income, under which every citizen would receive up to 1,500 euros a month.[32] Those models assume, either explicitly or implicitly, that the economy will continue to grow. Otherwise, there would simply not be enough money to pay out such huge amounts. The philosopher Richard David Precht is one of the advocates of a universal basic income (UBI) and is clear that 'there would need to be a booming economy and high productivity for all citizens in Germany to be able to receive a UBI'.[33] But our economy will not continue to boom if we only use as much as can be recycled.

As well as consumption being rationed, production would have to be controlled. Since green energy will be scarce, many branches of industry would have to shrink significantly, or disappear altogether. Aviation, banking, insurance, automobile companies, and parts of the chemicals industry, in particular, would have no great future. (See chapter 16.) Millions of people would become unemployed and have to look for a new job, for example in climate protection. This ecological transition could only take place in an ordered way if it were controlled by the state and if the secure future of all those affected could be guaranteed.

During World War II, Britain demonstrated how a government can effectively steer the economy through a radical transition. As already mentioned, the state did not intervene in individual companies, leaving owners and managers to decide how to run their businesses internally. The state simply dictated what was to be produced—and in what quantities. Businesses were then allocated the workforce and raw materials necessary to meet the state's goals. The British government exercised indirect control through its targeted allocation of resources.

Scarcity as a means of control: a principle that could work again. Only now, scarcity would apply not to labour and raw materials, but to green energy, which will not be sufficient to satisfy the demands of all branches of industry and other needs. The government would have to determine what the limited supply of green power should be used to produce. Medicines would probably be near the top of the list, and private cars would be near the bottom.

The objective would be a circular economy, in which only as much is produced as can be recycled. However, such a climate-neutral world would not be static. Technological innovation would still be urgently required: if energy efficiency could be increased, for example, more goods could be produced with the same number of wind turbines and solar panels.

Growth would return, but at a lower level. As paradoxical as it may sound: the economy has to shrink before it can be allowed to expand again. However, this possible growth would not have anything in common with today's capitalism, since the hierarchies would be turned upside down. Nature would dictate how much growth is possible—rather than growth dictating how much of the natural world remains intact.

These are distant goals. The first step would be organised shrinkage, with Britain's wartime economy as a proven model. The government steers, but companies remain in private ownership. This is not eco-socialism.[34] History has shown that state planning does not work if it also involves the abolition of almost all property ownership.

One final objection remains: Britain's wartime economy may be an interesting model, but we are not in a state of ecological war. We are not fighting the climate; we want to save it. There is a marked difference between World War II and the climate crisis. The British wanted to defeat an individual, Hitler, who seemed to be the personification of evil. The threat was also very present, as the Germans were just across the Channel after their defeat of France in 1940. Most importantly, though, the British wartime economy remained capitalist. The production of consumer goods shrank, but military industries expanded. There was no general farewell to growth—indeed, the overall economy grew by 27 per cent during the war.

The climate crisis is very different. The threat does not come from a specific person, but from a global chain reaction. The danger is not confined to individual nations; it threatens the entire planet. Also, the deadly threat is not immediately apparent. It often takes years or decades to unfold. And the change of direction would be far more drastic because protecting the climate necessitates a shrinking of the economy.

Those differences cannot be denied, and they are what make climate policy so difficult. Many people prefer to ignore the fact that our future is under threat. Very few people now deny that anthropogenic climate change is real—but does this mean we need to abolish capitalism altogether? That radical conclusion seems exaggerated and absurd to the vast majority of citizens.

Many people still labour under the misapprehension that they have a choice. If saying farewell to capitalism is so difficult, they reason, then let's just stick with it. But that choice is not available. There is no alternative for the industrialised countries. Either they end growth voluntarily, or the era of growth will end violently, when everything that forms the basis of our way of life has been destroyed.

Either way, capitalism will come to an end, and a new economic order will emerge. It can best be described as a 'survival economy', because it is about saving humanity from destruction.

CONCLUSION

The 'survival economy' has already begun

Humanity can only survive if it stops emitting greenhouse gases. That is very much easier said than done. Germany's economic output would need to shrink by at least 30 per cent. And that brings up the 'S'-word, which no politician wants to say out loud: sacrifice.

All political parties know they would immediately lose votes if they called for sacrifices. Even the tiniest restrictions are toxic, as the Greens experienced during the campaign for the 2013 parliamentary election in Germany, when they suggested designating every Thursday 'veggie day' in public-sector works canteens, with only plant-based options on offer. The idea was meant as an incentive to reduce meat consumption, not as a legislative proposal. But *Bild*, the conservative tabloid newspaper, immediately launched a countercampaign, running the headline 'The Greens Want to Ban Us from Eating Meat!'. The Green Party received only 8.4 per cent of the vote in that election, which shocked them so much that they have been portraying themselves as a 'party of freedoms' ever since. Their 2014 manifesto even included the statement, 'We really don't care whether people eat meat on Thursdays or not.'

All the other parties have a pathological fear of being labelled a 'party of prohibition'. The social-democrat health minister, Karl Lauterbach, stated that, 'Even the tiniest increase in the price of petrol is used to the full extent by the populists.'[1] Nothing must challenge the principle of 'the freedom of the road for free citizens', which the current Liberal finance minister, Christian Lindner, once summed up with the polemical statement, 'We will not save the planet by turning Germans into vegan cyclists.'[2]

There is no problem with parties only making demands they believe will win them votes. That's how democracy works. The parties do not lead their voters; they follow them. Change never comes from above; it always originates from below. However, there is no sign of a widespread change in attitude among the public. The vast majority of people are keen to cling on to the illusion that 'green growth' is possible. So political parties indulge that dream—all of them, from the Greens to the Christian conservatives.

A 'survival economy' is not currently politically enforceable, but it does not follow that the conclusion that capitalism must come to an end is incorrect. It would be a fatal mistake to restrict all thinking to what is likely to win a political majority. If that were the case, there would be no point in thinking at all—and the present could simply be renamed the future.

We still live in an affluent society and can barely imagine a general shortage of goods. The idea that state planning and rationing might be necessary seems strange to us. But we can already see the first signs of rationing on the horizon—in particular, of water. Germany will not become a desert in the future, but it will see an increase in the periods when hardly any rain falls across much of the country. Droughts like that of 2018 will no longer be rare exceptions, but regular occurrences. When precipitation is rare, the question immediately arises of who should have access to the scarce water supply—households, agriculture, or industry?[3]

The German government has already adopted a 'national water strategy' allowing for a 'water use hierarchy'—which is simply another name for rationing.[4] Water is already so scarce in eastern Brandenburg that supply companies want to curtail consumption. The water-supply company in Straussberg-Erkner has declared that people moving to the area from 2025 onwards will only be allowed to consume an average of 105 litres per person per day. Anyone exceeding that limit will face a fine, although how much has not been revealed.[5] Germans currently consume an average of 128 litres of water per day.[6] That means people in Straussberg-Erkner will have to seriously save water.

When important commodities become scarce, only the state can guarantee fair and efficient distribution by controlling and rationing the sparse amounts. The 'market' is no help at all. That became clear in Australia, which has faced extreme water shortages for a long time. At first, it was left to the private market to organise distribution. A kind of stock exchange for water utilisation rights was set up: every farmer was allocated his or her fair share of the available water resources, and some of the water rights could be traded on the market. If farmers needed more water, they could buy the rights to it on the market. Those who did not use up their full ration could sell the rights to the rest. The system was soon discontinued because people started speculating wildly with the water-utilisation rights, while the farmers were left fighting for their survival.[7]

On the financial markets, scarcity always leads to speculation, which pushes prices up, makes traders rich, and increases hardship. The state must intervene if all citizens are to get their fair share. Food could also soon become so scarce around the world that its distribution will have to be coordinated at the state level. The IPCC predicts that every degree of global warming will cut maize yields by around 7 per cent, those of wheat by 6 per cent, and of rice and soya by around 3 per cent.[8]

If there is to be enough food for everyone on the planet in future, it will have to be rationed. Leading scientists have already set out the ideal meal plan—called the 'planetary health diet'—which would feed every human being healthily and protect the environment at the same time. It provides each person with 2,500 calories a day: 500 grams of fruit and vegetables, 232 grams of whole grains or rice, 75 grams of legumes, 50 grams of potatoes, 50 grams of nuts, 250 grams of poultry, 13 grams of eggs, 31 grams of sugar, 50 grams of fat, and 28 grams of fish.[9]

At first glance, this menu may look rather meagre, but people in Germany would be far healthier if they adapted their eating habits. The current average daily calorie intake of German adults is not 2,500 but 3,500—and that is not good for their health. Sixty-seven per cent of men and 53 per cent of women are overweight, and almost a quarter are 'extremely overweight'.[10] Those extra pounds are not harmless; they increase the risk of conditions such as diabetes, cardiovascular disease, long-term inflammation, and cancer. Obesity is now the cause of almost 11 per cent of deaths in Germany.[11] Consuming less can be good for your health.

The 'survival economy' is not something in the distant future; the first signs of rationing are already with us. However, they are currently seen as individual emergency plans. They are expected to remain the exception while capitalism continues to expand. But that hope will fail because there will not be sufficient green energy to fuel 'green growth'.

Protecting the climate is only possible if the economy shrinks. Change is always scary, especially when it is combined with sacrifices. But we should not think of the future as bleak. An ecological circular economy can be pleasant. It would provide everything anyone needs for a successful life: stimulation, variety, knowledge, exchange, friendship, love, appreciation, fun, enjoyment, relaxation, play, and sport. As well as security, mobility, healthcare, work, and personal fulfilment.

Until now there has been no clear indication of how such an ecological circular economy can be achieved without triggering a severe economic crisis. There has been no concept for 'green shrinkage'. The 'survival economy' shows us how that transition could succeed without chaos breaking out. Businesses plan privately, but the state determines what should be produced and how scarce goods should be distributed. This concept is based on Britain's wartime economy, introduced in 1939, but it is not a carbon copy. It is now time for the end of capitalism.

Acknowledgements

Any book is only as good as its first proofreaders. Daniel Haufler (who has since died), Andrew James Johnston, Jörgen Pisarz, and Hugo Winters gave me a great deal of their time. As a historian, literary scholar, engineer, and economist respectively, they were an ideal team. This text would never have been possible without their knowledge, ideas, and objections.

bibliography

Bibliography

Abby, Edward, *The Journey Home: some words in defense of the American West* (Dutton 1977)

Agora Energiewende, Agora Verkehrswende, and Climate Neutrality Foundation, *Klimaneutrales Deutschland 2050* (Berlin 2020)

Agora Energiewende, Agora Verkehrswende, and Climate Neutrality Foundation, *Towards a Climate-Neutral Germany by 2045* (Berlin 2021)

Allen, Robert C., *The British Industrial Revolution in Global Perspective* (Cambridge University Press 2009)

Allen, Robert C., *Global Economic History: a very short introduction* (Oxford University Press 2011)

Allen, Robert C., *The Industrial Revolution: a very short introduction* (Oxford University Press 2017)

Appleby, Joyce, *Relentless Revolution: a history of capitalism* (Norton 2010)

Bach, Stefan, Andreas Thiemann, and Aline Zucco, *Looking for the Missing Rich: tracing the top tail of the wealth distribution* (DIW 2018, Discussion Papers 1717)

Bach, Stefan, Michelle Harnisch, and Niklas Isaak, 'Verteilungswirkungen der Energiepolitik — Personelle Einkommensverteilung. Endbericht.' Forschungsprojekt im Auftrag des Bundesministeriums für Wirtschaft und Energie ['Distribution Effects of Energy Policy — Personal Income

Distribution. Final Report.' Research Project Commissioned by the Federal Ministry for Economics and Energy] (Berlin, 23 November 2018)

Bähr, Johannes, *Werner von Siemens, 1816–1892: a biography* (Beck 2016)

Beckert, Sven, *Empire of Cotton: a new history of global capitalism* (Penguin 2015)

Berg, Axel, *Energiewende einfach durchsetzen. Roadmap für die nächsten zehn Jahre* [Getting the Energy Revolution Done: a roadmap for the next ten years.] (Oekom 2019)

Binswanger, Mathias, *Der Wachstumszwang. Warum die Volkswirtschaft immer weiterwachsen muss, selbst wenn wir genug haben* [The Growth Imperative: why the economy must keep growing even when we have enough] (Wiley 2019)

Bouverie, Tim, *Appeasement: Chamberlain, Churchill and the road to war* (Bodley Head 2019)

Brand, Ulrich and Markus Wissen, *The Imperial Mode of Living: everyday life and the ecological crisis of capitalism* (Verso 2021)

Braudel, Fernand, *Civilization and Capitalism 15th–18th Century, vol. I: the structures of everyday life* (Fontana Press 1985)

Braudel, Fernand, *Civilization and Capitalism 15th–18th Century, vol. III: the perspective of the world* (Fontana Press 1985)

Broadberry, Stephen, 'Lessons learned? British economic management and performance during the World Wars', in Broadberry, Stephen and Mark Harrison (eds), *The Economics of the Second World War: seventy-five years on* (CEPR Press 2020), pp. 30–39

Broadberry, Stephen and Kevin O'Rourke, *The Cambridge Economic History of Modern Europe, vol. 1, 1700–1870* (Cambridge University Press 2010)

Brüggemeier, Franz-Josef, *Sun, Water, Wind: development of the energy transition in Germany* (Friedrich Ebert Foundation 2017)

Brüggemeier, Franz-Josef, *Grubengold. Das Zeitalter der Kohle von 1750 bis heute* [Pit Gold: the age of coal from 1750 to the present] (Beck 2018)

Bundesministerium für Wirtschaft und Energie, *Energiedaten: Gesamtausgabe* [*Energy Figures: complete edition*] (Berlin 2019)

Büscher, Wolfgang, *Heimkehr* [Homecoming] (Rowohlt 2020)

Chancel, Lucas, Thomas Piketty, Emmanuel Saez, and Gabriel Zucman, *World Inequality Report 2022* (World Inequality Lab 2021)

Chang, Ha-Joon, *Kicking Away the Ladder: development strategy in historical perspective* (Anthem Press 2003)

Chang, Ha-Joon, *23 Things They Don't Tell You about Capitalism* (Penguin 2011)

Clark, Christopher, *Iron Kingdom: the rise and downfall of Prussia 1600–1947* (Penguin 2007)

Conrad, Sebastian, *German Colonialism: a short history* (Cambridge University Press 2012)

Daly, Herman E., *Beyond Growth* (Beacon Press 1996)

Darwin, John, *Unfinished Empire: the global expansion of Britain* (Penguin 2013)

Deaton, Angus, *The Great Escape: health, wealth, and the origins of inequality* (Princeton University Press 2013)

Dechema and FutureCamp (eds), *Roadmap Chemie 2050. Auf dem Weg zu einer treibhausgasneutralen Chemie in Deutschland* [Chemistry Roadmap: the path to greenhouse gas neutrality in the German chemical industry] (Berlin 2019)

Defoe, Daniel, *A Journal of the Plague Year* (1722)

Delina, Laurence E., *Strategies for Rapid Climate Mitigation: wartime mobilisation as a model for action?* (Routledge 2016)

Deutsche Umwelthilfe, *Versorgungssicherheit mit 100% Erneuerbaren Energien*, [Supply Security With 100% Renewable Energy Sources] (Berlin, November 2021)

Dörre, Klaus, *Rethinking Socialism: compass for a sustainability revolution* (Edward Elgar Publishing Limited 2021)

Eckert, Andreas, *Geschichte der Sklaverei. Von der Antike bis ins 21. Jahrhundert* [The History of Slavery: from the ancient world to the 21st century] (Beck 2021)

Edenhofer, Ottmar and Michael Jakob, *Klimapolitik. Ziele,*

Konflikte, Lösungen [Climate Policy: aims, conflicts, solutions] (Beck 2017)

Edgerton, David, *Britain's War Machine: weapons, resources, and experts in the Second World War* (Penguin 2012)

Ekardt, Felix, *Wir können uns ändern. Gesellschaftlicher Wandel jenseits von Kapitalismuskritik und Revolution* [We Can Change: social change beyond criticism of capitalism and revolution] (Oekom 2017)

Energy Brainpool, *Kalte Dunkelflaute. Robustheit des Stromsystems bei Extremwetter* [Cold Dunkelflaute: the robustness of the power system at times of extreme weather] (Berlin, 2017)

Food and Agriculture Organization of the United Nations, *The State of the World's Forests 2020: in brief* (Rome 2020)

Federal Agency for Civic Education/Federal Statistical Office, *Datenreport 2021* [Data Report 2021] (Bonn 2021)

Federal Agency for Nature Conservation, 'Mehr Flächen für Windenergie' — natur- und landschaftsverträglich verteilt ['More Areas for Wind Power' — Distributed in a Way That Is Compatible with Nature and the Landscape'] (Bonn 2021)

Federal Environment Agency, *Environmental Awareness in Germany 2018: results of a representative survey* (Dessau 2019)

Federal Environment Agency, *Repräsentative Erhebung von Pro-Kopf-Verbräuchen natürlicher Ressourcen in Deutschland (nach Bevölkerungsgruppen)* [Representative Survey of Per Capita Resource Consumption in Germany (By Population Group)] (Dessau 2016)

Federal Environment Agency, *Social Well-Being Within Planetary Boundaries: the precautionary post-growth approach* (Dessau 2018)

Federal Environment Agency, *Aktualisierung und Bewertung der Ökobilanzen von Windenergie- und Photovoltaikanlagen unter Berücksichtigung aktueller Technologieentwicklungen* [Update and Evaluation of the Environmental Impact of Wind Power and Photovoltaic Systems Amid Current Technological Developments] (Dessau 2021)

Federal Environment Agency, *Umweltschädliche Subventionen*

in Deutschland. Aktualisierte Ausgabe 2021 [Environmentally Damaging Subsidies in Germany, updated edition] (Dessau 2021)

Federal Environment Agency, *Erneuerbare Energien in Zahlen* [Renewable Energies in Figures] (Dessau, 2021)

Federal Ministry for Economic Affairs and Climate Action, *Jahreswirtschaftsbericht 2022* [Annual Economic Report 2022] (Berlin, 26 January 2022)

Federal Statistical Office, *Statistisches Jahrbuch 2019* [Statistical Yearbook 2019] (Wiesbaden 2020)

Federal Statistical Office, *Bautätigkeit und Wohnungen, Bestand an Wohnungen, Fachserie 5, Reihe 3*) [Federal German Statistical Office, Construction Activity and Housing, Housing Stock, special volume 5, series 3] (Wiesbaden 2021)

Fellmeth Ulrich, *Pecunia non olet. Die Wirtschaft der antiken Welt* [Pecunia Non Olet (Latin for 'money does not stink']: the economy of the ancient world] (Wissenschaftliche Buchgesellschaft 2008)

Flassbeck, Heiner, *Der begrenzte Planet und die unbegrenzte Wirtschaft. Lassen sich Ökonomie und Ökologie versöhnen?* [The Limited Planet and Unlimited Industry: can economy and ecology be reconciled?] (Westend 2020)

Foer, Jonathan S., *We Are the Weather: saving the planet begins at breakfast* (Farrar, Straus and Giroux 2019)

Fraunhofer Institute for Solar Energy Systems ISE, *Levelized Cost of Electricity: renewable energy technologies* (Freiburg 2021)

Fraunhofer Institute for Solar Energy Systems ISE, *Paths to a Climate-Neutral Energy System: the German energy transition in its social context* (Freiburg 2021)

Fücks, Ralf, *Green Growth, Smart Growth: a new approach to economics, innovation and the environment* (Anthem Press 2015)

Fuhrhop, Daniel, *Verbietet das Bauen! Streitschrift gegen Spekulation, Abriss und Flächenfraß* [Ban Building! A polemic against speculation, demolition, and voracious consumption of land] (Oekom 2020)

Galbraith, John Kenneth, *The Affluent Society* (Penguin 1999)

Gates, Bill, *How to Avoid a Climate Disaster: the solutions we have and the breakthroughs we need* (Allen Lane 2021)

German Association of Energy and Water Industries (BDEW), *Strompreisanalyse* [Electricity Price Analysis] (15 November 2021).

German Parliament, *Evaluierungsbericht der Bundesregierung über die Anwendung des Kohlendioxid-Speicherungsgesetzes sowie die Erfahrungen zur CCS -Technologie, Drucksache 19/6891* [Federal Government Assessment Report on the Application of the Carbon Dioxide Storage Act and Experiences with CSS Technology, Circular 19/6891] (21 December 2018)

Göke, Leonard, Claudia Kemfert, Mario Kendziorski, and Christian v. Hirschhausen, '100% Renewable Energy for Germany: coordinated expansion planning needed', *DIW Weekly Report* 29 and 30/2021, pp. 209–215

Göpel, Maja, *Rethinking Our World: an invitation to rescue our future* (Scribe 2023)

Gössling, Stefan and Andreas Humpe, 'The global scale, distribution and growth of aviation: implications for climate change'. In *Global Environmental Change*, 1 November 2020

Graeber, David, *Bullshit Jobs: a theory* (Allen Lane 2018)

Hasters, Alice, *Was weiße Menschen nicht über Rassismus hören wollen, aber wissen sollten* [What White People Don't Want to Hear about Racism, but Should Know] (Hanser 2020)

Henderson, Rebecca, *Reimagining Capitalism in a World on Fire* (Penguin 2021)

Hentschel, Karl-Martin, *Handbuch Klimaschutz. Wie Deutschland das 1,5-Grad-Ziel einhalten kann* [The Climate Protection Handbook: how Germany can meet its 1.5-degree goal] (Oekom 2020)

Herrmann, Ulrike, *Der Sieg des Kapitals. Wie der Reichtum in die Welt kam. Die Geschichte von Wachstum, Geld und Krisen* [The Triumph of Capital: how wealth came about—the history of growth, money, and crises] (Piper 2015)

Herrmann, Ulrike, *Kein Kapitalismus ist auch keine Lösung. Die*

Krise der heutigen Ökonomie—oder was wir von Smith, Marx und Keynes lernen können [No Capitalism is Not the Solution: the crisis in the modern economy—or, what we can learn from Smith, Marx, and Keynes] (Piper 2018)

Herrmann, Ulrike, *Deutschland, ein Wirtschaftsmärchen. Warum es kein Wunder ist, dass wir reich geworden sind*) [Germany, an Economic Fairy Tale: why it's no wonder we got rich] (Piper 2022)

Hesse, Jan-Otmar, 'Abkehr vom Kartelldenken? Das Gesetz gegen Wettbewerbsbeschränkungen als ordnungspolitische und wirtschaftstheoretische Zäsur der Ära Adenauer', in Hockerts, Hans Günter, and Günther Schulz (eds), *Der »Rheinische Kapitalismus« in der Ära Adenauer* ['An End to Anti-Trust Thinking? The law against restrictions on competition as a turning point in regulatory policy and economic theory in the Adenauer era', in *'Rhineland Capitalism' in the Adenauer Era*] (Ferdinand Schöningh 2016), pp. 29–50

Hirschhausen, Eckart von, *Mensch, Erde! Wir könnten es so schön haben* [Man, Earth! We could have it so good] (DTV 2021)

Hobsbawm, Eric, *The Age of Revolution: Europe 1789–1848* (Abacus 2010)

Hobsbawm, Eric, *The Age of Capital: 1848–1875* (Abacus 1997)

Hobsbawm, Eric, *The Age of Empire: 1875–1914* (Abacus 1994)

Holler, Christian, Joachim Gaukel, Harald Lesch, and Florian Lesch, *Erneuerbare Energien zum Verstehen und Mitreden* [How to Understand and Talk about Renewable Energy Sources] (Bertelsmann 2021)

Holthaus, Eric, *The Future Earth: a radical vision for what's possible in the age of warming* (HarperOne 2020)

Institute for Applied Ecology, *Wasserstoff sowie wasserstoffbasierte Energieträger und Rohstoffe. Eine Überblicksuntersuchung* [Hydrogen and Hydrogen-Based Energy Sources and Resources: a survey report] (Berlin 2020)

International Energy Agency, *The Role of Critical Minerals in Clean Energy Transitions* (Washington 2021)

Jackson, Tim, *Prosperity without Growth: foundations for the economy of tomorrow*, second edition (Routledge 2017)

Jackson, Tim, *Post Growth: life after capitalism* (Polity 2021)

Jensen, Annette, *Wir steigern das Bruttosozialglück. Von Menschen, die anders und besser wirtschaften* [Increasing Gross National Happiness: how humans can run a different and better economy] (Herder 2011)

Kennedy, Margrit, *Occupy Money: creating an economy where everyone wins* (New Society Publishers 2012)

Kern, Bruno, *Das Märchen vom grünen Wachstum. Plädoyer für eine solidarische und nachhaltige Gesellschaft* [The Fairy Tale of Green Growth: the case for a solidarity-based and sustainable society] (Rotpunkt 2019)

Kleinschmidt, Christian, *Wirtschaftsgeschichte der Neuzeit. Die Weltwirtschaft 1500–1850* [Economic History of the Modern Age: the global economy, 1500–1850] (Beck 2017)

Klingholz, Reiner, *Zu viel für diese Welt. Wege aus der doppelten Überbevölkerung* [Too Much for This World: ways to escape double overpopulation] (Edition Körber 2021)

Kocka, Jürgen, *Capitalism: a short history* (Princeton University Press 2016)

Kreutzfeldt, Malte, *Das Strompreis-Komplott. Warum die Energiekosten wirklich steigen und wer dafür bezahlt* [The Electricity Price Conspiracy: the real reason why energy prices rise and who really pays] (Knaur 2014:

Latif, Mojib, *Heißzeit. Mit Vollgas in die Klimakatastrophe—und wie wir auf die Bremse treten* [The Heat Age. headlong into the climate catastrophe: how to put on the brakes] (Herder 2020)

Lauterbach, Karl, *Bevor es zu spät ist. Was uns droht, wenn die Politik nicht mit der Wissenschaft Schritt hält* [Before It's Too Late: what will happen if politics doesn't keep up with science] (Rowohlt Berlin 2022)

Lepenies, Philipp, *The Power of a Single Number: a political history of GDP* (Columbia University Press 2016)

Levinson, Marc, *The Box: how the shipping container made the world smaller and the world economy bigger*, second edition (Princeton University Press 2016)

Li, Bowen, Sukanta Basu, Simon J. Watson, and Herman W. J.

Russchenberg, 'Brief Climatology of Dunkelflaute Events over and Surrounding the North and Baltic Sea Areas', in *Energies* 2021, 14, 6508

Lomborg, Bjorn, *False Alarm: how climate change panic costs us trillions, hurts the poor, and fails to fix the planet* (Hachette 2020)

McAfee, Andrew, *More From Less: the surprising story of how we learned to prosper using fewer resources — and what happens next* (Scribner 2019)

McKibben, Bill, 'A World at War: we're under attack from climate change — and our only hope is to mobilize like we did in WWII', *The New Republic*, 15 August 2016

McKinsey, *Net-Zero Germany: opportunities and challenges on the pathway to climate neutrality by 2045* (2021)

Maddison, Angus, *The World Economy: a millennial perspective* (OECD 2001)

Malm, Andreas, *Fossil Capital: the rise of steam power and the roots of global warming* (Verso 2016)

Malm, Andreas, *Corona, Climate, Chronic Emergency: war communism in the twenty-first century* (Verso 2020)

Marx, Karl, *Capital: a critique of political economy* (Penguin 1976)

Marx, Karl and Friedrich Engels, *The Communist Manifesto* (Penguin 2002)

Maxton, Graeme and Jorgen Randers, *Reinventing Prosperity: managing economic growth to reduce unemployment, inequality, and climate change* (Greystone 2016)

Mazzucato, Mariana, *The Entrepreneurial State: debunking public vs. private sector myths* (Anthem Press 2014)

Mazzucato, Mariana, *The Value of Everything: making and taking in the global economy* (Penguin 2019)

Mazzucato, Mariana, *Mission Economy: a moonshot guide to changing capitalism* (Allen Lane 2021)

Meadows, Dennis, Donella Meadows, Erich Zahn, and Peter Milling, *The Limits to Growth: a report for the Club of Rome's project on the predicament of mankind* (Universe Books 1972)

Milward, Alan S., *War, Economy and Society, 1939–1945* (Allen Lane 1977)

Monbiot, George, *Heat: how to stop the planet burning* (Allen Lane 2006)

Monbiot, George, 'Think Big on Climate: the transformation of society in months has been done before', *The Guardian*, 20 October 2021

Mundell, Robert, 'The Birth of Coinage', in *Columbia University Discussion Papers* (September 1999)

Neitzel, Sönke, *Deutsche Krieger. Vom Kaiserreich bis zur Berliner Republik—eine Militärgeschichte* [German Warriors: from the German Empire to the Berlin Republic—a military history] (Propyläen 2020)

Neubauer, Luisa and Alexander Repenning, *Beginning to End the Climate Crisis: a history of our future* (Brandeis University Press 2023)

Osterhammel, Jürgen, *The Transformation of the World: a global history of the nineteenth century* (Princeton University Press 2014)

Osterhammel, Jürgen and Niels P. Petersson, *Globalization: a short history* (Beck 2004)

Paech, Niko, *Liberation from Excess: the road to a post-growth economy* (Oekom 2012)

Parrique, T., Barth, J., Briens, F., Kerschner, C., Kraus-Polk, A., Kuokkanen, A., and Spangenberg, J.H., *Decoupling Debunked: evidence and arguments against green growth as a sole strategy for sustainability* (European Environmental Board 2019).

Parry, Ian, Simon Black, and Nate Vernon, 'Still Not Getting Energy Prices Right: a global and country update of fossil fuel subsidies', IMF Working Paper 21/236 (Washington 2021)

Pettifor, Ann, *The Case for the Green New Deal* (Verso 2019)

Phillips, Leigh, *Austerity Ecology & The Collapse-Porn Addicts: a defence of growth, progress, industry and stuff* (Zero Books 2015)

Phillips, Leigh and Michal Rozworski, *People's Republic of Walmart: how the world's biggest corporations are laying the foundation for socialism* (Verso 2019)

Phillipson, Nicholas, *Adam Smith: an enlightened life* (Penguin 2010)

Pinker, Steven, *Enlightenment Now: the case for reason, science, humanism, and progress* (Penguin 2019)

Pinzler, Petra and Günther Wessel, *Vier fürs Klima. Wie unsere Familie versucht, carbon dioxide-neutral zu leben* [Four for the Climate: how our family tries to be carbon dioxide-neutral] (Droemer 2018)

Pistor, Katharina, *The Code of Capital: how the law creates wealth and inequality* (Princeton University Press 2019)

Plöger, Sven, *Zieht Euch warm an, es wird heiß! Den Klimawandel verstehen und aus der Krise für die Welt von morgen lernen* [Wrap Up Warm, It's Going to Get Hot! Understanding climate change and learning for the world of tomorrow from the crisis of today] (Westend 2020)

Pötter, Bernhard, *Klimawandel. 33 Fragen—Antworten* [Climate Change: 33 questions—and answers] (Piper 2020)

Pötter, Bernhard, *Die grüne Null. Der Kampf um Deutschlands Zukunft ohne Kohle, Öl und Gas* [Green Zero: the battle for Germany's coal, oil, and gas-free future] (Piper 2021)

Precht, Richard David, *Freiheit für alle. Das Ende der Arbeit, wie wir sie kannten* [Freedom for All: the end of work as we know it] (Goldmann 2022)

Quaschning, Volker and Cornelia, *Energie-Revolution jetzt! Mobilität, Wohnen, grüner Strom und Wasserstoff. Was führt uns aus der Klimakrise—und was nicht?* [Energy Revolution Now! Mobility, living, green power, and hydrogen: what will lead us out of the climate crisis—and what won't?] (Hanser 2022)

Radkau, Joachim, *Nature and Power: a global history of the environment* (Cambridge University Press 2008)

Radkau, Joachim, *Technik in Deutschland. Vom 18. Jahrhundert bis heute* [Technology in Germany: from the 18th century to today] (Campus 2008)

Rahlf, Thomas (ed), *Deutschland in Daten. Zeitreihen zur Historischen Statistik* [Federal Agency for Civic Education, Germany in Figures: time series of historical statistics] (Bundeszentrale für politische Bildung 2015)

Rahmstorf, Stefan and Hans Joachim Schellnhuber, *Der*

Klimawandel. Diagnose, Prognose, Therapie [Climate Change: diagnosis, prognosis, therapy] (Beck 2018)

Raworth, Kate, *Doughnut Economics: seven ways to think like a 21st-century economist* (Random House 2017)

Reimer, Nick and Toralf Staud, *Deutschland 2050. Wie der Klimawandel unser Leben verändern wird* [Germany 2050: how climate change will change our lives] (Kiepenheuer & Witsch 2021)

Richters, Oliver and Andreas Siemoneit, *Marktwirtschaft reparieren. Entwurf einer freiheitlichen, gerechten und nachhaltigen Utopie* [Fixing the Market Economy: a blueprint for a liberal, just, and sustainable utopia] (Oekom 2019)

Ritchie, Hannah and Max Roser, 'Why did renewables become so cheap so fast?' (*Our World in Data*, 1 December 2020)

Rosling, Hans, *Factfulness: ten reasons we're wrong about the world—and why things are better than you think* (Flatiron Books 2019)

Russell, Ben, *James Watt: making the world anew* (Reaktion Books 2014)

Samtleben, Claire, 'Also on Sundays, women perform most of the housework and child care', *DIW Weekly Report 10/2019*, pp. 87–92

Schink, Nena, *Ich bin nicht grün. Ein Plädoyer für die Freiheit* [I Am Not Green: the case for freedom] (FinanzBuch 2021)

Schmelzer, Matthias and Andrea Vetter, *Degrowth/Postwachstum zur Einführung* [An Introduction to Degrowth/Post-Growth] (Junius 2019)

Schneidewind, Uwe, *Die Große Transformation. Eine Einführung in die Kunst gesellschaftlichen Wandels* [The Great Transformation: an introduction to the art of social change] (Fischer 2018)

Schor, Juliet, *True Wealth: how and why millions of Americans are creating a time-rich, ecologically light, small-scale, high-satisfaction economy* (Penguin 2011)

Schularick, Moritz, *Der entzauberte Staat. Was Deutschland aus der Pandemie lernen muss* [The Disenchanted State: what Germany must learn from the pandemic] (Beck 2021)

Schulmeister, Stephan, 'Carbon dioxide-Emissionen müssen stetig teurer werden — durch einen Preispfad für fossile Energie' ['Carbon dioxide emissions must always get more expensive — by means of a price path for fossil energy sources'], *Wirtschaftsdienst* 2020/10, pp. 812–14

Schulte, Ulrich, *Die grüne Macht. Wie die Ökopartei das Land verändern will* [Green Power: how the Green Party wants to change the country] (Rowohlt 2021)

Schumpeter, Joseph A., *The Theory of Economic Development: an inquiry into profits, capital, credit, interest, and the business cycle* (Transaction Publishers 2008)

Seba, Tony, *Clean Disruption of Energy and Transportation: how Silicon Valley will make oil, nuclear, natural gas, coal, electric utilities and conventional cars obsolete by 2030* (Clean Planet Ventures 2014)

Settele, Josef, *Die Triple-Krise. Artensterben, Klimawandel, Pandemien. Warum wir dringend handeln* müssen [The Triple Crisis: extinction, climate change, pandemics — why we must act urgently] (Edel 2020)

Sinn, Hans-Werner, *The Green Paradox: a supply-side approach to global warming* (The MIT Press 2012)

Skidelsky, Robert and Edward Skidelsky, *How Much Is Enough? Money and the good life* (Other Press 2013)

Smith, Adam, *An Inquiry into the Nature and Causes of the Wealth of Nations, first edition 1776. A selected edition* (Oxford University Press 2008)

Stelter, Daniel, *Ein Traum von einem Land. Deutschland 2040* [A Dream of a Country: Germany 2040] (Campus 2021)

Stimpel, Roland, *Wer langsam macht, kommt eher an. Verkehr abrüsten — Mobilität gewinnen* [Go Slow, Arrive Faster: disarm transport — gain mobility] (Edition Fuss 2021)

Straubhaar, Thomas, *Grundeinkommen Jetzt! Nur so ist die Marktwirtschaft zu retten* [Basic Income Now! The only way to save the market economy] (NZZ Libro 2021)

Tooze, Adam, *The Wages of Destruction: the making and breaking of the Nazi economy* (Penguin 2007)

Ulrich, Bernd, *Alles wird anders. Das Zeitalter der Ökologie* [Everything Is Changing: the ecological age] (Kiepenheuer & Witsch 2019)

Van de Mieroop, Marc, *The Ancient Mesopotamian City* (Oxford University Press 1997)

Vries, Peer, *Escaping Poverty: the origins of modern economic growth* (Vienna University Press 2013)

Wallace-Wells, David, *The Uninhabitable Earth: life after warming* (Penguin Random House 2019)

Waller, John, *The Real Oliver Twist: Robert Blincoe—a life that illuminates an age* (Icon Books 2005)

Way, Rupert, Matthew Ives, Penny Mealy, and J. Doyne Farmer, 'Empirically grounded technology forecasts and the energy transition', *INET Oxford Working Paper No. 2021–01* (14 September 2021)

Wealer, Ben, Simon Bauer, Leonard Gök, Christian von Hirschhausen, and Claudia Kemfert, 'High-priced and dangerous. Nuclear power is not an option for the climate-friendly energy mix', in *German Institute for Economic Research Weekly Report* vol. 9, Issue 30, pp. 235–43

Wehler, Hans-Ulrich, *Deutsche Gesellschaftsgeschichte, zweiter Band, 1815–1845/49* [A History of German Society, vol. II, 1815–1845/49] (Beck 1987)

Wehler, Hans-Ulrich, *Deutsche Gesellschaftsgeschichte, dritter Band, 1849–1914* [A History of German Society, vol. III, 1849–1914] (Beck 1995)

Welzer, Harald, *Alles könnte anders sein. Eine Gesellschaftsutopie für freie Menschen*) [Everything Could Be Different: a social utopia for free people] (Fischer 2019)

Wilkinson, Richard and Kate Pickett, *The Spirit Level: why more equal societies almost always do better* (Allen Lane 2009)

Wirth, Harry, 'Recent Facts about Photovoltaics in Germany' (Fraunhofer ISE, 3 April 2024)

Wuppertal Institute, *Climate-Neutral by 2035: key points of a German contribution to maintaining the CO2-neutral 1.5°c limit until 2035*. Discussion paper for Fridays for Future Germany, with the financial support of the GLS Bank (Wuppertal 2020)

Ziegler, Dieter, *Die industrielle Revolution* [The Industrial Revolution], 2nd edition (Wissenschaftliche Buchgesellschaft 2009)

Zweiniger-Bargielowska, Ina, 'Food Consumption in Britain during the Second World War', in Berghoff, Hartmut, Jan Logemann, and Felix Römer, *The Consumer on the Home Front: Second World War civilian consumption in comparative perspective* (Oxford University Press 2017), pp. 75–92

Notes

Introduction
1 Neubauer and Repenning, pp. 65 and 76.
2 Quoted in Lauterbach, p. 21.
3 Quaschning, p. 263.
4 Latif, pp. 23 ff.
5 Quoted in Neubauer and Repenning, p. 47.
6 Lauterbach, p. 14.
7 Holthaus, p. 40.
8 Sinn, pp. 127–28.

Chapter 1: A blessing
1 'Deutsche zweifeln am Kapitalismus' ['Germans Doubtful about Capitalism'], faz.net, 21 January 2020.
2 Osterhammel, p. 124. The worst-hit country was Ireland. Its population fell from 8.2 million in 1841 to just 4.5 million in 1901. At least one million people died of starvation; the rest migrated to America or England.
3 Osterhammel, p. 202.
4 Deaton, p. 82 ff. and p. 93. The average life expectancy of the English nobility did not begin to rise significantly until 1750. By 1850 it had reached 60 years. That average lifespan was not reached by commoners in Britain until 1930.
5 Deaton p. 148.
6 In 2016, the average healthy life expectancy in Germany was 67.3 years for women and 65.3 years for men.
7 Pinker, p. 82; Welzer, p. 22.
8 Pinker, p. 251.
9 The Apollo Guidance Computer could process between 50,000 and 100,000 instructions per second. In 2022, a good-quality

smartphone could be expected to have a processing speed of up to 16 billion instructions per second. That makes it 160,000 times faster (as calculated by Jörgen Pisarz).

10 Pinker, p. 251.

11 Chang 2011, p. 31.

12 Samtleben, p. 89.

13 For more on the life and work of Karl Marx, see Herrmann 2018, pp. 75 ff.

14 This statement is attributed to the American Marxist Fredric Jameson (Malm 2016, p. 278).

15 Prussia's first grammar school for girls opened in Cologne in 1903.

16 Statistisches Bundesamt, *Statistisches Jahrbuch 2019* [*Statistical Yearbook 2019*], p. 88.

17 Ibid., p. 93.

18 Maxton, p. 28 ff.

19 Between 1918 and 1928, women's right to vote in Britain was restricted to those who were older than 30 years of age and who owned a certain minimum amount of property.

20 Rosling, p. 201. This comparison is adjusted for purchasing power, meaning it takes into consideration how much can be bought in real terms for a unit of currency in each country.

21 Deaton, pp. xi and 101. Per-capita income is currently at approximately the same level as that in Great Britain around the year 1860.

22 Neubauer and Repenning, p. 164. Similarly, Raworth, p. 4.

23 Bach, Thiemann, and Zucco, p. 21.

24 Deaton, p. 102.

Chapter 2: England, 1760

1 Vries, pp. 44 ff.

2 Vries, p. 61. These examples are variations on an insight from the economist Josef Schumpeter (1883–1950), who described the revolutionary power of capital with the following words: 'Add successively as many mail coaches as you please, you will never get a railway thereby' (Schumpeter, p. 64).

3 The term 'industrialisation' has been in use since 1837. The first documented use of the expression 'Industrial Revolution' was in 1799 (Osterhammel, p. 909).

4 Parts of this chapter are the same as Herrmann 2015, pp. 34 ff.

5 Appleby, p. 10. Similarly, Osterhammel (p. 915), who quotes the British economic historian Patrick O'Brien: 'Nearly three centuries of empirical investigation and reflection by a succession of the very

best minds in history and the social sciences have not produced any kind of general theory of industrialisation.' The Dutch economic historian Peer Vries identifies 20 different theories that attempt to explain the birth of capitalism (see Vries 2013).

6 Private property ownership was under even more robust protection in France than in Great Britain, which proved to be problematic. In the Provence region, for example, lucrative irrigation projects could not be realised due to resistance from individual landowners. In Great Britain, by contrast, parliament was able to restrict the rights of landowners (Allen 2009, p. 5).

7 Pistor, p. 59. Roman civil law still shapes many of the legal systems of the world, via the 1900 German Code of Civil Law (*Bürgerliches Gesetzbuch*), which is still effective in Germany today and which formed the basis of the civil law codes of many modern states, including Japan, South Korea, Brazil, Greece, Estonia, Latvia, Ukraine, Switzerland, Italy, Portugal, and the Netherlands.

8 The Scottish economist Adam Smith (1723–1790) was the first to trace *The Wealth of Nations* back to the division of labour. He illustrated the principle using the example of a pin factory, in which he described precisely 18 manufacturing steps. Smith probably took his pin example straight from the work of the French Enlightenment scholar Denis Diderot, who also described 18 steps in the manufacture of pins in his 1755 *Encyclopédie*. For more on Smith's life and work, see Herrmann 2018, pp. 15 ff.

9 Fellmeth, p. 129. For more on the economic history of the ancient world, see also Herrmann 2015, pp. 20 ff.

10 Vries, p. 353.

11 For a more detailed description of the economy of Imperial China, see Herrmann 2015, pp. 25 ff.

12 Kocka [German edition], p. 49. For more on why capitalism is not the same as the market economy, see: Herrmann 2015, pp. 65 ff., and Herrmann 2018, pp. 139 ff.

13 Mercantilism was the predominant economic theory at the time, both in Britain and in continental Europe. Each nation strove to export as much as possible while minimising imports, in order to increase its stocks of gold and silver. High tariffs were imposed as a means of discouraging imports.

14 Vries, pp. 351 ff.

15 Vries, pp. 238 ff.

16 Hobsbawm 2010, p. 52; Beckert, pp. 149 ff. An estimated £400,000 was invested in the textile industry in the years

1809–1810—equivalent to just 1 per cent of the military spending of £45 million in the same period (Vries, p. 238).

17 Beckert, p. 75.

18 Allen 2009, pp. 184 and 207.

19 Ibid., p. 190.

20 Allen 2017, p. 37.

21 Arkwright's textile factories provided him with an annual income of £20,000—which his son raised to £40,000 (Allen 2017, p. 67). Some of the significant inventors in the history of industrial ceramics production also came from the lower social classes and had no scientific education (Allen 2017, p. 54).

22 Joel Mokyr and Hans-Joachim Voth, 'Understanding Growth in Europe, 1700–1870', in Broadberry and O'Rourke, pp. 7–42, here p. 37.

23 Beckert, p. 70.

24 Allen 2017, p. 70.

25 Allen 2009, pp. 192 ff..

26 Allen 2011, p 35; Kleinschmidt, p. 40. There are similar calculations for the spinning jenny. In England, it generated a return of 38 per cent, but only 2.5 per cent in France. In India, buying such a machine would have actually generated a loss, with a return of minus 5.2 per cent. That is why the spinning jenny initially only spread through England, where 20,070 were in operation by 1788 (Allen 2009, pp. 192 ff.).

27 Quoted in Braudel, vol. III, p. 562.

28 Braudel, Volume I, p. 197.

29 Before the decimalisation of the British currency in 1971, one pound was made up of 240 pence. The income of British day labourers in the late 18th century was recorded because the aristocratic social reformer Sir Frederick Eden wanted to know whether labourers could afford to buy grain after prices rose sharply. This resulted in the three-volume work *The State of the Poor*, which was published in 1797 (Allen 2009, p. 29).

30 The school fees for the two elder children were sixpence a week—the same amount that the father of the family spent on his beer (Allen 2009, p. 55).

31 Allen 2009, p. 35 ff.

32 Ibid., pp. 30 and 48.

33 Allen 2009, p. 48, and Allen 2017, p. 32.

34 Defoe 1722, p. 114.

35 Allen 2009, p. 68.

36 Ibid., p. 109 ff.

37 Ibid., p. 87.

38 Allen 2011, p. 28 ff. Almost the entire stock of British farmland was owned by just approximately 15,000 families (Allen 2017, p. 4).

39 Dan Bogart, Mauricio Drelichman, Oscar Gelderblom, and Jean-Laurent Rosenthal, 'State and Private Institutions', in Broadberry and O' Rourke, p. 78.

40 Allen 2009, p. 105.

41 Radkau 2008 (Campus), pp. 31 and 130 f. Around the year 1800, mining in the Ruhr Valley employed only 1,200 people. One problem was transportation: moving goods overland was expensive. As late as the mid-19th century, British coal, which was transported to Berlin by water, was still cheaper than competing coal from the Ruhr (Brüggemeier 2018, pp. 10 and 21).

42 Braudel, vol. I, pp. 368 ff. Even before industrialisation, between 1560 and 1800, coal consumption in England increased by a factor of 66 (Allen 2009, p. 81). The British were not the first to use coal industrially. Lignite was burned to fuel pottery kilns at Tiryns in Mycenaean Greece 3,600 years ago ('Industrialisierung in der Bronzezeit' ['Industrialisation in the Bronze Age'], *Süddeutsche Zeitung*, 23 December 2021. The innovation in England was that the entire economy was converted to coal use.

43 Quoted in Braudel, vol. III, p. 553. Cleveland's mention of Peru is a reference to the discovery in 1545 of the world's largest silver mine in Potosí. (Potosí is in present-day Bolivia, but was part of the Viceroyalty of Peru during Spanish colonial times.)

44 As early as the 1960s, the Indian historian Irfan Habib proposed the theory that wage gaps were the explanation for why India was not able to industrialise (see Braudel, vol. III, p. 505).

45 Russell, p. 145.

46 Marx, *Capital*, p. 353.

47 Ibid, p. 795.

48 On average, poor day labourers in the countryside lived twice as long as their city-dwelling peers, as the rural air was cleaner and diseases spread less easily (Waller, p. 4). However, even the poorest in Britain were still better off in the early phases of industrialisation than their continental counterparts. Recipients of alms in England were able to feed themselves around twice as well as average Italians in 1846 (Allen 2017, p. 66).

49 Allen 2011, p. 32. In the 1830s, Britain's cotton industry employed around 425,000 people (Allen 2009, p. 182).

Chapter 3: Essential energy

1 As early as 1690, the French physicist Denis Papin developed a proto steam engine in which a cylinder filled with water vapour, which then condensed, setting a piston in motion. Further developing that idea, the English engineer Thomas Savery invented a pistonless steam pump in 1698, which he called 'The Miner's Friend'. He was granted a patent for the machine until 1733, which meant Newcomen had to enter into a business partnership with Savery to market his steam engine.

2 Allen 2017, p. 45 f. Galileo Galilei (1564–1641) was the first to suspect that the atmosphere might have weight. He was also concerned with the problem of draining mines. He noticed that suction pumps were only able to raise mine water by around ten metres, and realised that some counterforce must be inhibiting the water's rise. His student Evangelista Torricelli later invented the mercury barometer for measuring air pressure.

3 Russell, pp. 73 ff.

4 Allen 2011, pp. 36 ff. They initially tried to optimise Newcomen's engine. The Scottish inventor James Watt gained world fame after patenting his separate condenser. Watt realised that constantly heating and cooling the entire metal cylinder wasted a lot of energy. Watt spatially separated the two processes. The cylinder always remained hot, and the steam was fed into a separate condenser, where it could cool to create the required vacuum. A different technology was introduced with the first steam locomotives—called the high-pressure steam engine. The steam was heated to temperatures well above 100 degrees Celsius so that its expansion created pressure. Atmospheric pressure was no longer involved in the process, and no condenser was necessary.

5 Braudel, vol. I, p. 424.

6 Hobsbawm 2010, p. 62.

7 Malm 2016, p. 22.

8 Hobsbawm 2010, p. 46. James Watt, for instance, thought his steam engines worked on the principle of 'latent heat'—a theory developed by his friend Joseph Black. Black's findings from the year 1762 were an important contribution to the development of thermodynamics but were irrelevant to the theory of steam power (Allen 2009, p. 6).

9 Radkau 2008 (Campus), p. 34. Here, Smith picks up on a legend that was already widely known at the time and that was supposed to have occurred in 1713. But the alleged child—by the name of Humphrey Potter—was in fact already 24 years old and an

experienced engineer at the time he automated the valves (see www. gracesguide.co.uk/Humphrey_Potter).

10 Phillipson, p. 131.

11 Joseph Black was later one of the two executors of Adam Smith's will. Black also made sure that James Watt had enough money initially to develop his steam engine, introducing him to the industrialist John Roebuck.

12 Quoted in Braudel, vol. III, pp. 538 ff.

13 Russell, p. 178.

14 Even many critics recognise the blessings brought by fossil-fuelled capitalism. See Monbiot, p. xi; Phillips, pp. 262 ff.

15 Plöger, p. 270.

16 Allen 2017, pp. 66 ff.

17 Hobsbawm 1994, p. 53.

Chapter 4: Every country was suddenly a 'developing country'

1 Russell, p. 220; Allen 2011, p. 58. Before industrialisation, only around three million pounds of cotton yarn were spun per year, compared to 85 million pounds in India (Allen 2009, pp. 182 ff). By 1800, the British had achieved a global market share of 30 per cent (Allen 2017, p. 42). Parts of this chapter are the same as Herrmann 2015, pp. 51 ff.

2 Great Britain maintained a strict ban on the export of machinery until 1842. However, construction plans were repeatedly smuggled out of the country for sale in continental Europe.

3 For more on Germany's economic development, see also Herrmann 2015, pp. 51 ff.

4 Radkau 2008 (Campus), pp. 82 ff.

5 Ibid., p. 82.

6 Allen 2017, p. 114.

7 Chang 2003, pp. 17 and 24 ff. The issue of tariffs was a source of constant conflict in the US. The 'industrial states' in the north favoured high import tariffs to protect their businesses from the English competition. The southern states, however, wanted free trade, since the export of agricultural products such as cotton or tobacco did not need to be protected. The American Civil War of 1861–1865 was fought not only over the issue of slavery, but also over import tariffs (Chang 2003, p. 27).

8 This explains why the British were the first to espouse free trade. In 1848, Great Britain still imposed tariffs on 1,146 different goods. By 1860, that number had plummeted to just 48 (Chang 2003, p. 23).

9   Wehler 1987, p. 125; Clark, p. 394.

10 Radkau 2008 (Campus), p. 33. This figure refers to the year 1825.

11 Wehler 1987, p. 623.

12 Ziegler, pp. 74 and 77 ff. Locomotive construction was concentrated from the outset in a few companies, which rose to become large corporations. Of the 729 locomotives in use in Prussia in 1853, 414 were built by Borsig. A distant second was Wöhlert, also a Berlin company, which built 34 of the locomotives (Radkau 2008 [Campus], p. 152).

13 Ibid., p. 151.

14 Wehler 1987, p. 622. By 1913, 63,000 kilometres of railways had been laid in Germany.

15 Ibid., pp. 97 ff.

16 Hobsbawm 1997, p. 282. Werner von Siemens set up his factory in 1847 with 10,000 thalers as start-up capital, which was an impressive sum at the time. A skilled worker in Berlin at the time earned a maximum of 300 thalers per year (Bähr, pp. 106 ff.).

17 The line between Magdeburg and Leipzig was approved at the beginning of 1836. Its capital was supposed to be 2.3 million thalers, but 5.2 million thalers of capital was subscribed within just two days. Seven million thalers was collected in just one day as capital for the line between Frankfurt on the Oder and Breslau (now Wrocław in Poland). When construction of the railway from Cologne to Krefeld required 2.4 million thalers in capital, 53 million was tendered immediately. And when the Thuringian Railway Company issued shares to the value of 16 million thalers, demand reached no less than 167 million thalers' worth (Wehler 1987, pp. 618 ff.).

18 Radkau 2008 (Campus), p. 130.

19 The Bessemer process could not be introduced everywhere in Germany, because it worked only with phosphorus-free iron. In 1876–77, the British inventor Sydney Thomas developed a process that also worked for iron with a high phosphorus content. It was first used in England in May 1879, and had already been introduced in Germany by September of the same year. Technology transfer was becoming increasingly rapid.

20 Ziegler, p. 75 ff. However, the new technology did not reach all areas of industry. In coalmines, most of the work underground was still done manually, and pit ponies were still the main means of transport. Their number increased rapidly until 1900 (Radkau 2008 (Campus), pp. 132 f).

21 Ziegler, pp. 108 ff.

22 See also Herrmann 2018, p. 115.

23 Hesse, pp. 29 ff.

24 Statistisches Bundesamt, *Statistisches Jahrbuch 2019* [*Statistical Yearbook 2019*], p. 528.

25 Radkau 2008 (Campus), p. 134.

26 Ibid., p. 272.

27 Ibid., pp. 176 ff.

28 Bähr, p. 76.

29 Ibid., pp. 240 ff

30 Radkau 2008 (Campus), p. 176.

31 Ibid., p. 182.

32 Ibid., p. 142. This list is taken from an official report to the British parliament in 1897. At that time, the British were concerned that German companies could squeeze British industry out of the world markets.

33 Radkau 2008 (Campus), p. 198.

34 Tooze, pp. 135 ff.

35 Ibid., p. 178. Tooze assumes that a farmer required at least 20 hectares of land to escape poverty.

36 Ibid., p. 138.

37 Maddison, p. 132.

38 For more on Germany's post-war economy, see Herrmann 2022.

39 Wenzlaff, Adriana, 'Made in Germany'— 125 Jahre Automobil' ['125 years of the automobile'], *Münchner Statistik*, 4th quarter, 2011, p. 21.

40 Rahlf (ed.), p. 231.

41 Radkau 2008 (Campus), p. 334.

42 *Statistisches Jahrbuch 2019* [*Statistical Yearbook 2019*], p. 494. According to the German Farmers' Association, there are currently around 600,000 euros' worth of machinery and buildings for every single job in the agricultural sector—a figure that continues to increase.

Chapter 5: Left behind forever?

1 Allen 2011, pp. 50 ff.

2 The general minimum wage in Bangladesh is 1,500 taka per month, but it is 5,300 per month in the garment industry. One US dollar is worth 86.6 taka (as of 4 May 2022). This means that garment workers earn around $61 a month (see www.minimum-wage.org/international/bangladesh).

3 Brand and Wissen, p. 54.

4   Allen 2011, pp. 136 ff. MITI stands for the Ministry of International Trade and Industry. Japan's economic boom came to an end in 1990 after the country slid into a disastrous real estate crisis. However, that crash was the trigger, not the cause of the decline in growth rates. The actual cause was the fact that Japan was now at the cutting edge of technology and could only grow as fast as technological progress allowed. But productivity in developed countries can only grow by a maximum of 1.5 per cent a year.

5   Mazzucato 2021, pp. 29 ff.

6   Allen 2011, pp. 128 ff.

7   Chang 2003, p. 67.

8   Allen 2009, p. 217. Germany's textile industry was typical in taking such technological shortcuts. It was generally a cottage industry until around 1850, when the 'fully integrated factory' suddenly took over. All phases of production were completely mechanised because the technology was now cheap enough. There were no intermediate stages in the transition from cottage industry to large-scale business (Radkau 2008 [Campus], p. 83).

9   Fewer than 2 per cent of girls live in countries such as Afghanistan or South Sudan, where schooling for women is almost non-existent (Rosling, p. 29).

10 McAfee, p. 194; Pinker, pp. 95 and 257.

11 McAfee, p. 169, quoting the aeronautical engineer Peter Diamandis.

12 Rosling, p. 92; Klingholz, pp. 272 ff.

13 Klingholz, p. 275.

14 These figures are adjusted for purchasing power parity, which means they already take account of the fact that prices in Bangladesh are significantly lower than in Germany and that a dollar buys far more in Bangladesh than in Germany.

15 The countries of the Global South know they need to grow their markets. That was the reason for the establishment of the AfCFTA in 2019. It aims to reduce all trade barriers on the African continent. Eritrea is the only African country not participating. The AfCFTA has the right approach, but it will not change the fact that Africa lags behind in technology. Africa lacks a powerful central government such as China's to systematically control the process of industrialisation.

16 Osterhammel and Petersson, p. 64.

17 It would be important for such a minimum wage to apply only to export goods such as textiles. If a general minimum wage were introduced that also applied to the internal markets of the Global South, the result would be inflation in many countries, because the higher

wages would not be matched by any domestic offer. Or, to put it in technical terms, real wages cannot outstrip a country's productivity.

18 Currently, almost 140 states have agreed to a global minimum tax rate of 15 per cent for large corporations with an annual turnover of 750 million euros or more. That would generate an estimated 150 billion euros in additional tax revenues around the world. The project consists of two innovations. First, if tax havens levy corporate tax at a lower rate than 15 per cent, profits can be taxed subsequently wherever the company is headquartered. That would result in an expected increase in tax revenues of 1.6 to 6.2 billion euros a year for Germany (Ifo Institute, press release, 18 March 2022). Second, profits would have to be taxed where they are generated. Until now, they have been taxed only in the location of the company's headquarters. That would benefit large emerging economies, in particular. Germany legislated to introduce the minimum tax on 15 December 2023. However, a global minimum tax rate can do nothing to prevent the rich from continuing to shift their private income to tax havens.

19 Faisal Islam, 'G7: rich nations back deal to tax multinationals', BBC News, 6 June 2021, www.bbc.com/news/world-57368247.

20 China is the best example of the extent to which the West can benefit when a once-poor country industrialises by initially relying on protectionism. The People's Republic has now become Germany's most important trading partner. In 2023, Germany imported goods to the value of 157.2 billion euros from China, and exported 97.3 billion euros' worth in the other direction (www.destatis.de/EN/Themes/Economy/Foreign-Trade/trading-partners.html).

Chapter 6: Exploitation and war are not necessary

1 See, for example, Phillips, pp. 257 ff.

2 Most of the slaves in Ancient Greece came from the Black Sea region, the Balkans, and Asia Minor. The majority were war captives, but targeted kidnapping raids and piracy also took place. The Ancient Romans took their slaves from the same regions, but also enslaved Greeks and Germanic people. Another important aspect of ancient slavery was self-sale: poor Romans sold themselves as slaves as a way of securing their own survival (Eckert, pp. 25 ff).

3 Ibid., pp. 11 ff.

4 Ibid., p. 41. Between 1530 and 1780, hundreds of thousands of Europeans were enslaved by North Africans — and vice versa. Perhaps the most famous victim was Miguel de Cervantes, author

of *Don Quixote*, who spent five years in captivity in Algiers before
a ransom was paid for his release. It was not until the mid-18th
century that European fleets were advanced enough to resist the
pirate states of North Africa.

5   Allen 2011, p. 97.

6   Eckert, pp. 36 ff.

7   Ibid., p. 3.

8   A European invasion of the African coast was hampered by the
heavy seas and the almost-ubiquitous hidden sandbanks. Europeans
therefore preferred to lie at anchor offshore and rely on local
boatsmen to ferry them to land. An additional hazard came from the
fact that West African rulers often exchanged their slaves for guns,
and were able to arm themselves to such an extent that conquering
their territories became impossible. Local rulers were not weakened
militarily until the British banned the slave trade in 1808 and the
supply of weapons to Africa dried up (Darwin, pp. 43 ff).

9   A romanticised view of Africa can be found, *inter alia*, at Hasters,
pp. 30 and 57.

10 Eckert, p. 50. Countless people also died in Africa itself as a consequence of slaving raids, as slaving intensified and prolonged existing
conflicts on the continent (Eckert, p. 94).

11 Ibid., pp. 51 ff.

12 Eckert, p. 52. England outlawed the slave trade in 1808. However,
the population of enslaved people in the US continued to rise
because of the number of children born into slavery.

13 In the mid-18th century, Maryland, Virginia, and North Carolina
were the biggest tobacco producers in the world, and employed an
enslaved workforce of 145,000. Some 40,000 enslaved labourers
worked in rice production further south, in Georgia and South
Carolina (Ibid., pp. 68 ff.).

14 Ibid., pp. 70 ff.

15 Vries, p. 255.

16 See Smith, p. 411.

17 In 1807, one cotton plantation in Mississippi is said to have
generated an annual return of 22.5 per cent on invested capital
(Beckert, p. 117).

18 Allen 2011, p. 72.

19 The British also realised that slave labour did not pay on home soil,
either. Textile manufacturers initially tried to run their spinning mills
with disenfranchised orphaned children. This 'white slavery' developed as a result of overcrowding in England's parish workhouses.

The orphans were given over to the factory owners, who only had to provide board and lodging for them. But even though most of the children were not given enough to eat and suffered lifelong damage to their health, their labour was still too expensive. They constantly tried to escape, and were unmotivated and careless in their work. As factory owners realised, it was far cheaper to employ children who still lived with their parents, and to pay them a regular wage. That is why child labour, but not child slavery, became commonplace (Malm 2016, pp. 131 ff.).

20 Beckert, p. xv.

21 Vries, p. 254.

22 Marx, p. 915. For a similar modern view, see Phillips, p. 257.

23 Ibid., p. 918. Marx does not limit his category of 'primitive accumulation' to colonies and slavery, but also includes all factors he considers to have been necessary to make capitalism possible in the first place. For him, those are the abolition of mandatory guild membership; the end of serfdom; the 'genesis of the capitalist farmer'; the privatisation of the commons; the transformation of arable land into pastureland for sheep grazing; the 'colossal spoliation of church property' after the Reformation; 'stock-exchange gambling and the modern bankocracy'; 'laws to push down workers' wages'; and national debt (see chapter 24 of *Capital*).

24 Ibid., p. 924. This view still exists today: Beckert, p. 63.

25 Beckert, p. 63; Eckert, p. 89.

26 Vries, p. 257; Eckert, p. 49.

27 Vries, p. 257; Kocka, pp. 58 ff.

28 See, for example, Hasters, pp. 62 ff. and 170 ff.; Brand and Wissen, p. 74; Kleinschmidt, p. 19.

29 Quoted in Vries, p. 247.

30 Vries, p. 249. These figures are so-called silver equivalents, which means that they also include gold deposits, converted to their equivalent value in silver, to give an idea of the scale.

31 Vries, pp. 250 ff. There was also little interest in European goods in Russia or the Arab World, for example. From 1600 to 1800, 400 tonnes of silver were exported to the Middle East, 459 tonnes went to the Baltic countries and Russia, and 461 tonnes ended up in the Far East. Furthermore, a large proportion of the silver remained in the Americas to cover the local costs for mining and transportation. This means there was more silver per capita in South America than in Europe—which did not trigger industrialisation, because all the wealth was concentrated in the hands of a few large landowners (Allen 2011, pp. 76 ff.).

32 Vries, pp. 250 ff.

33 Ibid., p. 247.

34 Herrmann 2018, pp. 59 ff. Prolonged droughts set in on the Gangetic Plain from 1769 onwards. The resulting crop failures hit particularly hard because the land had been given over to growing crops for export. Rather than cultivating grain, farmers were forced to grow poppies for the production of opium, which the British East India Company sold on to China at great profit. That meant grain stores were empty when the droughts began. Rather than transferring grain supplies from other parts of India, the British ignored the emergency, concerned only for their own profits. They taxed local farmers all the more heavily to make up for losses incurred by the drop in the opium harvest. Up to one-third of the Bengali population starved to death.

35 Often, a posting to India lasting just a few years was enough to enable British colonial officers to return to England with mindboggling wealth. In Britain, they commonly became known as 'nabobs', from the Bengali word for 'ruler'. They were thoroughly hated for using their looted Indian wealth to buy up old aristocratic estates and secure themselves seats in parliament. They eventually formed their own lobby in the House of Commons, and used their power to preserve the privileges of the East India Company.

36 Vries, p. 271. This figure includes the US and the Caribbean, so India alone was even less significant. See also Osterhammel and Petersson, p. 42.

37 Chang 2003, p. 45.

38 Vries, pp. 271 and 301. European grain production tripled between 1815 and 1913, while the population only doubled.

39 Smith, p. 308.

40 Brand and Wissen, p. 83.

41 Osterhammel and Petersson, p. 71. This does not include the colonial possessions of Russia or the Ottoman Empire.

42 The first German colony was founded as early as 1683 by the Prussian Frederick William, Elector of Brandenburg, in what is now known as Ghana. Named 'Gross Fredericksburg' after him, it consisted of an approximately 30-kilometre-long strip of coastline. The whole venture quickly failed, and the colony was officially abandoned in 1717.

43 Conrad, pp. 86 ff. Of the approximately 14,000 German troops involved, around 1,500 died in battle or as a result of disease.

44 Ibid., p. 87.

45 Ibid., pp. 97 ff.

46 Ibid., p. 21.

47 Levinson, p. 15; Conrad, p. 18.

48 The issue of whether Germany was solely to blame for World War I is still a matter of historical debate. The theory of 'sole responsibility' is supported by the fact that the German generals did not develop any kind of defensive strategy, planning rather to 'defend' Germany by attacking Belgium and France. So, for the Germans, there was no alternative to war—while the French, for example, organised their national force along purely defensive lines.

49 In his 1910 book, *The Great Illusion*, the English journalist Norman Angell demonstrated that war in Europe would be 'commercial suicide'. The book was a bestseller and was translated into 15 languages within just one year.

50 See www.sahra-wagenknecht.de/de/article/487.kapitalismus-heisst-krieg.html

51 Bilmes, Linda and Joseph Stiglitz, *The Three Trillion Dollar War: the true cost of the Iraq conflict* (Norton 2008).

52 The price of a barrel of oil was $32 in 2003. At that time, the US imported 9.3 million barrels a day. That means the US spent almost $109 billion a year on imported oil. However, the Iraq War caused a global oil shortage, almost doubling its price. If the war were really about access to oil, that would mean it completely backfired for America.

53 As in industry, capital investment increases constantly in the military. Ten times more money was spent for every killed enemy in the Korean War, from 1950 to 1954, than in World War II. However, high capital investment is not necessarily a guarantee of victory, as the Vietnam War from 1955 to 1975 showed (Milward, p. 170).

54 Among the most important developments in the steel industry are the puddling process of 1784, the Bessemer process of 1856, the Siemens-Martin process of 1864, and the Linz-Donawitz process of 1950.

55 Radkau 2008 (Campus), p. 267. The main effect of the constant wars in Europe was to make each country keen to copy the technological advances of its neighbours as quickly as possible so as not to fall behind militarily. Thus, war is one of the reasons innovations spread so rapidly in Europe. Military conflict cannot, however, explain why so many technological innovations came about in the first place.

Chapter 7: Expansion or collapse

1 The figure of 2.8 per cent annual growth refers to the period from 2000 to 2019. The Covid-19 pandemic caused a slump of minus 3.1 per cent.

2 Klingholz, p. 258; Raworth, pp. 247 ff.

3 Abbey, p. 183.

4 Earth Overshoot Day is calculated each year by the Global Footprint Network. It is the date on which the consumption of renewable resources by people in a particular country first exceeds nature's ability to replenish them in that year.

5 Chancel et al., p. 196.

6 Brand and Wissen, p. 2.

7 See www.statistics.gr/en/statistics. The Greek economy continued to shrink until 2016—and has barely recovered since. The Covid-19 crisis caused it to slump by 9 per cent in 2020.

8 See https://blogs.lse.ac.uk/greeceatlse/2021/03/10/discussing-the-brain-drain. For more on the European debt crisis, see Herrmann 2022, pp. 233 ff. It was unfortunate for Greece that the eurozone pursued precisely the wrong policy: there were no stimulus packages, instead of which the state was instructed to cut spending, which only served to deepen the crisis. A fatal downward spiral began. The unemployed were no longer able to spend on consumption, forcing even more shops and businesses to close. That led to a further drop in demand, creating even more unemployment.

9 Jackson 2021, p. xv.

10 See www.wu.ac.at/mobile-first/news/details/detail/was-hat-corona-bis-jetzt-den-oesterreichischen-staat-gekostet/ ['How Much Has Covid-19 Cost the Austrian State So Far?']. The figure of 70 billion euros takes into account the tax shortfalls due to Covid-19.

11 See www.admin.ch/gov/de/start/dokumentation/medienmitteilun-gen.msg-id-84265.html ['Covid-19: Expenditure Up to the End of June']. The figure of 40 billion francs refers only to spending related to Covid-19, such as reduced-hours compensation. Tax shortfalls due to the pandemic are not included.

12 Klingholz, p. 260; Phillips, p. 59; Kern, p. 190.

13 Binswanger, pp. 101 ff.

14 For a complete history of money, see Herrmann 2015, pp. 109 ff.

15 Mundell, p. 5.

16 Van de Mieroop, p. 212.

17 Promissory notes later lost their appeal and were eventually replaced in the Middle Ages by bills of exchange, which were invented in the

Arab world. They are based on a simple idea: the seller of a commodity allows customers to defer payment—mostly for three months—which is tantamount to a short-term loan. This transaction is recorded in a bill of exchange issued by the seller and accepted by the buyer. During its term of validity, the bill can be passed on to others as a means of payment. Over the centuries, bill transactions became increasingly sophisticated, especially as merchants soon realised they could issue bills of exchange without an underlying transaction. Rather than trading in goods, they immediately created credit—and therefore also money.

18 Binswanger, p. 12 and 50; Jackson 2021, pp. 28 ff.
19 Kennedy, p. 14.
20 Ibid., p. 15.
21 Binswanger, pp. 95 ff.
22 Galbraith 1999, pp. 217 ff.
23 Schmelzer and Vetter, p. 38.
24 The global economic crisis that began in 1929 led to a new economic theory based on the insights of John Maynard Keynes. The British economist was the first to offer a systematic description of the way states can remedy economic crises by taking on debt and creating additional demand. For more on Keynesian theory, see Herrmann 2018, pp. 181 ff.
25 Mazzucato 2019, pp. 220 ff.
26 To mention just a few suggestions for how GDP could be reformed or expanded: the United Nations has set out 17 Sustainable Development Goals (SDGs), including gender equality, and access to clean water and sanitation. The UN also makes use of the Human Development Index created by the winner of the Nobel Prize for Economics, Amartya Sen. It measures how likely individuals are to achieve their full potential. The OECD, for its part, publishes the Better Life Index, which also takes into account such aspects as civic engagement and work-life balance. Another alternative indicator is the National Welfare Index, which also measures income inequality, the value of domestic work, and also such things as the cost of damage due to greenhouse gas emissions, traffic accidents, and air pollution.
27 For the third time in 2024, under economics minister Robert Habeck of the Green Party, Germany's annual government economic report was not purely oriented towards GDP, but also included social and environmental indicators. They included, for example, such aspects as 'women in leadership positions', 'lowering groundwater nitrate

levels', and 'intergenerational educational mobility'. This range of indicators is not complete, however, and is due to be expanded in the next annual economic report. Also, the aim is not to replace GDP with these indicators, but to expand it (Federal Ministry for Economic Affairs and Climate Action, pp. 121 ff.).

Chapter 8: The price of prosperity

1   See https://ourworldindata.org/grapher/years-of-fossil-fuel-reserves-left
2   Rahmstorf and Schellnhuber, pp. 48 ff.
3   Ibid., p. 47.
4   See www.tagesschau.de/inland/deutschlandtrend/deutschlandtrend-1645.html. The sceptics are found mainly among supporters of the far-right AfD party, only 60 per cent of whom believe that climate change is caused by humans.
5   Rahmstorf and Schellnhuber, p. 26.
6   Latif, pp. 84 ff.
7   Over the past 10,000 years, global temperatures have fluctuated by only one degree above or below the mean temperature of 14 degrees.
8   Some sceptics claim that climate change is due purely to changes in solar activity. However, this view is clearly wrong, as solar activity has been diminishing for the past 40 years. In 2008 and 2018, the Sun's luminosity reached new lows—while global temperatures hit record highs. So, in fact, the opposite of the sceptics' belief is true: without that weaker solar luminosity, the Earth would probably be even hotter than it is now. (Rahmstorf and Schellnhuber, pp. 39 ff.)
9   Interview with Anders Levermann in *taz*, 29 November 2020.
10 Rahmstorf and Schellnhuber, p. 25; Raworth, p. 48.
11 Neubauer and Repenning, p. 60.
12 Ibid., p. 75.
13 Lomborg, p. 3.
14 Ibid., p. 4.
15 Foer, p. 187. Similarly in Ulrich, pp. 145 ff.
16 'Das Weltklima gerät aus den Fugen' ['The Global Climate Goes Awry'], *Der Spiegel*, 11 August 1985, p. 122.
17 'Mauern gegen das Meer' ['Walls Against the Sea'], *Süddeutsche Zeitung*, 30 October 2021. However, the Meteorological Institute does admit that sea levels could rise by two metres by the year 2100: www.knmi.nl/kennis-en-datacentrum/achtergrond/knmi-klimaatsignaal-21
18 'Dem Untergang geweiht' ['Doomed to Drown'], *Süddeutsche Zeitung* 13 October 2021.

19   CNN: https://edition.cnn.com/2020/01/13/world/climate-change-oceans-heat-intl/index.html.

20   Rahmstorf and Schellnhuber, p. 59.

21   'Dem Untergang geweiht' ['Doomed to Drown'], *Süddeutsche Zeitung*, 13 October 2021.

22   Sea-level rise has been measured by satellite since 1993. In that time, 42 per cent of the rise has been caused by thermal expansion of the water, while 21 per cent came from the melting of mountain glaciers. The Greenlandic icesheet contributed 15 per cent, and 8 per cent was due to ice loss in the Antarctic (Rahmstorf and Schellnhuber, p. 63).

23   Deutsche Presse-Agenture, 5 May 2020.

24   'Welche Zukunft darf es sein?' ['Which Future Would You Like?'], *Süddeutsche Zeitung*, 15 November 2021.

25   Monbiot, pp. 9 ff. The deforestation of the Amazon is accelerating the desertification process. Seventeen per cent of its area has so far been deforested, and the figure is already 20 per cent for the Brazilian Amazon specifically. When around 25 per cent of the trees are gone, the rainforest will no longer be able to produce rain, and will begin to dry out (Plöger, p. 227).

26   Reimer and Staud, p. 323.

27   Many of the effects of climate change were either not foreseen at all or were predicted wrongly. For example, scientists believed that the stratosphere over the Arctic was 'really clean', but in autumn 2021 a study showed that smoke particles had accumulated in huge amounts at an altitude of seven kilometres after widespread forest fires in Siberia. Those particles could destabilise the ozone layer, exposing the Earth to more dangerous UV radiation from the Sun. See https://acp.copernicus.org/articles/21/15783/2021/acp-21-15783-2021-discussion.html.

28   See https://agupubs.onlinelibrary.wiley.com/doi/10.1029/2019GL082187.

29   Rahmstorf and Schellnhuber, p. 59. In 2018, 76 per cent of climate change was due to carbon dioxide, of which 66 per cent came from fossil fuels and 10 per cent came from agriculture and forestry. Seventeen per cent of climate change was caused by methane, 5 per cent by nitrous oxide, and 2 per cent by fluorinated gases ('Dumping Greenhouse Gases in the Atmosphere', MCC press release, 10 November 2021).

30   It was not only in Canada that forests went up in flames in the summer of 2021, but also in the US states of Oregon, Washington,

California, Arizona, Nevada, and Utah. Those fires released enough carbon dioxide into the atmosphere to entirely make up for the shortfall in US emissions due to the Covid-19 lockdowns, when public life came to a standstill.

31 'Zahlen liefern keinen Grund zur Entspannung' ['Figures Give No Cause to Relax'], *taz*, 10 November 2021

32 See https://crowtherlab.pageflow.io/cities-of-the-future-visualizing-climate-change-to-inspire-action.

33 In the dry year 2020, Brandenburg registered only 511.4 litres of precipitation per square kilometre. In Saxony-Anhalt, that figure was 499.9 litres. Bavaria, by contrast, received 861 litres, and 816 litres fell in Baden-Württemberg. The next year saw much higher rainfall, but the pattern was the same: Brandenburg received 600.6 litres; Saxony-Anhalt, 582.4 litres; Bavaria, 926.8 litres; and Baden-Württemberg 980.9 litres (German Meteorological Service, *Climate Status Report Germany*).

34 Rahmstorf and Schellnhuber, p. 53.

35 Deutscher Wetterdienst, *Faktenpapier Extremwetterkongress* ['German Meteorological Service, *Fact Paper for the Extreme Weather Congress*'], October 2021, p. 10.

36 Latif, pp. 40 ff.

37 Interview with the hydrologist Dietrich Borchardt, *taz*, 6 July 2020.

38 Büscher, p. 117.

39 It was known as early as 1833 that spruce monocultures attract bark beetles. A forest guardian from Hanover reported in that year that such pure stands of trees provided a feast for an 'army of insects' (Radkau 2008 ([CUP], p. 215).

40 'Angriff auf den Wald' ['Attack on the Forest'], *Süddeutsche Zeitung*, 7 August 2021.

41 'Das Problem ist, dass wir Holz verschwenden' [The Problem Is That We Waste Wood'], *Süddeutsche Zeitung*, 2 October 2020.

42 German Parliament, p. 19.

Chapter 9: The carbon dioxide will not go away

1 The figure of 420 carbon dioxide molecules per million air particles was measured in April 2022. That value was a new record, as the seasons have a great influence on the concentration of carbon dioxide, which is always highest in April. Plants photosynthesise carbon dioxide into oxygen, but deciduous trees of course have no leaves in winter. Since the vegetation in the northern hemisphere accounts for the majority of the world's plant mass, the northern seasons have

a very powerful effect. The lowest carbon dioxide values are always measured in September. In 2021, the September value was around 413 carbon dioxide molecules per million air particles.

2   See www.umweltbundesamt.de/sites/default/files/medien/publikation/long/3447.pdf, p. 6.

3   See www.umweltbundesamt.de/themen/wasser/gewaesser/grundwasser/nutzung-belastungen/carbon-capture-storage#positionspapiere-des-umweltbundesamts.

4   Quaschning, p. 123.

5   So far, there is only one conceivable possibility for making energy-intensive carbon dioxide capture economically viable. It involves using the captured carbon dioxide for 'tertiary oil recovery'. This technology has been in use in the US for almost 50 years. Carbon dioxide is injected into the oilfields to push out the remaining oil reserves that cannot be reached using conventional drilling methods. The carbon dioxide used for this comes from natural sources, but it could be replaced with carbon dioxide captured from fossil-fuelled power plants. However, that would not reduce the amount of carbon dioxide in the atmosphere. On the contrary: the additional oil extracted this way would eventually be burned, releasing even more greenhouse gases (German Parliament, pp. 11, 25).

6   'See www.geoengineeringmonitor.org/2024/01/geo-map-ccs-jan-2023.

7   German Parliament, p. 49.

8   Göpel, p. 105; Wallace-Wells, p. 169.

9   German Parliament, pp. 9 ff. The University of Freiburg recently calculated how much energy it would take to remove carbon dioxide directly from the air, taking into account the entire life cycle of such a filter, from manufacture to scrapping. If the filters are run on natural gas, they produce 0.3 tonnes of carbon dioxide equivalents for each tonne of carbon dioxide captured. It is currently more efficient to avoid emitting the carbon dioxide in the first place (Informationsdienst Wissenschaft, 29 October 2021).

10 Calculated by Jörgen Pisarz.

11 Quoted in Sinn, pp. 299 ff. A maximum of 900 gigatonnes of carbon dioxide could be stored in old gas and oil reserves around the world. Former coalmines could contain 200 gigatonnes, which comes to a total of 1,100 gigatonnes of carbon dioxide.

12 This figure again refers to carbon dioxide equivalents. Methane, nitrous oxide, and fluorinated greenhouse gases are converted into carbon dioxide according to their effect on the climate.

13 The carbon dioxide is naturally compressed when it is stored deep underground by the increased pressure and heat in the Earth's interior. The optimum depth is at least 800 metres (www.bgr.bund. de/EN/Themen/Nutzung_tieferer_Untergrund_carbon dioxideSpeicherung/carbon dioxideSpeicherung/FAQ/faq_inhalt_en.html).

14 German Parliament, p. 13.

15 Ibid., p. 14.

16 The storage capacity of depleted gasfields in Germany is about 2.7 billion tonnes of carbon dioxide. With a storage capacity of just 130 million tonnes of carbon dioxide, depleted oil reservoirs are too small to play a role (www.bgr.bund.de/EN/Themen/ Nutzung_tieferer_Untergrund_carbon dioxideSpeicherung/carbon dioxideSpeicherung/FAQ/faq_inhalt_en.html).

17 See www.umweltbundesamt.de/daten/klima/treibhausgas-emissionen-in-deutschland/kohlendioxid-emissionen#kohlendioxid-emissionen-im-vergleich-zu-anderen-treibhausgasen. These figures refer to carbon dioxide equivalents. Nitrous oxide and methane are converted into carbon dioxide according to the risk they pose for the climate.

18 See www.lbeg.niedersachsen.de/energie_rohstoffe/co2speicherung/ co2-speicherung-935.html#english. There is a legitimate concern that saltwater could rise towards the surface if carbon dioxide is forced into the aquifers under pressure. A similar effect has already been observed in North Hesse. Alkaline solutions resulting from potash mining in the Fulda district were pumped into a Plattendolomit (mudstone layer) formation at a depth of 400 to 500 metres. The saltwater in the formation was displaced and rose, and has now contaminated the local drinking water wells (German Parliament, p. 15).

19 Sinn, p. 301.

20 Pötter 2021, p. 214. In Ketzin, a total of 67,271 tonnes of carbon dioxide were stored in a saline aquifer between 20 June 2008 and 29 August 2013 (German Parliament, p. 11). The project was coordinated by the German Research Centre for Geosciences in Potsdam. There were originally three more such projects in Germany, but they were soon abandoned before any carbon dioxide was ever pumped into the ground. The energy giant RWE carried out research in North Frisia, and Vattenfall in eastern Brandenburg, and the joint research project CLEAN, including the energy companies GDF Suez and Vattenfall, among others, was active in the Altmark region of Saxony-Anhalt. All three projects failed due to resistance from the

local community (German Parliament, p. 6).

21 German Parliament, p. 23. Sleipner is located 260 kilometres to the west of Norway, at about the same latitude as Stavanger.

22 Geoengineeringmonitor.org. The German research mission CDRmare is currently attempting to ascertain how secure storage beneath the seabed really is. ('Der Ozean als carbon dioxide-Schlucker' ['The Ocean as a Carbon Dioxide Absorber'], *Süddeutsche Zeitung*, 29 March 2022

23 'Weg mit dem Klimakiller' ['Getting Rid of the Climate Killer'], *Süddeutsche Zeitung*, 10 December 2021. A total storage capacity of 200 billion tonnes of carbon dioxide is assumed for the North Sea as a whole (Pötter 2021, p. 222).

24 Orca is a joint venture: the Swiss company Climeworks filters the carbon dioxide out of the air, while the Icelandic company Carbfix has developed the technology to inject it into subsurface basalts.

25 German Parliament, p. 14.

26 'Begraben in der Tiefe des Gesteins' ['Buried in the Depths of the Rock'], *taz*, 23 October 2021.

27 Way et al., p. 9. The search for new ways to store carbon dioxide is far from over. The German research mission CDRmare is currently investigating the possibility of adding lime to the North and Baltic Seas to enable their water to absorb more carbon dioxide from the atmosphere. Around five tonnes of lime would be needed to absorb every tonne of carbon dioxide. However, it is unclear whether the lime would later precipitate out. Some are also considering fertilising the oceans to promote the growth of plankton and algae, which can bind carbon dioxide. A preliminary trial in the Antarctic Ocean had mixed results: a species of algae bloomed that can be toxic under certain circumstances ('Der Ozean als carbon dioxide-Schlucker' ['The Ocean as a Carbon Dioxide Absorber'], *Süddeutsche Zeitung*, 29 March 2022).

Chapter 10: Nuclear power is still a mistake

1 Deutsche Presse-Agentur, 19 October 2021. At the same time, 48 per cent believe the decision to phase out nuclear power was correct. Respondents were highly divided along party political lines: 59 per cent of conservative (CDU/CSU) and liberal (FDP) voters, and 91 per cent of far-right AfD voters were against phasing out nuclear power. Conversely, 79 per cent of Green voters, 64 per cent of far-left Die Linke voters, and 62 per cent of social-democrat (SPD) voters were in favour.

2 Phasing out nuclear power was first approved in 2000 by the Social Democrat-Green coalition government led by chancellor Gerhard Schröder. The Stade nuclear power plant went offline in 2003, followed by the reactor in Obrigheim in 2005. The rest of the country's plants received permission to produce a residual amount of electricity, meaning they would have been gradually closed down between 2015 and 2020. The conservative–liberal coalition led by Angela Merkel reversed those decisions, and, on 28 October 2010, extended the working life of the plants by eight to 14 years. There was then an abrupt about-turn in policy after the accident in Fukushima. Eight nuclear power plants were decommissioned in 2011, with the remaining nine reactors gradually taken offline by April 2023.

3 See www.infratest-dimap.de/fileadmin/_migrated/content_uploads/dt1106_bericht.pdf, p. 11. Germany has not completely withdrawn from nuclear power. There is still one research reactor active in Garching near Munich, a fuel-rod factory in Lingen, and a uranium-enrichment plant in Gronau, both near the Dutch border. All three have unlimited operating licences.

4 Even nuclear power plants are not completely climate-neutral, because preparing the fuel rods and the disposing of the waste causes carbon dioxide emissions. Germany's nuclear power plants produced about 32 grams of carbon dioxide per kilowatt hour of electricity. For comparison, burning lignite produces up to 1,100 grams per kilowatt hour (Pötter 2020, p. 58).

5 Flassbeck, pp. 116 ff.; Sinn, pp. 252 ff,; Pinker, pp. 146 ff.; McAfee, p. 110; Phillips, pp. 199 ff.; Stelter, p. 226.

6 The Ministry for Nuclear Affairs was renamed the Ministry for Scientific Research in 1962, and became the Ministry for Education and Science in 1969.

7 Brüggemeier 2017, p. 7.

8 Bundesministerium für Wirtschaft und Energie, *Energiedaten: Gesamtausgabe, Energy Figures: complete edition*] (Berlin 2019), p. 14. These figures refer to primary energy consumption.

9 Wealer et al., p. 236.

10 'Neue Atomkraft mit grünem Segen' ['New Nuclear Power with the Blessing of the Greens'], *taz*, 3 February 2022.

11 Despite the huge cost of the new Flamanville nuclear power plant, France is planning to build six more reactors of this type, as announced by President Emmanuel Macron in February 2022. However, the importance of nuclear power in France is still likely to decrease. It currently has 56 reactors in operation, of which

one-third are more than 40 years old and are approaching the end of their useful lives ('Vive l'Atomkraft!' ['Long live Nuclear Power!'] *Süddeutsche Zeitung*, 11 February 2022).

Another European pressurised water reactor is under construction at Hinkley Point in the United Kingdom; it was due to go online in summer 2026, but is now expected to be finished in 2031. When construction began in 2016, its cost was estimated at £18 billion—but that has already risen to at least £41 billion. The project will only be profitable because the British government guarantees an electricity feed-in tariff of 10.5 cents per kilowatt hour, which is well above the market price for electric power ('Britischer Meiler kostet mehr' ['British Reactor to Cost More'], *Frankfurter Rundschau*, 3 February 2021). Two European pressurised water reactors began operating in Taishan, China, in 2018 and 2019 respectively. Taishan-1 had to be switched off again in July 2021 due to vibrations and radioactive gas leaks (Neue Atomkraft mit grünem Segen' ['New nuclear power with a green blessing'], *taz*, 3 February 2022).

12 Between 2010 and 2019, the price of a megawatt hour of solar-generated electricity fell from US$378 to $68. In the same period, the cost of nuclear-generated power rose by $59—from $96 to $155 per megawatt hour (Ritchie and Roser, p. 14).

13 See www1.wdr.de/daserste/monitor/sendungen/atom-deal-100.html.

14 See https://pris.iaea.org/PRIS/WorldStatistics/WorldTrendNuclear PowerCapacity.aspx.

15 See www.iea.org/reports/key-world-energy-statistics-2021/ supply. The figures refer to the year 2019 and to primary energy consumption.

16 See https://pris.iaea.org/pris/.

17 Just over 50 nuclear power plants are currently under construction around the world, approximately half of which are being built by the state-owned Russian concern, Rosatom. Most construction projects are in the red. This includes four reactors in Turkey, which have generated an estimated loss of $22 billion for Rosatom.
('Kernenergie auf Pump' ['Nuclear Power on the Never-Never'], *Süddeutsche Zeitung*, 22 December 2021

18 See www.iea.org/reports/world-energy-investment-2021/executive-summary.

19 See www.manager-magazin.de/finanzen/versicherungen/ a-761954.html

20 One of the companies planning to build such mini nuclear plants

is the British technology giant Rolls-Royce. It has earmarked £195 million of its own funds for such projects, and has received state subsidies of £210 million. The company plans to have a prototype model ready within ten years, which should produce enough electricity to supply one million households (Deutsche Presse-Agenture, 9 November 2021). Another mini reactor is planned in Romania, to be built by the US company NuScale. It will be a light-water reactor (Deutsche Presse-Agenture, 5 November, 2021).

21 Gates, pp. 86 ff.; Pinker, p. 330.
22 Radkau 2008 (Campus), p. 11.
23 Ibid., p. 366.
24 Ibid., p. 367. The average capacity of nuclear power plants is just under 1,000 megawatts.
25 'The Controversial Future of Nuclear Power in the US', *National Geographic*, 4 May 2021.
26 'See https://maritime-executive.com/editorials/russia-s-floating-nuclear-plant-plugged-in-at-pevek.
27 Quaschning, p. 108. This calculation includes reserves and resources—all conceivable uranium deposits. It is also based on nuclear power covering only an estimated 50 per cent of the global demand for energy. If that proportion were higher, uranium reserves would be depleted even more quickly and would not last even ten years.

Chapter 11: Unfortunately unreliable

1   Latif, p. 26.
2   Plöger, p. 260.
3   Berg, pp. 61 ff.
4   Malm 2016, p. 159.
5   Radkau (Campus) 2008, pp. 232 ff
6   Seba, p. 173.
7   Federal Environment Agency, 'Renewable energies in figures' (17 November 2021).
8   Initially, nuclear power was discussed as an alternative to solar energy, but nuclear power never became established in spaceflight, and only a small number of nuclear-powered satellites were ever built (Radkau [Campus] 2008, p. 41.
9   See http://californiasolarcenter.org/old-pages-with-inbound-links/history-pv.
10 Seba, p. 25; Ritchie and Roser, p. 14.
11 'Obama auf Jimmy Carters Spuren' ['Obama Follows in Jimmy

Carter's Footsteps'], *Süddeutsche Zeitung*, 11 October 2010. However, Carter's successor, Ronald Reagan, had the collectors removed immediately after taking office.

12 Jensen, p. 41.

13 Pötter 2020, pp. 95 ff.

14 The EEG levy hit households particularly hard because approximately 2,000 energy-intensive industrial companies were excluded from paying it, either partially or completely, so as not to endanger their competitiveness. That included such enterprises as aluminium-smelting plants, but also such entities as local public transport providers, and the meteorological service, which relies on electricity-intensive computers. Those industrial companies made up only 4 per cent of all businesses, but accounted for 20 per cent of overall electricity consumption (Brüggemeier 2017, p. 24). A popular trick among companies was to simply buy up the power plants that supplied them with electricity so that the power counted as having been produced in-house by the company—and therefore was not subject to the EEG levy (Kreutzfeldt, p. 49).

15 Bach, Harnisch, and Isaak, p. 16.

16 Wirth, p. 18.

17 Wirth, p. 16.

18 Federal Agency for Civic Education, p. 246.

19 Federal Environment Agency 2019, pp. 32 and 38. The current centre-left (Social Democrat-Green-Liberal) coalition government has since reformed taxes on energy: the EEG levy was abolished in mid-2022. This was financed by a rise in the carbon tax. However, that does nothing to change the social imbalance, since the carbon tax is also a tax on consumption, thereby placing the greatest burden on low-income households.

20 Small photovoltaic modules mounted on private roofs in southern Germany generate one kilowatt hour for 5.81 to 8.04 eurocents. The cost is somewhat higher in northern Germany, at 7.96 to 11.01 cents (Fraunhofer ISE, *Levelized Cost of Electricity: renewable energy technologies*, p. 17). That makes private solar modules about as cheap as conventional electricity generation. In 2021, German households had to pay an average of 7.93 cents per kilowatt hour—if we consider only the pure electricity price. The final price charged to consumers was 32.16 cents, with the difference being made up of taxes, fees, and network charges (German Association of Energy and Water Industries (BDEW), *Strompreisanalyse* [*Electricity Price Analysis*] (15 November 2021).

21 Fraunhofer ISE, *Levelized Cost of Electricity*, p. 17. One reason the price of solar panels has fallen so sharply is that they are technically relatively easy to manufacture. That is also the reason they are no longer produced in Germany, but primarily in China.

22 Wirth, p. 44. The irradiation sum rises to 3.5 kilowatt hours per day and square metre if the solar panels are south-facing and inclined by 30 per cent to the horizontal.

23 Wirth, p. 37. The nominal efficiency of commercial solar panels has now reached 21 per cent, but they degrade with use — due to such factors as soiling, electrical line resistance, and losses during the necessary conversion of direct current to alternating current.

24 See www.ise.fraunhofer.de/en/key-topics/integrated-photovoltaics/floating-photovoltaics-fpv.html.

25 See www.ise.fraunhofer.de/en/key-topics/integrated-photovoltaics/building-integrated-photovoltaics-bipv.html.

26 'Himbeeren und Sonne auf knappen Flächen' ['Raspberries and Sun in Scarce Spaces'], *taz*, 25 June 2020.

27 German Meteorological Service, 'Current annual course of global radiation 2021'. However, seasonal differences between summer and winter are not the only fluctuations; the weather also varies from year to year. In 2021, less global insolation than the long-term average was measured in Germany in January, May, July, August, and November, while more than average was measured in the other months of that year. Only December 2021 showed the same amount of solar irradiance as the previous year.

28 Jensen, pp. 40 ff.

29 See https://strom-report.de/windenergie.

30 See www.destatis.de/EN/Press/2022/03/PE22_116_43312.html.

31 Federal Environment Agency, 'Renewable energies in figures' (17 November 2021). Solar panels can be used to generate either heat or electricity. In 2020, solar thermal energy covered 0.384 per cent of Germany's final energy consumption. Photovoltaics accounted for 1.92 per cent.

32 Ibid.

33 'Wir überwinden alte Vorurteile' ['We Will Overcome Old Prejudices']. Interview with Robert Habeck, *Süddeutsche Zeitung*, 25 November 2021.

34 Pötter 2021, p. 63.

35 Section 6 of the amended Renewable Energy Sources Act (EEG) of 27 July 2021 provides for an annual payment to municipalities located within 2.5 kilometres of a wind farm of a maximum of 0.2

eurocents per kilowatt hour fed into the grid. The size of the payment depends on how much of the municipality's area is located within that radius—and on the local wind conditions. However, municipalities can reckon with 25,000 to 30,000 euros on average. Even before that legislative amendment, wind turbines were lucrative for many municipalities because they can charge rental fees for access routes, cables, and land use.

36 Federal Ministry for Economic Affairs and Climate Action, 'Germany's Current Climate Action Status' (20 January 2022), p. 13.

37 'Mit dem 2-Prozent-Ziel zum 1,5-Grad-Ziel' ['Achieving the 1.5-Degree Goal With the 2-Per-Cent Goal'], *taz*, 15 January 2022.

38 See www.dwd.de/DE/leistungen/windkarten/deutschland_und_bundeslaender.html.

39 Göke et al., p. 210.

40 Nature and landscape conservation regulations would allow 2.7 per cent of the land area in Saxony and 1.5 per cent in Bavaria to be given over to wind-power production. In Germany as a whole, around 3.6 per cent of land would be suitable (Federal Agency for Nature Conservation, p. 6).

41 'Kampf gegen Windmühlen' ['Fighting Against Windmills'], *Süddeutsche Zeitung*, 16 February 2022.

42 Kompetenzzentrum Naturschutz und Energiewende, Flächenverfügbarkeit für die Energiewende (Berlin, 17 March 2020). At somewhere between 37,000 and 67,000, the total number of turbines will remain manageable, as their performance capacity is constantly increasing. Researchers believe wind turbines will reach an average output of 3.5 megawatts in future.

43 Different studies into photovoltaics also result in differing expansion targets for the year 2045, ranging from around 240 to 510 gigawatts. Most studies assume an installed capacity of 300 to 450 gigawatts (Wirth, pp. 5 ff.).

44 One kilowatt hour of onshore wind-generated electricity currently costs 3.94 to 8.29 eurocents; offshore wind parks produce the same amount for 7.23 to 12.13 cents (Fraunhofer ISE, *Levelized Cost of Electricity*, p. 4).

45 Wirth, p. 44. Ground-mounted photovoltaics achieve 980 full-load hours; roof-mounted units reach 910 hours.

46 There are currently around 1,500 offshore wind turbines off Germany's North Sea and Baltic coasts, with an installed capacity of almost eight gigawatts. That could rise to 7,000 turbines with an installed capacity of 70 gigawatts—enough to cover a maximum of

15 per cent of Germany's overall energy consumption in the future (Quaschning, p. 87).

47 See www.agora-energiewende.org/data-tools/agorameter/chart/today/ power_generation/01.01.2024/29.02.2024/monthly.

48 Wirth, p. 53.

49 Reimer and Staud, p. 274.

50 Some writers place their hopes in wind power from abroad rather than electricity from the desert. The two climate researchers Rahmstorf and Schellnhuber dream of a 'trans-European network' connecting the coasts of Scotland, Norway, Morocco, and Mauretania, as well as northern Russia and Kazakhstan, where there are many onshore locations (in sparsely populated areas) that can provide more than 3,000 full-load hours. They envisage prices of less than five cents per kilowatt hour—including line costs (Rahmstorf and Schellnhuber, p. 106).

51 Quaschning, pp. 141 ff.

52 Ibid., p. 147 bases this calculation on cables with a transmission performance of two gigawatts, but which can only work at 70 per cent capacity. At the same time, he assumes a large drop in the demand for energy in Germany, without which far more than 100 cables would be required.

53 The world's first liquid hydrogen carrier ship is the *Suiso Frontier*, which was built by the Japanese conglomerate Kawasaki. The project is part of a state research plan to investigate how large quantities of green hydrogen can be imported to Japan from Australia in the future.

54 There are currently natural gas pipelines from Algeria and Morocco to Spain, and from Tunisia and Libya to Italy.

55 Alternatively, it would be possible to combust the hydrogen directly, for example in fuel cells for cars. However, that would be equally inefficient.

56 Franz Alt, 'Nur Glück gehabt' ['Just Been Lucky'], *taz*, 22 January 2022.

Chapter 12: The storage problem

1 Fraunhofer ISE, *Levelized Cost of Electricity*, p. 2.

2 The necessary infrastructure for electric car batteries to be used to stabilise the electricity supply is not yet in place. Their batteries work with direct current, but the grid works with alternating current.

3 Gates, p. 79.

4 Plans to build Europe's biggest pump-storage station in Atdorf in the southern Black Forest were dropped in 2017.

5   Holler et al., pp. 141 ff. Research is now underway to find alternatives to pumped-storage plants, while using the same principle. One idea is to sink hollow concrete spheres in the sea. When electricity is scarce, water is allowed to fill the spheres, driving a turbine as it enters. When there is an oversupply of electricity, the surplus is used to pump the water back out of the spheres. Gravity batteries are another variation on this idea. A large number of concrete blocks are positioned near a crane so that in times of abundance, surplus power can be used to drive the crane's electric motor to raise and stack the blocks on top of each other to form high towers. When power is needed, the blocks are lowered back to the ground, and the motor works as a generator to convert the energy released back into electricity.

6   Agence France-Presse, 27 May 2021.

7   Deutsche Presse-Agenture, 1 October 2021.

8   Edenhofer and Jakob, p. 111; Wirth, pp. 64 ff.

9   Quaschning, p. 94.

10 Wirth, loc. cit.

11 Quaschning, p. 91.

12 Wirth, p. 57.

13 German Meteorological Service, 'Wetterbedingte Risiken der Stromproduktion aus erneuerbaren Energien durch kombinierten Einsatz von Windkraft und Photovoltaik reduzieren' ['Reducing weather-related risks to electricity production from renewable energies with a combination of wind power and photovoltaics'], press release, 6 March. More detailed analysis later showed that periods of *dunkelflaute* almost always occur in November, December, or January, and that in 30 to 40 per cent of cases they affect several European countries at the same time, because they are caused by large areas of high pressure (Li et al., p. 9).

14 Energy Brainpool, p. 9.

15 The efficiency of electrolysers is 70 to 80 per cent, at best (Quaschning, p. 129). This means that 20 to 30 per cent of the environmentally friendly electricity is lost when green hydrogen is produced. In order to make it storable, the hydrogen must then be compressed, resulting in the loss of approximately a further 10 per cent of the energy. This is compounded by losses during storage, which can be considerable (Institute for Applied Ecology, p. 33). Huge amounts of energy are lost again when the hydrogen is reconverted into electricity in gas power stations to bridge periods of *dunkelflaute*, because gas turbines are only 30 per cent efficient.

Combined cycle gas turbine power plants have a greater level of efficiency, at 50 per cent. But such CCGT plants would be so much more expensive to build that it would not make economic sense, especially since they are only supposed to be employed on very few days. In any case, it can be assumed that at least 65 per cent of the electricity would be lost when it is stored in the form of hydrogen. The electrolysers themselves would also contribute to the loss of green electricity, further reducing overall efficiency. Two scenarios are conceivable in principle. In the first, there are only very few electrolysers. That would mean more wind turbines and solar power plants were required to keep the electrolysers as well utilised as possible. In the second, there are many electrolysers. In this case, less excess wind and solar power capacity is required. The best case is somewhere in between those two extremes, with around 5.4 per cent of the green electricity remaining unused (Energy Brainpool, p. 21).

16 As part of its 'National Hydrogen Strategy', the German government aims to raise the capacity of electrolysers for the production of green hydrogen to five gigawatts by 2030 and ten gigawatts by 2035. An initial seven billion euros have been earmarked to fund this objective.

17 Quaschning, p. 127.

18 The current installed capacity of conventional power plants is around 85 gigawatts. In future, flexibly controllable gas-fired power plants with a capacity of 100 to 160 gigawatts will be needed (Fraunhofer ISE, *Paths to a Climate-Neutral Energy System*, p. 27).

19 One interesting issue is that of who is going to finance the gas-fired power stations that will run so rarely. The organisation Environmental Action Aid Germany (Deutsche Umwelthilfe) believes the market will regulate itself: at times of *dunkelflaute*, power would be so scarce that energy prices would skyrocket—creating massive windfall profits for gas suppliers, which could then be used to finance the power plants (Deutsche Umwelthilfe, pp. 3 ff. and 20). Such an analysis may be correct in theory, but it completely ignores the practical realities of energy supply. Since periods of *dunkelflaute* cannot be predicted reliably, gas suppliers would not know when they can expect that extra income. Whenever there happened to be an extended period without *dunkelflaute*, such companies would quickly face a liquidity crisis. Conversely, it is not realistic to expect customers to accept sudden extreme increases in electricity prices. Many energy-supply companies would face bankruptcy and

might therefore stop buying power — leaving the gas suppliers sitting on their costs as the economy collapses. The only option therefore is for governments to guarantee gas suppliers a fixed income if they build a power plant. That would mean it was no longer the electricity that was being paid for, but the provision of production capacities.

20 Germany would require battery capacities of 50 to 400 gigawatt hours; for electrolysers, the required installed capacity would be 50 to 130 gigawatts (Fraunhofer ISE, *Paths to a Climate-Neutral Energy System*, pp. 27 ff.). The large margins in predicted demand are due to the influence of behavioural changes — that is, in how much people cut back on energy use.

21 Hentschel, p. 64. Similarly: Energy Brainpool, pp. 22 ff.

Chapter 13: The energy transformation will be expensive, not cheap

1 Skidelsky and Skidelsky, p. 128.

2 Way et al., p. 1.

3 Fraunhofer ISE, *Paths to a Climate-Neutral Energy System*, p. 53. (The figures are based on the 'reference' scenario, which assumes that citizens' consumer behaviour will not change.) The economist Daniel Stelter rightly points out that it cannot be assumed that only luxury goods are bought as Christmas presents. In many families, presents represent necessary spending — for example, on children's clothing (Stelter, p. 236).

4 Ritchie and Roser, p. 15.

5 Way et al., p. 3. A total of 2,905 different forecasts for the years 2010 to 2020 were evaluated. The only accurate predictions were those that dispensed with their own assumptions and assumed a continuation of the existing trend.

6 The production costs are sinking for solar panels, wind turbines, and batteries, but the efficiency of those technologies is hardly rising at all. This contrasts with computers, for example, which have become both far cheaper and much more powerful. It has become common practice among experts to describe these two different phenomena as 'Moore's Law' and 'Wright's Law'. In 1936, the American aeronautical engineer Theodore Paul Wright described the way products become cheaper as more units are manufactured — thanks to the experience and knowledge gained. Such a 'learning curve' has been observed in a total of 66 different branches of technology, and applies to the manufacture of solar panels and batteries (Ritchie and Roser, p. 10). The co-founder of Intel, Gordon Moore, formulated a 'law' in 1965 which

said that the processing power of computers doubles every year. (This has since been adjusted to a period of 18 months to two years.) The phenomenon is only observed in integrated circuits, as highlighted by Microsoft co-founder Bill Gates: 'A computer chip made today has roughly one million times more transistors on it than one made in 1970, making it a million times more powerful ... When crystalline silicon solar cells were introduced in the 1970s, they converted about 15 per cent of the sunlight that hit them into electricity. Today they convert around 25 per cent.' (Gates, pp. 45 ff.)

7   A Ford Model T cost all of $370 in 1914. Adjusted for inflation, that's the equivalent of $11,624 in 2024. The current price of a VW Golf GTD is 43,815 euros.

8   See www.iea.org/reports/key-world-energy-statistics-2021/supply. In 2019, 1,427 terawatt hours of electricity were produced by wind power around the globe, and 681 terawatt hours were produced by solar power. That corresponds to 7.6 exajoules of energy. Globally, a total of 606 exajoules of energy were consumed.

9   See www.iea.org/reports/electric-vehicles. In 2019, there was a global total of around 10 million electric cars.

10 International Energy Agency, pp. 5 ff.

11 International Energy Agency, pp. 8 ff. Like everyone else, the IAE can only work with possible scenarios, which inevitably yield differing results. The uncertainties are illustrated by the case of cobalt. Worldwide demand could increase by a factor of eight by 2040, but it could also increase by a factor of 30 if every country switches to climate-neutral energy sources.

12 International Energy Agency, pp. 11 ff.

13 The biggest lithium reserves are found in the salt lakes of Bolivia, Argentina, and Chile. The salt-laden water is pumped to the surface, where it evaporates. That means no fresh water is used in the actual extraction of the lithium. However, when the salt water is pumped out, the resulting negative pressure can cause fresh water to flow into the cavity, further exacerbating the lack of fresh water in those very arid regions. However, it would be unfair to accuse lithium-extraction activities alone of ruining the environment. Almost all raw materials have dubious environmental credentials. That is particularly true of fossil fuels.

14 International Energy Agency, p. 12. In 1930, the average copper content of ore was 1.8 per cent. Today, the global average is only 0.5 per cent. That means three times as much ore must be mined to extract the same amount of copper as in 1930 (Parrique et al., p. 35).

15 Seba, pp. 2 ff.
16 Meadows et al., pp. 55 ff.
17 McAfee, p. 120.
18 International Energy Agency, p. 14.
19 Fücks, p. 97; Statista, reserves of copper worldwide 2010 to 2020; www.usgs.gov/centers/national-minerals-information-center/ historical-statistics-mineral-and-material-commodities.
20 Quaschning, pp. 169 ff.; Fücks, p. 109; McAfee, pp. 107 ff.
21 Statista, Reserves of rare earths.
22 See www.bgr.bund.de/EN/Gemeinsames/Produkte/Downloads/ Informationen_Nachhaltigkeit/seltene%20erden_en.pdf?__blob= publicationFile&v=4
23 www.boerse.de/historische-kurse/Kupfer/XC0005705501
24 Parrique et al., p. 20. This UN figure encompasses all raw materials, including water and agricultural products.
25 Quaschning, p. 172; [www.heraeus.com/en/hpm/company/hpm_ news/2020_hpm_news/09_milestone_for_green_hydrogen.html
26 The German company Duesenfeld claims it can already recycle 91 per cent of a battery cell (www.duesenfeld.com/recycling.html).
27 Today, 62 per cent of steel is recycled, but that barely puts a dent in consumption. Since high-quality steel can currently contain a maximum of one-third of old scrap without impacting the quality, recycling can only stretch existing reserves by seven to twelve years (Parrique et al., p. 48).
28 Valuable metals are already recycled. Globally, 85 per cent of gold, 60 per cent of both platinum and nickel, 50 per cent of silver, 45 per cent of copper, 42 per cent of aluminium, 37 per cent of chromium, and 36 per cent of zinc and cobalt are recycled. However, lithium and rare earths are very rarely reused, with less than 1 per cent being recycled (International Energy Agency, p. 34). Recycling of batteries is particularly inadequate, which the EU wants to tackle with a directive. From 2026, it intends 90 per cent of all cobalt, copper, and nickel, and 35 per cent of lithium, to be recycled.
29 International Energy Agency, p. 15.
30 International Energy Agency, p. 11. Technology optimists ignore the cost of raw materials when they talk about the energy transition, which is all the more remarkable because, when it comes to fossil fuels, they like to quote the cost of extracting coal or gas to explain why their production costs do not fall (Way et al., pp. 2 ff.; Ritchie and Roser, pp. 12 ff.).
31 'Arbeitskräftemangel im Klimaschutz' ['Labour Shortage in Climate

Protection'], *Frankfurter Allgemeine Zeitung*, 21 May 2021.

32 Federal Environment Agency 2021, 'Aktualisierung und Bewertung der Ökobilanzen von Windenergie- und Photovoltaikanlagen', p. 33; Wirth, p. 50; Quaschning, pp. 200 ff.

33 See https://pvcycle.de/reuse/. Many studies are over-optimistic in assuming that solar modules have an average useful life of 30 years (Wirth, p. 6). But in reality, the panels wear out within 20 years ('Mehr Solarstrom, mehr Solarmüll' ['More Solar Power, More Solar Trash'], *taz*, 26 February 2022).

34 Federal Environment Agency 2021, 'Aktualisierung und Bewertung der Ökobilanzen von Windenergie- und Photovoltaikanlagen', p. 35. Depending on their location, wind turbines make up for the energy required to manufacture and dispose of them within 2.5 to eleven months.

Chapter 14: The dream of 'decoupling' will not work

1 Germany's primary energy consumption is made up of combustion of fossil carbons in the chemical industry amounting to 776 petajoules; conversion losses in power stations of 2,404 petajoules; and 569 petajoules of consumption in the energy sector. Of the remaining 9,056 petajoules of final energy consumption, 2,536 petajoules were consumed by industry; 2,770 petajoules by traffic and transport; 2,408 petajoules by domestic households; and 1,342 by commerce, trade, and services (Wirth p. 54). These figures are taken from the year 2019 in order to exclude the special effects of the Covid-19 pandemic, which began in 2020.

2 This is a slight variation on the information contained on the German Wikipedia page 'Liste der Größenordnungen der Energie'. (The equivalent English-language page is called 'Orders of magnitude (energy)', but it does not contain the pyramid comparison.)

3 Agora Energiewende et al. 2021, p. 21; Göke et al., pp. 211 ff.; Wuppertal Institute, p. 33.

4 Agora Energiewende et al. 2020, pp. 10 ff.

5 Calculation based on figures published in Wirth p. 54—see note 1.

6 Currently, only 3.3 per cent of German domestic energy consumption is covered by solar thermal energy, ambient heat ,and geothermal energy ('Household energy consumption for housing continued to increase in 2019', *Destatis*, 13 August 2021).

7 Underfloor heating is particularly efficient, because floors provide a large area with which to heat a room. This means the heating water does not need to be at as high a temperature as in less efficient

conventional radiators, which are small by comparison and so require very hot water to heat interior spaces.

8   Heat pumps can also make use of the sewer system, since wastewater can be as warm as 20 degrees. Berlin's municipal water company has already launched several test projects. The city has around 580 kilometres of suitable sewers. The electricity provider E.ON estimates that up to 14 per cent of the entire country's heating requirements could be met using heat from wastewater in this way ('Wärme aus der Kanalisation' ['Heat from the Sewers'], *Süddeutsche Zeitung*, 12 July 2021).

9   Agora Energiewende et al. 2020, p. 83; Göke et al., p. 211. There is one hitch, however. Although heat pumps normally require little power to run, they turn into energy guzzlers on cold days. This is because the new technology extracts heat from the ambient air or the ground. When the temperature outside is low, heat is provided by the electricity supply alone, and electricity is scarce and expensive in winter. Since the ground is better at retaining heat, energy experts recommend prioritising ground-source heat pumps over air-source pumps.

10 Calculated on the basis of note 1.

11 See www.tuev-nord.de/de/privatkunden/verkehr/auto-motorrad-cara-van/elektromobilitaet/wirkungsgrad. These high levels of efficiency only apply to battery-driven vehicles. Hydrogen-powered vehicles are extremely inefficient, consuming up to three times as much electricity, due to conversion losses. Twenty to 30 per cent of the electricity used to produce the hydrogen is lost in the process; a further 25 per cent is required to compress and transport the hydrogen. Once in the vehicle, the hydrogen is converted back into electricity by a fuel cell, with the loss of another 40 per cent (Quaschning, pp. 129 ff.). The inefficiency of hydrogen-powered vehicles is due to immutable and unavoidable physical limitations. Despite that, this technological dead-end has received hundreds of millions of euros in state funding. Millions have been pumped into it from publicly funded innovation programs, in addition to which German carmakers received 187 million euros. The results have been meagre. In June 2021, there were only 1,261 fuel cell-driven cars in the whole of Germany ('Zähe Zelle' ['Tough Cell'], *Süddeutsche Zeitung*, 2 August 2021). This funding madness is explained by the fact that fuel cells resemble combustion engines, so German carmakers hoped to be able to keep making big profits using their traditional technologies.

12 Klingholz, pp. 189 ff.; Seba, pp. 104 ff.; Holler et al., p. 27.

13 As efficient as electric vehicles are, they falter in winter particularly, when energy is already scarce, because the cold adversely affects their batteries' electrical conductivity. That means the batteries must be warmed, which consumes additional energy. The vehicle's interior also needs to be specially heated, so the driver and passengers don't get cold, because there is no excess heat for this, unlike in combustion vehicles. This leads to a reduction in the range of electric cars in winter of around 20 per cent, as calculated by Germany's main automobile association, the ADAC. Under such circumstances, electric cars are barely more efficient than diesel motors ('Wenn der Akku dauerfröstelt' ['When Batteries Constantly Feel the Cold'], *Süddeutsche Zeitung*, 29 January 2022).

14 Gates, p. 135.

15 Göpel, p. 100.

16 Plöger, p. 275.

17 Another problem with electric cars is that they still need tyres, which become worn. Around 500 grams of material is worn away per tyre per year, releasing microplastics into the environment (von Hirschhausen, p. 228).

18 Wuppertal Institute, p. 80; Quaschning, p. 174; Agora Energiewende et al. 2020, p. 93.

19 Agora Energiewende et al. 2020, p. 88. There are various models for flexible private car use. 'Carsharing' is based on individual vehicles being used by several drivers at different times. 'Ridesharing' is when several people travel together in one vehicle to a common destination. 'Ridepooling' describes a vehicle being used at the same time by several people who get in and out at different destinations.

20 See www.destatis.de/EN/Press/2019/04/PE19_139_811.html.

21 Ibid., p. 60 places its hopes in an increase in car exports.

22 Quaschning, p. 182; Plöger, p. 279.

23 See www.zukunft-mobilitaet.net/172138/flugverkehr/flugreisen-haushalte-personen-einkommen-oekonomischer-status-haeufigkeit.

24 Gössling and Humpe, p. 1.

25 See https://co2.myclimate.org/en/calculate_emissions.

26 Göpel, pp. 153 ff.

27 Gates, pp. 14 ff. and 59. In recent years, kerosene cost an average of $2.22 per gallon in the US, while biofuels for jets cost $5.35. One gallon is equal to 3.785 litres.

28 Fücks, p. 191.

29 'Technisch machbar, aber noch teuer' ['Technically Possible But Still Expensive'], *taz*, 1 July 2021.

30 Quaschning, p. 189.
31 Schulte, p. 189.
32 Quaschning, pp. 190 ff. Scientists at Stanford University have suc-
   ceeded in developing a catalyst that increases the efficiency of the
   process by which carbon dioxide molecules are split and turned into
   synthetic petrol by a factor of a thousand. The catalyst is made of
   ruthenium coated with porous plastic ('Stanford engineers create a
   catalyst that can turn carbon dioxide into gasoline 1,000 times more
   efficiently', *Stanford News Service*, 9 February 2022). However, this
   new process is energy-intensive and would also not change the fact
   that carbon dioxide is very difficult to extract from the air.
33 Planes would have to fly at lower altitude, since the denser the
   atmosphere is, the more water vapour it can absorb. That would
   result in fewer icy cirrus clouds. However, there is more air resistance at lower altitudes, which would increase both flight times and
   fuel requirements (Quaschning, pp. 190 ff.).
34 Pure hydrogen is a conceivable alternative to synthetic kerosene.
   Airbus aims to release a plane fuelled by liquid hydrogen by 2035.
   However, the necessary fuel tanks require so much space that they
   would take up a third of the plane. Also, water vapour would still be
   produced, creating climate-damaging condensation trails.
35 Pinzler and Wessel, p. 82.
36 See www.lufthansagroup.com/en/responsibility/climate-
   environment/climate-protection-goals.html.
37 If climate studies mention aviation at all, they get tangled up in
   contradictions. A typical example is the scenario presented by the
   Climate Neutrality Foundation. On the one hand, the text points
   out explicitly that 'so-called non-carbon dioxide effects' such as
   condensation trails have so far proved to be an insoluable problem.
   'It must be stressed that these climate effects remain, even when
   carbon dioxide-free fuel is used.' (2020, p. 99.) Still, it is claimed
   that it is compatible with climate-protection goals to aim to increase
   the number of German airline passengers by 1 per cent a year—only
   for the number to fall again by 2 per cent a year between 2040 and
   2050 as flights become 50 per cent more expensive due to the price
   of green kerosene (2020, p. 91). If those projected figures are correct, German air travel would increase by a total of 4 per cent by
   2050.
38 See www.bdl.aero/en/topics-and-positions/the-importance-of-air-
   transport/aviation-provides-more-than-800000-secure-jobs-in-ger-
   many/

39 See www.oecd-ilibrary.org/sites/508bfb5b-en/index.html?itemId=/content/component/508bfb5b-en. In 2018, 1,992 billion tonnes of crude oil, 1,292 billion tonnes of coal, and 1,023 billion tonnes of refined oil products, as well as 461 billion tonnes of gas, were transported by ship. A total of 11 billion tonnes of freight are transported across the oceans every year, which is the equivalent of 1.5 tonnes for every person on Earth.

40 For a detailed history of globalisation, see Herrmann 2015, pp. 97 ff. Globalisation did not begin with the shipping container. Its origins go back to the 15th century, when the first ocean-going sailing ships were developed.

41 See www.fraunhofer.de/en/research/current-research/hydrogen-how-to-stay-mobile/hydrogen-suitable-for-powering-trucks-ships-trains-aircrafts.html

42 The world's biggest shipping company, Mærsk, has forged ahead and commissioned eight container ships from Korea that can run on both traditional fuel and methanol. It still remains unclear, however, where the green methanol is going to come from. The shipping company believes in the power of the market: 'Mærsk is committed to solving the chicken-and-egg dilemma (i.e. no one builds ships propelled by green fuel technology before there is sufficient green fuel available and no one is producing green fuels for shipping until there is demand) by placing a significant order for ships ready to run on green methanol, thus creating a demand for it.' (https://shipandbunker.com/news/world/811784-maersk-parent-firm-sees-chicken-and-egg-dilemma-for-methanol-bunkering.)

43 Hentschel, p. 84.

44 Agora Energiewende et al., 2020, p. 65. Converting steelworks to climate-neutral operation would cost around 30 billion euros (Federal Ministry for Economic Affairs and Energy, *The Steel Action Concept*, Berlin 2020, p. 6). The German steelmaking industry turned over 43 billion euros in 2023.

45 Wuppertal Institute, p. 70. A car weighing one tonne contains 600 kilos of steel, ten kilos of cast iron, 90 kilos of aluminium, 100 kilos of plastic, and 1.6 metres of electric cables. (www.automotive.at/automotive/woraus-besteht-eigentlich-ein-auto-45022).

46 Dechema and FutureCamp (eds), p. 9. Re-equipping the chemical industry would cost around 68 billion euros (p. 77). The chemical industry not only consumes a very large amount of energy in its production processes, but it also uses fossil carbon as a base material. For example, plastics, paints, solvents, and herbicides are produced

from a light crude oil called naphtha. This could conceivably be replaced with synthetic naphtha. Once again, it would be manufactured by combining green hydrogen with carbon dioxide, which is a very energy-intensive process. It would be chemically similar to green kerosene or methane, but with a far a more complex molecular structure.

47 Agora Energiewende et al. 2020, p. 71.

48 Ibid., p. 70, footnote 13. Nonetheless, this study still fails to explain fully why the figure it places on the energy requirements of the chemical industry is so much lower than that quoted by the industry itself. It contains calculation errors. On the one hand, it excludes the energy requirements for imported green naphtha (p. 70, footnote 13), explaining the discrepancies with the chemical industry's own estimates. But, on the other hand, it explicitly includes the electric power consumed to import the naphtha in the overall requirements of 372 terawatt hours (p. 71). This contradiction is repeated in the latest study from the year 2021 (*Towards a Climate-Neutral Germany by 2045*), albeit this time on p. 54, footnote 13 and p. 55. (No full English version. The English version of this as mentioned in the bibliography is an executive summary, so doesn't include these detailed calculations. The page number(s) refer(s) to the German edition.)

49 Wuppertal Institute, pp. 66 and 68.

50 Dechema and FutureCamp (eds), p. 74.

51 Gates, pp. 99 ff.

52 Sixty per cent of the carbon dioxide emissions generated by the cement industry come from the calcination process by which lime is turned into cement. The remaining 40 per cent stem from the heat required for this.

53 Rahmstorf and Schellnhuber, p. 130; Holthaus, p. 142.

54 Timber has doubled in price since 2019 (as of 14 July 2024).

55 The world has lost 178 billion hectares of forest since 1990. That's equivalent to an area five times the size of Germany, and amounts to 4.4 per cent of total global forest cover (FAO, pp. 7 and 12). Germany's health minister, Karl Lauterbach, nonetheless believes that wood is the building material of the future. He argues that if we ate less meat, less animal feed would be needed, freeing up agricultural areas for reforestation (p. 159). That may be the case, but those trees would take another 100 years to grow to a size useful for the construction industry.

56 Clay buildings can currently reach 13 metres in height.

57 Fücks, p. 176.

58 The process that converts carbon dioxide into stone and binds it permanently could be used to reduce emissions in the cement industry. The resulting magnesium and calcium silicates could then be added to the cement. However, that would only reduce emissions by eight to 33 per cent, and all mineralisation plants would have to be subsidised by the state ('Geschäftsmodelle für die carbon dioxide-Mineralisierung' ['Business models for carbon dioxide mineralisation']), *idw*, 15 March 2022.

59 Fuhrhop, p. 75.

60 Reimer and Staud, pp. 238 ff.

61 'Sie sorgen für Zersiedelung' [They Create Urban Sprawl'], Interview with Anton Hofreiter, *Spiegel*, 13 December 2021.

62 See https://berlinspectator.com/2021/02/17/germany-the-single-family-home-and-an-odd-discussion.

63 Fuhrhop, p. 44.

64 Ibid., p. 45, quoting the architect Günther Moewes.

65 Ibid., pp. 95 ff. The refurbished building consumes 95.8 kilowatt hours of energy per year and square metre; a passive house requires at least 100 kilowatt hours, but that figure can be as high as 112.3 kilowatt hours if the passive house is constructed on greenfield land, necessitating longer journeys to work or to shop. These figures include consumption during modernisation/construction and the continuing running requirements of the buildings.

66 Federal Statistical Office 2021, p. 6.

67 See www.destatis.de/EN/Themes/Society-Environment/Population/Households-Families/_node.html.

68 The last census of buildings and housing was carried out in 2022. At that time, there were 1.9 million empty residential units (www.zensus2022.de/DE/Aktuelles/PM_Zensus_2022_Ergebnisveroeffentlichung_Wohnungen_Leerstand.html).

69 Berlin levies a tax on second homes equivalent to 15 per cent of the net basic rent (without heating and other costs). In 2017, 17,000 second-home owners were subject to this tax. However, foreign second-home owners are not subject to it, which means the statistics are incomplete. Anecdotal evidence shows that for a long time it was very popular in other EU states to buy up apartments in Berlin because they were considered so cheap.

70 Fuhrhop, p. 110.

71 See www.umweltbundesamt.de/daten/private-haushalte-konsum/wohnen/wohnflaeche#zahl-der-wohnungen-gestiegen. This figure

does not take vacant housing into account.

72 See www.handelsblatt.com/politik/deutschland/mieter-und-eigen-tuemer-wohnraum-in-deutschland-so-gross-ist-ihre-wohnung-im-vergleich/26929832.html ['Living Space in Germany: how big is your apartment by comparison?'].

73 See www.destatis.de/DE/Themen/Branchen-Unternehmen/Bauen/Tabellen/betriebe.html.

74 Currently, only 1 per cent of Germany's buildings are insulated per year. If Germany is to become climate-neutral by 2045, 4 per cent would need to be insulated per year.

75 Agora Energiewende et al. 2020, p. 12.

76 Edenhofer and Jakob, p. 56. Rahmstorf and Schellnhuber quote similar figures, with annual global economic growth of 1.9 to 3.8 per cent slowing by only 0.06 per cent per year due to the transition to green energy (p. 103).

77 Agora Energiewende et al. 2020, p. 15. The authors cite a study published by the Federation of German Industries (BDI) in 2018, called *Climate Paths for Germany*. It assumes accumulated additional growth of 0.9 per cent if greenhouse gas emissions are cut by 95 per cent by the year 2050 (p. 102). However, this study is extremely self-contradictory when it comes to the details. For example, it predicts that climate protection will boost the automobile industry by 0.4 per cent (p. 104), but it fails to explain where that growth is supposed to come from. Elsewhere, the study predicts that the number of cars in Germany will have to decrease by 11 per cent—to 41 million—by 2050 (p. 179). This assumption is in fact extremely optimistic, as most studies predict that there will only be enough green electricity available to run a maximum of 30 million cars.

78 Fraunhofer ISE, November 2021, p. 55.

79 Fücks, p. 24.

80 Federal Environment Agency 2018, p. 36.

81 Wuppertal Institute, p. 58.

Chapter 15: Why technological innovation and digitisation cannot save the climate

1   Theories of decline are older than capitalism. Humans have always been uneasy about their own hubris. The Bible recounts the story of the failed building of the Tower of Babel, and Greek myths tell of the fall of Icarus.

2   Quoted in McAfee, p. 180. To this day, nothing has changed in this respect, and bad news still sells especially well. The data

analyst Kalev Leetaru examined all *New York Times* articles published between 1945 and 2005, as well as newspaper archives from
another 130 countries, for the period, and found that the basic tone
of those texts became increasingly negative over time (Pinker pp. 50
ff.).

3   Marx's work can be divided into two phases. As a young man, he
was a philosopher and a revolutionary who hoped the political system would be overthrown. It was in this spirit that he wrote the
Communist Manifesto in 1848. However, the revolution failed in
Germany and throughout Europe. No real parliamentary democracy
developed anywhere, and from July 1849, at the latest, monarchs
were back firmly on their thrones everywhere. It was disappointment at this failure that turned Marx to economics, and he began
searching for contradictions within capitalism itself which would
bring about the fall of that economic system. He—completely correctly—described the 'coercive law of competition': it is attractive
for each individual entrepreneur to purchase new machinery that
is more productive than that of his competitors, because when a
manufacturer produces his goods more cheaply, he can sell them
more cheaply and make more profit. Competitors must catch
up immediately, or else they will be priced out of the market. So
they also invest in new machinery. At some point, most markets
will be saturated and unable to absorb any additional goods. Only
those companies with the lowest production costs will survive this
cutthroat competition. They are mostly large companies that profit
from the phenomenon that modern economists call 'economies of
scale'. The greater the number of units manufactured, the lower the
cost of the technology per unit produced.

Marx was the first economist to point out that capitalism
tends to create oligopolies: small companies are priced out of the
market until only a limited number of big firms dominate an entire
branch of industry. Marx welcomed these concentration processes.
He hoped capitalism would bring about its own downfall—when
the capitalists all ousted each other, leaving only a few companies.
'One capitalist always kills many,' which would make the revolution
easier, according to Marx. Eventually, 'the mass of the people' would
remove 'a few usurpers'. 'The expropriators will be expropriated.' As
we know from history, things turned out differently. Although Marx
accurately predicted the oligopoly of large companies, that did not
bring about the downfall of capitalism. (For a detailed description of
Marxist theory, see also Herrmann 2018, pp. 106 and 125 ff.)

4 Quoted in Herrmann 2018, p. 128.
5 Wehler 1995, p. 84.
6 Quoted in McAfee, p. 58.
7 Ibid., p. 61.
8 Quoted in Gates, pp. 113 ff. Similarly, Lomborg, p. 168.
9 Gates, p. 114. People still go hungry in India, although there is enough food for them. Of India's 1.4 billion inhabitants, around 189 million do not have enough to eat. This is due to the continued marginalisation and exploitation of lower-caste and indigenous people.
10 Lomborg, pp. 168 ff. Ehrlich also gained fame due to a wager that he lost spectacularly. The US economist Julian Simon challenged him to name five metals with a total value of $1,000, which he believed would soon become scarce and therefore would increase considerably in price. Ehrlich chose chromium, copper, nickel, tin, and tungsten. The wager ran from 1980 to 1990. At the end of that period, the inflation-adjusted price of all five metals had fallen, and Ehrlich paid Simon the difference, amounting to $576.07. Ehrlich would also have lost the bet if he had chosen petrol, sugar, coffee, cotton, wool, or phosphates. All raw materials had fallen in price, despite a population rise of 800 million over the same period (Fücks, pp. 99 ff.). It later turned out that Ehrlich had only lost by chance. Raw materials prices had risen in most other ten-year periods (Jackson, pp. 13 ff.). After 2000, raw materials prices tripled, and even increased fivefold in 2021, due to chain-of-supply problems connected with the Covid-19 pandemic (BGR-Preisindex metallische Rohstoffe [Federal Institute for Geosciences and Natural Resources (BGR), 'Price Index for Metal Resources']).
11 The Club of Rome was founded in 1968 to promote interdisciplinary research into the future of humanity. It was initiated by the Italian industrialist Aurelio Peccei and the Scottish OECD director, Alexander King. *The Limits to Growth* was the result of a study carried out at the MIT, led by Donella and Dennis Meadows, and based on the pioneering work of Professor Forrester and others in the field of System Dynamics. The study was funded to the tune of one million deutschmarks by the Volkswagen Foundation.
12 Meadows et al., p. 23.
13 "Grenzen des Wachstums' gehört zurück ins Bücherregal' ['*The Limits to Growth*' Belongs Back on the Bookshelf'], *Süddeutsche Zeitung*, 14 March 2022.
14 Meadows et al., pp. 56 ff.
15 Ibid., p. 142.

16 *The Limits to Growth* predicted that the atmospheric concentration of carbon dioxide would reach 380 parts per million by the year 2000 (Ibid., pp. 60 ff.). That value was reached in 2005.

17 Meadows et al., p. 81. There was great concern at the time that the world could warm uncontrollably due to heat pollution from industry, power plants, and domestic buildings. The danger was thought to be about as great as that posed by greenhouse gas emissions. We now know that heat pollution contributes only about 3 per cent to global warming (www.n-tv.de/wissen/Abwaerme-veraendert-Klima-article10020821.html).

18 Meadows et al., p. 145.

19 Radkau 2008 (Campus), pp. 186 ff.

20 Seba, p. 129.

21 Radkau 2008 (Campus), p. 208. In 1893, the Academy refused to install a Chair of Agricultural Technology.

22 Seba, p. 101.

23 Ritchie and Roser, p. 10; Radkau 2008 (Campus), p. 406.

24 Ibid., p. 406.

25 Levinson, pp. xiii ff.

26 Seba, pp. 38 ff.

27 *Süddeutsche Zeitung*, 5 May 2021.

28 Radkau 2008 (Campus), p. 429.

29 Seba, p. 39. The UN has designated 19 November as World Toilet Day to help improve sanitation around the world.

30 Pinker, p. 331.

31 Daly, p. 28.

32 Paech, p. 49.

33 Daly, p. 42. One of the reasons for the confusion surrounding 'qualitative growth' is the way GDP is calculated. Economic performance is measured by prices; the material basis is not accounted for, which leads to the misconception that it is not important. Since only cash flows are counted, two different phenomena can lead to a rise in GDP: either increasing the quantity of products sold, or increasing their quality, allowing manufacturers to demand higher prices for them. Thus, while increasing quality can increase GDP, it does not follow conversely that purely qualitative growth exists (Daly, p. 28).

34 Pinker, p. 135.

35 Plöger, p. 263; Parrique et al., p. 45. As always, these are carbon dioxide equivalents, meaning that the greenhouse effects of other gases has been converted in to the equivalent amount of carbon dioxide.

36 Plöger, p. 265.
37 Researchers distinguish between different kinds of rebound effect. First, the 'direct rebound effect' occurs when saving raw materials leads to more of the same product being consumed. This can be observed in the automobile industry, when, for example, more fuel-efficient cars are driven more often, faster, or over longer distances. Second, the 'indirect rebound effect' occurs when resources freed by an efficiency improvement are re-allocated to another type of consumption. And, third, the 'macroeconomic rebound effect' occurs when machines become so cheap that they are used to manufacture a wide range of products. This was the case for steam engines, and is also observed in the case of robots and computerisation (Parrique et al., pp. 36 ff.).
38 'Wir sehen uns beim Yottabyte' ['See You Again When We Reach the Yottabyte'], *taz*, 20 March 2021.
39 Klingholz, pp. 247 ff.
40 Wuppertal Institute, p. 75.
41 Gössling and Humpe, p. 1.
42 Stimpel, pp. 111 ff.
43 Munich Airport, Annual Traffic Report 2021 (Munich 2022), p. 5.
44 'Helfen Videokonferenzen dem Klima?' ['Is Video Conferencing Good for the Climate?'], *Süddeutsche Zeitung*, 4 December 2021.
45 Quaschning, p. 163; Lauterbach, p. 22.
46 Stimpel, pp. 152 ff.
47 Federal Environment Agency 2018, p. 82.
48 Wuppertal Institute, p. 58, footnote 42.
49 Neubauer and Repenning, p. 230.
50 Paech, pp. 80 ff.
51 Ibid., p. 9.
52 'Wie viel carbon dioxide verbrauchen Bühnen, Museen und Bibliotheken?' ['How Much Carbon Dioxide Is Used by Theatres, Museums, and Libraries?'], *Tagesspiegel*, 24 February 2022.

Chapter 16: Green shrinkage

1 Quaschning, p. 10.
2 Statistisches Bundesamt, Volkswirtschaftliche Gesamtrechnungen. Inlandsproduktberechnung. Lange Reihen ab 1970 [Federal Statistical Office, *National Accounts: calculation of gross domestic product. Long series from 1970*] (Wiesbaden 2022), p. 14.
3 Welzer, pp. 66 ff.
4 'Bullshit jobs' should not be confused with 'shit jobs', such as

working at McDonald's: they are important, but badly paid. With bullshit jobs, the situation is completely the other way around (Graeber, pp. 14 ff.).

5 Graeber, pp. xxii and 14. While 37 per cent of respondents in the UK thought their own jobs were pointless, 50 per cent considered their work worthwhile. Thirteen per cent said they didn't know.

6 The term recycling gives the impression that 100 per cent of all waste is reused. The German Green Party's Toni Hofreiter expressed this illusory concept wonderfully: 'A copper atom does not break down. It can be integrated into an electric motor ten million times in succession.' (Schulte, p. 195.) It is true that copper can be recycled extremely well without losing quality even after several cycles of use. But the same is not true of all materials, unfortunately. Recycled plastics, for example, are only suitable for low-grade uses, while paper can be reused three to six times at the most before it is turned into cardboard and eventually biofuel (Parrique et al., p. 46). Recycling itself also consumes energy. There can be no such thing as a perfect circular economy. Even such a system requires new raw materials, albeit fewer than are used in our current 'throwaway society'.

7 Pettifor, p. 67.

8 Schor, p. x; Raworth, p. 264; Paech, pp. 111 ff.

9 Schor, p. 119.

10 Ibid., p. 151.

11 Ibid., p. x.

12 'Von Rädern und Büchern' ['Of Bikes and Books'], *taz*, 25 September 2021.

13 Schor, p. 13.

14 Ekardt, pp. 128 ff.

15 Welzer, p. 78.

16 All speculative trading is based on derivatives. The basic principle was invented in ancient times and is actually quite sensible because these instruments enable future cash flows to be planned reliably. Airlines are a good example. They sell plane tickets far ahead of time, and their prices are, of course, based on their costs. One significant cost item is kerosene fuel. No one knows today how much oil will cost in the future, and those transactions are carried out in dollars, whose exchange rate also cannot be predicted, so airlines buy oil and currency derivatives to set a fixed price at the time of purchase, thus hedging the risks of those unknown costs. The catch, however, is that derivatives themselves can also be traded speculatively without

the need for them to be underpinned by basic business activities, such as providing passengers with flights. The statistics clearly show that this pure gambling is normal practice today: in 2023, the nominal value of all over-the-counter derivatives traded around the world was $657 trillion (www.bis.org/publ/otc_hy2405.pdf). Total global economic output for the year 2021 was only $85 trillion. That means there are far more derivatives in the world than there are goods. (For a detailed history of speculative financial trading, see Herrmann 2015, pp. 142 ff.)

17 McKinsey, p. 8.

18 Deutsches Aktieninstitut (German Equities Institute), Shareholder Numbers 2021 (19 January 2022). Some 46.6 per cent of those with a net monthly salary of more than 4,000 euros own shares. However, there is a broad gap even among the wealthy. The richest 1 per cent of the German population alone holds around 36 per cent of the total national wealth—mostly in the form of corporate shares (Bach, Thiemann, and Zucco, p. 19).

19 Savings accounts and cash alone amount to around three trillion euros in Germany. Overall financial assets stand at around 7.8 trillion euros. That includes shares, fixed-rate securities, life insurance policies, and other assets.

20 Fücks, p. 18. Here, Fücks is quoting Martin Jänicke, the longtime director of the Environmental Policy Research Centre at the Free University of Berlin.

21 Schneidewind, pp. 161 ff.

22 Neubauer and Repenning, p. 235.

23 Jackson 2017, p. 174.

Chapter 17: The failure of economists

1 Henderson, pp. 36 and 222.

2 For a more detailed description of Keynes' theories, see Herrmann 2018, pp. 181 ff.

3 Keynes himself once predicted that productivity would be so high in the year 2030 that people in industrialised Western nations would only have to work for 15 hours a week (J.M. Keynes, 'Economic Possibilities for Our Grandchildren', 1930). In the degrowth movement, this is sometimes interpreted as Keynes having somehow showed the way to end capitalism by reducing working hours. This interpretation is not supported by the short text itself. In his essay, Keynes describes the end of neither growth nor industrialisation. He wrote his essay in the midst of the global economic crisis. His

outlook for the next 100 years was meant to reassure his contemporaries that economic growth would soon return. He described how their grandchildren would be so rich in 2030 that they would barely have to work at all and would be able to devote all their time to leisure activities. Keynes correctly predicted growth rates, but working hours were not reduced as much as they could have been. Instead, many unnecessary jobs were invented—including the aforementioned 'bullshit jobs'.

4   For a more detailed description of neoclassical economic theory, see Herrmann 2018, pp. 139 ff. and 205 ff.

5   The best critique of neoclassical economics is still that of Joseph Schumpeter (1883–1950), who was a conservative economist himself. For a detailed description, see Herrmann 2018, pp. 146 ff.

6   Carbon taxation is a kind of environmental tax. Every tonne of carbon dioxide emitted has a price, which is intended to rise slowly but steadily. Germany recently introduced a carbon dioxide tax on heating and other fuels, which stood at 30 euros per tonne in 2022, and is set to rise to 55 euros by 2025. From 2026 onwards, the price of carbon dioxide emissions will be decided at auction, although a price corridor of 55 to 65 euros will still apply for the year 2026. This means that Germany has not chosen a pure carbon tax, but has decided also to launch a national certificate trading system. Carbon dioxide certificates are a licence to pollute. First, the state determines the total amount of emissions allowed per year, and issues the corresponding number of certificates; businesses that want to emit carbon dioxide will need to possess certificates to that amount, or buy them on the exchange market. Carbon dioxide emission prices would therefore not be set by the state, but by the market. To increase innovative pressure, the amount of permissible emissions will fall year by year, so pollution rights (certificates) become scarcer.

The EU introduced an emissions certificate trading system for power stations and some industrial plants in 2005. The system has also applied to intra-European flights since 2012. However, this covers only 45 per cent of greenhouse gas emissions, as road traffic, many businesses, and real estate properties are not included in the system. Furthermore, there was an oversupply of certificates at the beginning of the scheme, so the price of carbon dioxide emissions had reached only a risible five euros per tonne by 2017, and the climate-protecting impact was zero. Following reforms, the cost of carbon dioxide emissions in the EU rose significantly, and now stands at 70.67 euros per tonne (as of 2 July 2024). The disadvantage of such a certificate-trading system is that prices can fluctuate heavily on the market—depending on the economic climate at the time. Another problem is the mass involvement of speculative trading. Even in 2012, the total volume of carbon dioxide transactions was more than 33 times bigger than the industry's need for certificates (Schulmeister, p. 813).

Since oil and gas prices also fluctuate heavily, businesses are unable to make reliable calculations about the future cost of using fossil fuels, which means they also cannot predict whether it would be economically advantageous to invest in climate-neutral technology. This has led to the proposal of a third option, in which the state does not tax carbon dioxide emissions, and instead imposes a fixed price path for oil, gas, and coal. A hypothetical example: the EU could determine that the price of a barrel of oil will rise to 200 euros by 2030. If the price on the international markets only happens to be 100 euros by then, the EU would pocket the difference of 100 euros. A border adjustment would be introduced to prevent European businesses being disadvantaged in international competition: exports would be excluded from this pricing system, and imports would also have to pay the energy tax. This border adjustment system would not have to be invented from scratch, as it already applies for value-added tax (Schulmeister, pp. 813 ff.).

7   Stelter, p. 216; Schularick, p. 97; Edenhofer and Jakob, pp. 70 ff.; Lomborg, pp. 154 ff.; Pinzler and Wessel, p. 278; Flassbeck, pp. 82 ff.; Fücks, pp. 177 ff.; Raworth, p. 213; Neubauer and Repenning, pp. 151 ff.; Henderson, p. 222; McAfee, pp. 249 ff.; Plöger, p. 223; Richters and Siemoneit, p. 112.

8   Edenhofer and Jakob, pp. 70 ff.

9   Welzer, p. 235.

10 Plöger, p. 68; Latif, p. 168. Switzerland's carbon dioxide levy is not imposed on diesel or petrol. It only applies to heat generation in households, industry, and power production. A VOC (volatile organic compounds) tax is also levied on paints, varnishes, and cleaning products. One-third of the state revenues generated by those levies goes on modernising old buildings, while the rest is paid out to the Swiss population. That came to 64.20 francs per person in 2024. (www.bafu.admin.ch/bafu/de/home/themen/klima/fachinformationen/verminderungsmassnahmen/co2-abgabe/rueckverteilung/umweltabgabe-rueckverteilung-2021.html).

11 See www.government.se/government-policy/swedens-carbon-tax/swedens-carbon-tax. In Sweden, the carbon tax applies to all fossil

fuels. It also applies to industry, which has paid the same tax rate as households since 2018. The carbon tax revenues flow straight into the state coffers, rather than being redistributed to citizens, as they are in Switzerland.

12 International comparisons are tricky because the data sets used for each country can differ greatly. If 'ecological footprint' is taken as the criterion, the results show that Sweden uses 6.3 'global hectares' per person, Switzerland uses 4.3 global hectares per person, and Germany 4.7. The maximum limit for sustainability is 1.6 global hectares per capita (https://data.footprintnetwork.org). The results turn out differently if the carbon footprint of goods consumed is taken as the criterion (imports are counted, exports are excluded). Then, the Swiss have the worst results among these three nations, with 13.5 tonnes of carbon dioxide per capita. For Germans, the figure is just under ten tonnes, and only 6.8 tonnes for the Swedes (https://ourworldindata.org/co2/country/sweden?country=SWE~DEU~CHE).

13 The figures are fiddled to a certain extent when it comes to the carbon tax—especially in Sweden. The official tax rate is 114 euros per tonne of carbon dioxide, but there are so many exceptions that the average rate is actually less than 30 euros per tonne (www.oecd.org/tax/tax-policy/brochure-taxing-energy-use-2019.pdf, p. 6).

14 See www.bft.de/daten-und-fakten/benzinpreis-zusammensetzun.

15 Germany's main automobile association, the ADAC, publishes regular surveys of car fuel prices in Europe: www.adac.de/verkehr/tanken-kraftstoff-antrieb/ausland/spritpreise-ausland (as of 6 May 2022). Those lists show that fuel prices are high all over Europe, while it should be borne in mind that wages are much lower in some of those countries than in Germany. If purchasing power is taken into consideration, the countries with the highest car fuel prices are Bulgaria, Romania, Lithuania, and Croatia (www.focus.de/finanzen/news/benzinpreise/deutschlands-problem-sind-nicht-die-spritkosten-8–05-euro-pro-liter-wen-die-benzinpreise-in- europa-wirklich-erdruecken_id_72883068.html).

16 Employees only have to pay tax on company cars of 1 per cent of the car's list price per month. For example: A Porsche Cayenne costs 99,600 euros. That is equivalent to a monetary advantage of 996 euros a month. If the employee pays the top tax rate of 42 per cent, the real costs are 418.32 euros per month.

17 Federal Environment Agency 2021, p. 66.

18 There are astonishing differences between individual EU states

when it comes to carbon dioxide emissions from new fossil-powered cars. For the most part, those differences can be explained by the different proportions of electric cars (https://teslamag.de/news/ marktforscher-elektroautos-co2-emissionen-eu-geringer-sechs-laen-der-unter-100-gkm-37251).

19 To date, Germany has not managed to introduce a true energy repayment scheme. Instead, one type of energy tax was replaced by another: the so-called EEG surcharge (a levy imposed as part of the 'Law on Renewable Energy Sources) was abolished in July 2022, and subsidies for green electricity are now funded from carbon dioxide emission prices. The disadvantage of this system is that it does not result in social redistribution: the poorest sections of society remain the most heavily impacted by energy consumption taxes. Although the poorest spend the least on energy overall, their income is so small that electricity and heating costs make up a relatively large part of their budget.

20 Schor, p. 3; Pettifor, p. 152; Berg, p. 91; Richters and Siemoneit, p. 111; Pötter 2020, p. 88; Seba, p. 181; Wirth, p. 14; Hirschhausen, p. 287; Malm 2016, p. 369; Latif, p. 27; Monbiot 2006, p. 55; Edenhofer and Jakob, p. 87.

21 Parry et al., p. 2.

22 Parry et al., p. 7.

23 Germany's Federal Environment Agency also considers the IMF's definition to be problematic. The word 'subsidy' really refers to targeted support given to individual groups by the state finance system. That aspect is lost when all environmental costs are summed up together and passed on to society as a whole (Federal Environment Agency 2021, pp. 18 ff.).

24 The state also receives around 9.4 billion euros a year from vehicle taxes. On the other side, it spent about 14 billion euros on road construction. This shows that motor traffic generates far more income than costs for the state.

25 However, there are subsidies that lower the overall amount received by the state from traffic-related taxes. Foremost among those is the tax relief on company cars, which—as described in this chapter—generates a yearly tax deficit of 3.1 billion euros. Another such subsidy is the tax allowance for commuters, which cost the state around six billion euros in 2018 (Federal Environment Agency 2021, p. 63).

26 Ibid., pp. 60 ff.

27 Climate-protection activists occasionally claim that green energy

has never been subsidised at all, because, until 2021 at least, the money did not come directly from the state, but via the environmental energy levy paid by the customers of electricity suppliers (Wirth, p. 17). This purely technical distinction is meaningless from an economic point of view. Both are instances of subsidies, because it makes no difference to citizens whether they have to pay a tax or an environmental energy levy. Their net income is reduced by the state's targeted support of those who own solar panels and wind turbines.

28 Schink, pp. 57 ff

Chapter 18: A model

1   McKibben 2016.
2   Malm 2020, pp. 6 ff.; 'Jeder kämpft für sich allein' ['Everyone Fights for Themselves'], *taz*, 7 April 2020.
3   Wallace-Wells, p. 169.
4   Malm 2020, p. 12.
5   McKibben 2016.
6   Foer, p. 8.
7   McKibben 2016; Monbiot 2006, p. 98; Foer, p. 8.
8   Monbiot 2021.
9   McKibben 2016.
10 Delina, p. 3. Similarly Pettifor, pp. 98 ff.
11 Foer, p. 9. On average, each person in Germany currently consumes 57 kilos of meat per year.
12 Delina, p. 79.
13 See www.statista.com/statistics/1031678/gdp-and-real-gdp-united-states-1930–2019. These figures refer to growth in the period from 1939 to 1945, although the US did not enter the war until December 1941. This is done to make comparisons with Britain easier.
14 Delina, p. 79; Tooze, p. 406.
15 Broadberry, p. 30.
16 The share of military spending in Britain's economic output averaged 53 per cent between 1940 and 1945. Imports of military goods in that period totalled 12 per cent on average (Tooze, p. 406). The number of imports was limited due to the lack of sufficient transport ships.
17 'Hoffnung heißt Handeln' ['Hope Means Action'], interview with Jane Goodall, *Süddeutsche Zeitung*, 22 December 2021.
18 Bouverie, p. xi. The French lost 1.7 million in World War I, 1.8 million Russians died, and German deaths exceeded two million.

19 Ibid., p. 35.
20 Ibid., pp. 51 ff.
21 Ibid., p. 103.
22 Ibid., p. 116.
23 Ibid., p. 89.
24 Ibid., pp. 182 ff.
25 Ibid., p. 223. The Sudeten region was home to 2.8 million German speakers, but also 800,000 Czech speakers. Not all the German speakers, including Social Democrats and Jews, wanted to 'return to the Reich'.
26 Ibid., p. 324.
27 Ibid., p. 253.
28 Neitzel, p. 127; Tooze, p. 454.
29 Edgerton 2012, p. 2. Per capita, the British were about 40 per cent better off than the Germans in 1939 (Tooze, pp. 136 ff.).
30 Ibid., pp. xvi and 67 ff.
31 Ibid., p. 70.
32 Broadberry, p. 34.
33 Milward, p. 42; Broadberry, p. 34.
34 Milward, pp. 121 and 234.
35 Milward, p. 127.
36 Work on national accounting began at around the same time in the US and Great Britain, after the Wall Street Crash in 1929. That severe recession pushed questions to the forefront that had not previously interested anyone. How many people were actually unemployed? Did people have enough money to survive? How far had production fallen? And in which branches of industry? The US Senate commissioned a later winner of the Nobel Prize for Economics, Simon Kuznets, to calculate the United States' national income for the years 1929 to 1932. He found that it had fallen by half. Industry had shrunk by 70 per cent overall, and by 80 per cent in the construction industry. Only the public sector had grown. Keynes knew of those calculations, but initially found them uninteresting. As late as 1939, he wrote in his *General Theory* that the purpose of 'such things as net real output and the general level of prices ... should be to satisfy historical ... curiosity'. But the outbreak of World War II raised similar questions to those that arose after the economic crisis of 1929, and the British needed to calculate their national income. However, Keynes made a crucial change to the methodology: he shifted the focus to production, and the modern concept of GDP was born (See Lepenies, pp. 57 ff.; Mazzucato

2019, pp. 81 ff.).

37 Milward, pp. 233 ff. Around a million fewer people were employed in civilian industries during the war than in peacetime (Edgerton 2012, p. 296).

38 In total, 6.9 per cent of Britain's capital assets were destroyed in the war. This figure includes sunk cargo ships and their freight (Edgerton 2012, p. 297).

39 Zweiniger-Bargielowska, pp. 78 ff. Germany attempted to blockade British imports using submarine warfare in the Atlantic. It did not succeed. In 1941, Germany sank 5 per cent of Britain's import goods. By 1944, that success rate had fallen to just 0.4 per cent.

40 Edgerton, p. 159. Civilian imports fell by 30 per cent in 1942, by 23 per cent in 1943, and by 20 per cent in 1944, compared to figures from 1938.

41 Milward, p. 250.

42 Zweiniger-Bargielowska, p. 79.

43 Zweiniger-Bargielowska, p. 80. Many pastures were converted to arable farmland in order to grow more food. The amount of arable land grew by 66 per cent between 1939 and 1944. That meant the county produced 31 per cent less meat—but 200 per cent more grain (Milward, p. 252).

44 See www.nhs.uk/better-health/lose-weight/calorie-counting.

45 Edgerton, p. 171.

46 However, only wholemeal bread was available, to which the British developed a lasting aversion that continues to this day. Highly desired white bread was forbidden in order to preserve scarce grain supplies. Bread was rationed after the war because Britain additionally had to supply its occupied zone in western Germany—where the need was extreme. In the Ruhr Valley area, the amount of food available per person per day was only 900 calories at times.

47 Zweiniger-Bargielowska, pp. 77 ff. The black market played almost no role, as the British had enough to eat. In addition, the government could easily control the flow of food since the majority still had to be imported and so could be registered in the ports. Imports still accounted for 59 per cent of Britain's food during the war. Britain's Ministry of Food therefore was not faced with the problem of having to patrol countless small farms looking for hidden crops. Only fresh eggs were a problem, since they were all produced domestically: more than half 'disappeared' on the way to the official distribution points.

48 Zweiniger-Bargielowska, p. 89. Between 1939 and 1945, the

maternal mortality rate fell from 3.13 to 1.8 deaths per 1,000 births, while neonatal mortality fell from 51 to 46 per 1,000 births. However, babies from the poorest sections of society were still twice as likely to die as the children of the elite.

49 The issue of eating out at restaurants caused such resentment among the broader population that meals were limited to two courses and to a price of five shillings (Zweiniger-Bargielowska, p. 84).

50 'Jeder kämpft für sich allein' ['Everyone Fights for Themselves'], *taz*, 7 April 2020.

51 Broadberry, p. 30. The fall in consumption of more than 30 per cent during World War II was more severe than in World War I, when consumption fell by 'only' 22 per cent.

52 Deutsche Bundesbank, *Lange Zeitreihen. Zur Wirtschaftsentwicklung in Deutschland* [*Deutsche Bundesbank Long Term Series on Economic Development in Germany*] (March 2022), p. 4. Comparisons with the former West Germany can only serve as approximate guides, as they do not include statistics from communist East Germany. The 'five new federal states' have been included in the statistics since 1990.

53 'Sie können Schweinebraten essen' ['You Can Have Your Sunday Roast'], interview with Anton Hofreiter, *taz*, 10 July 2021.

54 Large companies plan constantly, leaving nothing to chance. The aim of large concerns is a company-internal 'vertical integration': they try to control all stages of production, from raw materials to sales. They do not always produce everything themselves. They often use 'outsourcing', as the practice has become known. But those apparently independent suppliers are kept on a very short leash and are subject to the interests of the larger concern. A winner of the Nobel Prize for Economics, Herbert Simon, once asked how an unsuspecting Martian might describe our economy. Would it assume that Earthlings lived in a market economy? Probably not. Instead, it might come to the conclusion that Earthlings had an organised economy in which most economic activity is coordinated within the boundaries of companies — rather than by the market relations between companies (*Journal of Economic Perspectives*, vol. 5, no. 2, spring 1991, 'Organizations and Markets').

Chapter 19: Our future lives

1 Even Keynesians occasionally believe that only private businesses can be innovative: Flassbeck, p. 38.

2 Mazzucato 2014, p. 95.

3   Gates, p. 185.

4   Mazzucato 2021, p. 55.

5   Radkau 2008 (Campus), p. 164.

6   Mazzucato 2021, p. 34; Radkau 2008 (Campus), p. 366; Edgerton 2019, p. 116.

7   This reveals another weakness of GDP calculations: it considers the state as only incurring costs. Its figures largely ignore the fact that a significant proportion of economic activity is only possible because of the state. (For a detailed criticism, see Mazzucato 2019, pp. 85 ff. and 241 ff.)

8   Rosling, p. 198; Deaton, p. 67.

9   Deaton, pp. 122 ff.

10 The International Energy Agency points out that states must issue clear and strong signals about the energy transition so that new mining operations to provide sufficient lithium can be set up in time, for example (IEA, p. 14).

11 The carbon budget approach seems hypermodern, but similar ideas have been around since the 18th century, when fears of a firewood shortage circulated in Germany. Ideas emerged of a 'total wood state', in which everything in life would depend on the availability of wood (Radkau 2000 [Campus], p. 232). However, it was soon realised that there was a sufficient supply of wood, and the energy concerns vanished.

12 'Wir brauchen radikale Maßnahmen' ['We Need Radical Measures'], interview with Volker Quaschning, *taz*, 11 November 2021.

13 See https://data.worldbank.org/indicator/EN.ATM.carbon dioxideE.PC.

14 Ibid

15 The world's population will soon reach its peak, as the global birthrate is currently less than 2.5 children per woman. That compares to five live births per female in 1965. The birth rate is falling because most infants now survive. This apparent paradox is explained by the fact that couples use family planning when they can be confident that their newborn babies will survive to adulthood. They no longer have to have as many offspring as possible to ensure that at least a few of their children will survive. Successful family planning is also dependent on the education of (future) mothers. Despite the current low birth rate, the world's population will continue to grow for a time—because the children who have already been born will live longer (Rosling, pp. 79 ff.).

16 Ulrich, p. 192.

17 Chancel et al., p. 18.
18 Ibid., p. 27.
19 Ibid., p. 195.
20 Ibid., p. 196.
21 Federal Environment Agency 2016, p. 16.
22 Pinzler and Wessel, p. 282.
23 Quoted in Monbiot 2006, p. 43.
24 Lauterbach, p. 165.
25 See www.mpg.de/15510963/lachgas-landwirtschaft-klimawandel.
26 Settele, pp. 66 ff. The loss of insects in well documented in Germany: from 1989 to 2016, entomologists from Krefeld counted local insect populations in 63 German nature-protection areas.
27 Ibid., pp. 19 ff. In spring 2018, to demonstrate how irreplaceable insects are, a supermarket in Hanover removed all products from its shelves that would not exist without pollination: apples, coffee, chocolate, orange and mixed fruit juice, fruit yoghurt, jam, ready-meals, frozen pizzas, various ice cream flavours, cosmetics, dried fruit, and cotton-based clothing. About 60 per cent of its product range was gone. They named the event 'No bees, empty shelves'. Even gummy bears were gone, as they are coated with beeswax to stop them sticking together.
28 Ibid., pp. 151 ff.
29 Ibid., p. 69.
30 Ibid., p. 254.
31 Wilkinson and Pickett, pp. 81 ff.
32 The philosopher Richard David Precht suggests 1,400 to 1,500 euros a month, which every German citizen over the age of 18 would be entitled to receive (Precht, pp. 391 ff.). Precht makes explicit reference to the Swiss economist Thomas Straubhaar (Precht, p. 397), who, however, believes the universal basic income should be set at 1,000 euros a month, to which children would also be entitled—'from infancy to old age' (Straubhaar, pp. 25 ff.). The climate-protection activist Luisa Neubauer also envisages a basic income of 1,500 euros a month; although it is unclear whether she believes that money should be paid out to every person in Germany or only adults (Neubauer and Repenning, p. 229).
33 Precht, p. 402.
34 Introducing a new version of Britain's wartime economy would mean the end of capitalism, because it is based on an organised shrinking of the economy—but private ownership would still exist. However, there are many writers who advocate for various kinds of climate

socialism. For example, the Swedish Marxist Andreas Malm calls for 'ecological war communism', which would be democratic but oriented ecologically to the Soviet Union—so a kind of Leninism without Lenin (Malm 2020, p. 167). The central flaw in this approach is the fact that there has never been a Soviet-type centrally planned economy that was also democratic. Such economies are always dictatorships. Also, one of the main features of the planned economy in the Soviet Union was that it was far more environmentally destructive than under capitalism. Ultimately, aside from in the military, it fostered no technological innovation, as the ubiquitous control of the state stifled any individual initiative.

Innovations will be needed in the future battle against the climate crisis. The sociologist Klaus Dörre therefore proposes 'democratic-sustainable socialism', consisting principally of self-governing cooperatives. However, such a form of society has never existed anywhere. Additionally, Dörre also assumes continued growth. He does recognise 'transformation conflicts', but only in individual fossil-based branches of industry such as open-cut mining for lignite. For the economy as a whole, he believes the 'sustainability revolution' is 'comparable to the first Industrial Revolution' (Dörre, p. 86). Thus, Dörre's model completely fails to offer any kind of approach to steering a shrinking economy.

The two Canadian socialists Leigh Philips and Michal Rozworski propose a kind of democratic socialism based on the internal planning processes of the US retail giants Walmart and Amazon. The flaw in this approach is that is confuses business economics and macroeconomics. More importantly, Philips and Rozworski also assume that continued economic growth will be possible. The climate disaster is of only marginal interest to them. Only the Austrian socialist Bruno Kern says clearly that the economy will have to shrink in the future—and therefore advocates for a kind of 'ecosocialism'. Kern believes in robust state planning, and is also convinced that climate protection can only succeed if private ownership is radically restricted. Under his system, only 'individual … independent, family-run businesses and … cooperatives' will be allowed, which would be forbidden to take on employees (Kern, pp. 176 ff.). There is also no functioning historical model for this kind of socialism. Most importantly, though, it can be expected that resistance to the necessary massive wave of expropriations would overshadow any concerns about climate protection.

Conclusion: The 'survival economy' has already begun

1 Lauterbach, p. 154.
2 Quoted in Schulte, pp. 159 ff.
3 Disputes over access to water are not new. They are as old as our sedentary lifestyle. The word 'rival' comes from the ancient Latin for 'person using the same stream' (Radkau 2000 (CUP), p. 88).
4 See www.bmuv.de/fileadmin/Daten_BMU/Pools/Broschueren/ nationale_wasserstrategie_2023_en_bf.pdf.
5 See www.zfk.de/wasser-abwasser/wse-deckelt-bei- neukunden-abnahmemenge.
6 See www.destatis.de/DE/Presse/Pressemitteilungen/Zahl-der-Woche/ 2022/PD22_12_p002.html
7 Lauterbach, pp. 194 ff.
8 Reimer and Staud, p. 255; Lauterbach, p. 164.
9 See https://eatforum.org/content/uploads/2019/01/EAT-Lancet_ Commission_Summary_Report.pdf.
10 See www.rki.de/DE/Content/Gesundheitsmonitoring/Themen/ Uebergewicht_Adipositas/Uebergewicht_Adipositas_node.html.
11 See https://ourworldindata.org/obesity.